a Wee Bow for
Jedd.

GW01606807

A Northamptonshire Garland

A Northamptonshire Garland

An Anthology of Northamptonshire Poets with Biographical Notes

COMPILED AND EDITED BY

TREVOR HOLD

Northamptonshire Libraries

Published by
Northamptonshire Libraries
27 Guildhall Road
Northampton NN1 1EF

Biographical entries
© Trevor Hold 1989, and
Northamptonshire Libraries 1989

ISBN 0 905391 13 6

Typeset in Melior and Souvenir
by Stanley L Hunt (Printers) Ltd
Midland Road, Rushden
Northamptonshire NN10 9UA

Designed by Bernard Crossland

COVER ILLUSTRATIONS

Front cover: Margaret Compton, wife of the 2nd Marquis of Northampton. Raeburn's portrait (1813) shows her accompanying herself at the harp, probably singing one of the Gaelic folksongs that she learnt at her childhood home on the Isle of Mull [Marquis of Northampton].

Back cover: Portrait of John Clare, Northamptonshire's 'Peasant Poet' in 1844, by Thomas Grimshaw.

In Praise of Northamptonshire

Mountains move minds; their towering heads
reveal
Depths of sky. Forests too, whose aspect
Giddies the sight with unremitting vastness;
Lakes, coasts and seas: all these impress
Our disenchanted souls. We still
Respond to the grandeur of each prospect.

But it is to that unassuming shire
Where I was born that my own spirit flies,
Homing to her parks and ancient trees,
The sandstone manor and the weathered spire,
The steady river ambling to the seas.
Wherever I may live, my exiled eyes
Will seek that landscape and those gentle skies.

TREVOR HOLD

CONTENTS

'What the Visitors had to Say'

A Garland of Northamptonshire Poets

A Mixed Bunch

LIST OF ILLUSTRATIONS

page numbers indicate facing pages

ABOUT THE AUTHOR

TREVOR HOLD was born at Northampton in 1939 and educated at Northampton Grammar School and the University of Nottingham, where he studied music. After a short spell as music master at Market Harborough Grammar School, he held appointments as Lecturer in Music at the Universities of Aberystwyth (1963-5) and Liverpool (1965-70). In 1970 he was appointed to the staff of the Department of Adult Education, University of Leicester, which enabled him to move back to Northamptonshire, and he has lived with his family in the village of Wadenhoe ever since. In 1989 he retired from fulltime teaching in order to devote himself to writing and composition.

He began composing music at the age of nine and poetry in his early teens, and ever since has practised both arts. His music is regularly performed in the concert hall and on the BBC, and more recently on record, and he has published two collections of poetry, *Time and the Bell* (1971) and *Caught in Amber* (1981). His poetry and music reflect his deep affection for and knowledge of his native county, its countryside and history, its writers and poets.

INTRODUCTION

In his introduction to *Shorter Poems of the Eighteenth Century*, Iola Williams states that the first duty of the anthologist is 'to state the rules that he has set himself, their reasons, and the occasions on which he has broken those rules'. Here are the ground rules that I set myself in *A Northamptonshire Garland*. Firstly, what is it? It is an anthology of poetry written by Northamptonshire poets between 1450 and 1950. Excluding 'Anon.', there are ninety-six poems by sixty-eight different poets.

What do I mean by 'Northamptonshire poet'? Let us take the phrase like a charade, word by word, then together. By 'Northamptonshire' I mean the County of Northampton and the old Soke of Peterborough. John Clare was born at Helpston, *Northamptonshire* (not, God forgive us! Cambridgeshire): the County boundary changes of 1974 can never alter that fact. By 'poet', I mean someone who has published poetry in book form. With restrictions of space I have had to make this the rule. It does however exclude numerous writers who have contributed to newspapers and magazines. The pages of, for instance, *The Northamptonshire Mercury, The Northampton and County Independent* and *The Northampton County Magazine* are scattered with poems, some of them very good. Most poets however show their seriousness of purpose by eventually publishing in book form. By 'Northamptonshire poet', I mean either a poet born in the County or a poet who lived for a considerable time in the County. The first category includes John Askham, W. L. Bowles, Ann Bradstreet, John Clare, John Dryden, Henry Kingsley and Thomas Randolph; the second, Philip Doddridge, Digby Dolben, George De Wilde, Charles Kingsley, Marianne Farningham and George Whyte-Melville. Immediately there arises a problem. Some poets in the first category did not remain here for very long. In the case of Henry Kingsley, he was taken, cot and all, to Devonshire before he was twelve months old. Certainly De Wilde, Doddridge and Whyte-Melville are far more qualified to be called 'Northamptonshire poets' than he. Indeed so is Henry's more famous brother, Charles. Though not born here, he spent six crucially formative years of boyhood (from the age of four to eleven) at Barnack, and the fenland scenery was to imprint itself on his later writings, notably *Hereward the Wake* and that marvellously evocative essay in *Prose Idylls*, 'The Fens'. I've allowed two exceptions to my rule of qualification: Mark Akenside and Felicia Hemans. Both resided in the County for less than two years, but their short stays were poetically productive and important in their developments as poets. Akenside set up as a rival medical practitioner to Northampton's sitting incumbent, Dr. John Stonhouse, and was well acquainted with Philip Doddridge. Felicia Hemans wrote a sonnet in praise of Fawsley Park and, as one of her biographers has pointed out, almost certainly got her inspiration for *The Stately Homes of England* from her sojourn here.

But to continue my ground rules: no poets are included who were born after 1900. This is not for lack of material—far from it. I could have expanded my selection considerably, forwards as well as within my imposed time-scale, without detriment to quality, if practicalities of space and cost had allowed. But, inevitably, difficulties of assessment and objectivity arise with poets recently dead or still living.

Wherever possible I have chosen poems with local subject-matter, particularly in the cases of poets in my second category. But my final touchstone has been poetic merit. I came across many poets during my research—not only 'peasant-poets', but parson- and schoolmaster-poets too—whose poetry at best rose to competent versifying, at worst dropped to the most atrocious doggerel. Some of these writers would interest the social historian, but not the reader of poetry. I have made one or two exceptions, to prove the point if it needs proving, notably Elizabeth Brown, the 'cottage-girl' from Woodend, a few of whose *Lines on the Coronation of Her Most Gracious Majesty Queen Victoria* I include. My excuse is that of the admirers of the poetry of William McGonagall. At some nebulous point, difficult to discern, 'bad poetry' crosses the line to become 'good bad-poetry'. Elizabeth Brown, I feel, has crossed this line and has an indisputable touch of the 'McGonagalls'.

The question will already have surfaced in the minds of many readers: does Northamptonshire have any poets of national importance? Two poets, I think it will be agreed, are outstanding on anyone's list: our national Poet-Laureate, John Dryden, and our County's unofficial laureate and, many would say, England's finest nature-poet, John Clare. On a slightly lower step of the Pantheon come: Thomas Vaux, one of the most admired poets of Tudor England; Anne Bradstreet, who emigrated from Northampton with her husband to become America's first female poet; Thomas Randolph, one of Ben Jonson's favourite 'sons'; Molly Leapor, in many people's view one of the finest female poets of the eighteenth century; Digby Dolben, whose poetry, edited by Robert Bridges, was published in Oxford University Press' standard edition; and W. L. Bowles, a poet much admired by Coleridge and his friends. Amongst our County's lesser luminaries–fascinating glow-worms in the byways of literature–are such poets as Peter Hausted, John Askham, Mildmay Fane and Robert Wild. Admittedly, except for Clare and Dryden, none of these are household names, and even those whose names will be recognised, like Doddridge, Whyte-Melville and the Kingsleys, will be better known in contexts outside poetry. But compared with our county neighbours, Northamptonshire has done very well. Only Warwickshire, with Shakespeare, Drayton, Landor and Brooke, has a more impressive progeny.

Choice of poem and number of poems chosen are necessarily subjective. Most poets are represented by a single poem; those poets whom I consider of importance, by two; those of specially high quality, three. Only two poets have more than three: Dryden four and Clare five. This indicates my own personal view of our two major poets: others would probably have reversed the representation.

Within these tight restraints I have endeavoured to include as wide a variety of poetry as possible. Poets range chronologically from Anthony Woodville (b. *c*1442) to George Harrison (d. 1950). For most poets, the writing of poetry is an 'out-of-office-hours' activity. Very few of the authors represented here were full-time writers in that they earned their livelihood from writing. The 'day-jobs' of our authors were remarkably diverse. As well as the expectedly large batch of clerics, these include: doctors, farm-workers, journalists, librarians, schoolmasters, shoemakers, landed gentry, a civil servant, a diplomat, a hairdresser, a solicitor, a miller, a ribbon-weaver–even a professional astronomer. One poet has the dubious distinction of having stood trial for murder. (He was, I hasten to add, honourably acquitted.) Geographically I have tried to cast the net as wide as possible –from Barnack (Kingsleys) and Helpston (Clare) in the north-east to Aynho (Marmion and Wild) and King's Sutton

(Bowles) in the south-west, from Little Bowden (Jane West)—yes, until 1888 Little Bowden was part of Northamptonshire—in the north, to Grafton Regis (Woodville) in the south. As Appendix B shows, there are very few villages in the County which have not produced their resident poet at one time or another. Though the county town has its expected share in the anthology, statistically some villages are more 'poetical': for example, Castle Ashby provides three poets and Aynho and tiny Easton Maudit two apiece.

I have also endeavoured to keep a reasonable balance between the sexes. Considering how few women poets were published before the nineteenth century, fourteen out of a total of sixty-eight is an impressive tally. Five of these poetesses—Mary Alcock, Anne Bradstreet, Hester Chapone, Felicia Hemans and Mary Leapor—produced poetry of the highest quality.

Finally, a plea: the fact that the majority of these poets will be completely unknown should not deter. I have a low threshold of boredom. These poems have all been thoroughly scanned and sieved by reading and re-reading, and I have only allowed through the sieve those poems which have given me enjoyment. There are many little gems, ranging from the humorous, such as Eleanor Westley's attempt to write to a friend foiled by constant 'Porlockian' interruptions, to the poignantly sad 'balet' written by Anthony Woodville on the eve of his execution; from Anne Bradstreet's touching tribute to her husband to Talbot Keene's witty 'House Rules'; from Mildmay Fane's celebration of a happy country life at Apethorpe to Thomas Bell's heart-felt lament at the lot of the Barnwell village schoolmaster. Some poems will be of particular interest to local historians, notably John Plummer's anti-Trades Union song, 'Scab! Scab!! Scab!!!', John Merry's song celebrating the downfall of a local banker, 'Marriott & Co.', and Ferdinando Archer's account of the Great Fire of Northampton. It seems a great pity that such poems, the result of much thought and artistic care, living words from a past age, should be hidden away behind the closed covers of books on a library shelf, inaccessible except to the inquisitive scholar. The aim of this anthology is to bring to the public attention a sample of this work. Small and insignificant as it may seem, these poets and their poetry represent an important aspect of our local heritage and as such a part of our national heritage.

In preparing this anthology, I have adopted a simple

format. Poets are represented in alphabetical order, which ensures more variety than the alternative chronological order. For each poet I have supplied a biographical note and brief 'assessment' followed by a representative poem or poems, including source and date of first publication. Annotations given by the poets in the original publications are identified in parenthesis by the words (Author's note). Titles of poems are the poet's own except for those bracketed which are mine. Poems without titles, the poet's or mine, are identified by their opening line in quotation marks. There are two appendices: Appendix A is a select bibliography of Northamptonshire poets, 1450–1900, including the sixty or so whose poetry I looked at but did not include in the anthology. Appendix B is a gazetteer of poets and places, which should prove helpful in locating local writers. Finally, I have added a section of anonymous and traditional verse from the County, ranging from children's rhymes to churchyard epitaphs, taking in *en route* place-name rhymes, lace-tells, sampler verse, election broadsides, proverbs, charms and weathersaws. It will act, I hope, as a welcome leavening to the more solid matter of the Garland proper.

TREVOR HOLD
Wadenhoe

September 1989

ACKNOWLEDGEMENTS

I would like to express my thanks to the following individuals for their help in making this anthology possible: Marion Arnold and the staff of the Northamptonshire Studies Collection, Northampton Central Library, who gave me unstinted help during my frequent forays to their library shelves; Victor A. Hatley, always generous with his unsurpassable knowledge of local Northampton history, who was prepared to seek out answers to even my most recondite questions and who checked through my final typescript; my colleague R. L. Greenall who published some of my early researches in *Northamptonshire Past and Present;* Dr. Keith Brooker whose own researches on Northamptonshire writers gave me valuable leads; David Powell, with whom I discussed this project some eighteen years ago and whose own articles have been invaluable starting-points; the staff at Northamptonshire Record Office, Delapre Abbey, for their help and advice; my wife, Susan Hold, who read through the typescript, dotting the 'i's and crossing the 't's; and finally Mr. John Munro, County Leisure and Libraries Officer, without whose encouragement and support this anthology would not have risen from its typescript. I must add the following rider to these acknowledgements: any errors which may have crept into the anthology are in the final instance my own. Of the many printed sources I consulted, the following were particularly useful. (Abbreviations used in the anthology are given in brackets):

SAMUEL ALLIBONE, *Dictionary of English Literature,* 1858–71 (Allibone)

ANN BAKER, *Glossary of Northamptonshire Words and Phrases,* 1854 (Baker)

JOHN BRIDGES (ed. PETER WHALLEY), *The History and Antiquities of Northamptonshire,* 1791

JOHN COLE, *Popular Biography of Northamptonshire,* 1839 (Pop. Biog.)

ALICE DRYDEN, ed., *Memorials of Old Northamptonshire,* 1903 (Memorials)

HERBERT A. EVANS, *Highways and Byways of Northamptonshire and Rutland,* 1918

H. I. LONGDEN, *Northamptonshire and Rutland Clergy,* 1938-52 (Longden)

H. J. MASSINGHAM, ed., *Seventeenth Century English Verse,* 1920

ARTHUR MEE, ed., *Northamptonshire (The King's England),* 1945 (Mee)

NICHOLAS PEVSNER, *Northamptonshire (The Buildings of England)*, 1961 (Pevsner)
JUSTIN SIMPSON, *Obituary and Records for the Counties of Lincoln, Rutland & Northampton*, 1861 (Simpson)
JULIET SMITH, *Northamptonshire (A Shell Guide)*, 1968
THOMAS STERNBERG, *The Dialect and Folk-lore of Northamptonshire*, 1851 (Sternberg)
JOHN TAYLOR, *Bibliotheca Northantonenis*, 1884
JOHN TAYLOR, *Antiquarian Memoranda and Biographies*, 1901
LESLIE STEPHEN, ed., *Dictionary of National Biography*, 1885–91
ANTHONY À WOOD, *Athenae Oxonienses . . .*, 1691–2, 1721. Each 2 vols. (Anthony à Wood)

I also found valuable material in the following newspapers, magazines, directories and journals:

Northampton and County Independent
Northampton County Magazine, 1928–33 (NCM)
Northampton Mercury
Northamptonshire Notes and Queries, 1885–95 (NNQ)
Northamptonshire Past and Present, 1948– (NP&P)
Whellan's Northamptonshire Directories, 1849 and 1874 (Whellan)

POEMS

Northamptonshire Libraries are grateful to the following for permission to reproduce poems or parts of poems. The Board of Trinity College, Dublin and the Council of the Early English Text Society for *The Northampton play of Abraham and Isaac*, TCDMS 432 (formerly D.4.18) fols 75v-81; and Patrick Leigh Fermor for his poem *Northamptonshire Fields*.

In some cases it has proved impossible to identify copyright holders, and Northamptonshire Libraries apologise if any have inadvertently been omitted from this list.

ILLUSTRATIONS

Northamptonshire Libraries are grateful to the following for permission to reproduce illustrations. Her Majesty the Queen for Holbein's drawing of Thomas, Lord Vaux, from the Royal Library, Windsor Castle; The National Portrait Gallery for portraits of William Bowles, Charles Kingsley, Henry Kingsley and George John Whyte-Melville; Lambeth Palace Library for portraits of Edward IV and Earl Rivers (M265. fvi); The Marquis of Northampton for the portrait of Margaret Compton (front cover illustration) and the photograph of the monument to Spencer Compton in Castle Ashby Church; Mr. Frank Thompson for the photograph of George Harrison; and Mr. R. Greenall for the portrait of Mildmay Fane.

'What the visitors had to say'

An Introductory Bouquet

ANON

The following couplet comes from a poem by an anonymous Shropshire poet which lists the characteristics of each county in turn. (John Holloway gives the entire poem in *The Oxford Book of Local Verse*, 1987, No. 327.):

Northamptonshire, full of love
Benethe the gyrdyll and noth above . . .

MICHAEL DRAYTON

(1563–1631)

Michael Drayton's *Polyolbion*, 'a choreographical description of all the tracts, rivers, mountains, forests, and other parts of Great Britain', appeared complete in thirty 'Songs' in 1622. Northamptonshire is described in the 23rd Song. This is the introductory 'Argument':

From furious Fights Invention comes,
Deaf'ned with noise of rattling drums,
And in the Northamptonian bounds,
Shows Whittlewood's, and Sacie's grounds;
Then to Mount Hellidon doth go,
(Whence Charwell, Leame, and Nen do flow)

The Surface which of England sings,
And Nen down to the Washes brings;
Then whereas Welland makes her way,
Shows Rockingham her rich array:
A Course at Kelmarsh then she takes,
Where she Northamptonshire forsakes.

Polyolbion, 1622

(The literal meaning of the final couplet is: 'Invention' describes a hare-course before leaving Northamptonshire for another county.)

ROBERT BLOOMFIELD

(1766–1823)

The Suffolk-born 'peasant-poet', Robert Bloomfield, visited Wakefield Lodge, the home of the Duke of Grafton in Whittlebury Forest, in August 1800. Here are extracts from the poem that he wrote afterwards for the benefit of his children:

Lines occasioned by a visit to Whittlebury Forest

Genius of the Forest Shades,
Lend thy pow'r, and lend thine ear!
A stranger trod thy lonely glades,
Amidst thy dark and bounding Deer;
Inquiring Childhood claims the verse,
O let them not inquire in vain;
Be with me while I thus rehearse
The glories of thy Sylvan Reign.

Thy Dells by wintry currents worn,
Secluded haunts, how dear to me!
From all but Nature's converse borne,
No ear to hear, no eye to see.
Their honour'd leaves the green Oaks rear'd,
And crowned the upland's graceful swell;
While answering through the vale was heard
Each distant Heifer's tinkling bell . . .

When morning still unclouded rose,
Refresh'd with sleep and joyous dreams,
Where fruitful fields with woodlands close,
I trac'd the births of various streams.
From beds of Clay, here creeping rills
Unseen to parent Ouse would steal;
Or, gushing from the northward Hills,
Would glitter through Tove's winding dale.

Rural Tales, Ballads and Songs, 1801

REVD. E. WHITE

(fl. 1798)

The village of Potterspury is a mere crow's flight from Wakefield Lodge. It was here that the Rev. E. White was pastor for a brief period (1798–1800): not a week too short from the tone and contents of his poem:

At Pury then, I join a rustic throng,
Blockish as inattentive. Not the house
Of God himself could awe them. In comes Hodge
As gently as a trooper; plump he squats
In his accustomed seat. The farmer snores;
His son looks big, and dashing as a lord;
And ere the blessing closes with 'Amen',
An impious hubbub bounces on your ear;
And faster than they entered, all rush out.
But not with prayerful silence; no one asks,
With pensive earnestness, 'Am I the wretch
Thus guilty, or thus pardoned? Is heaven mine?'
But talk of weather, and the growth of corn,
The state of markets, and the price of pigs;
How horses, poultry, eggs, and butter sold?
Or scandal; the most trifling village news;
Such themes the intervals of worship fill.

Ye visit their abodes in the fond hope
Of finding life. You are discovered: one
In the stable lurks; one slinks behind a stack,
Anxious to 'scape the parson, who perchance
Might start religion. Join their social throng;
Or at the dining board, or cheerful tea,
Bring in the subject of the last discourse—
The wisest cannot recollect the text!

But each devoutly tries: one fumbler thumbs
The bible; and what you in David read
Is certainly (they all conclude) in John.

Peasants have human souls; and he is blest
Who plucks but one from mis'ry and despair.
The rude and simple are to Jesus dear.
But when both young and long instructed shew
A vicious dominance, but female free!
When any name but that of Christ is sweet,
And any theme more grateful than his love;
Who'd plough a rock? or water a dead tree?
Or toil with souls gross-hearted,–sermon-proof?–
Perplexed, dispirited, as useless here,
In spite of house and orchard, and some friends
Affectionate, and Fitzroy's transient smile,
I sigh for liberty, and fain would fly.

So oft we loathe the oaks ourselves desired,
And of our chosen gardens grow ashamed.

Perhaps ashamed of his exasperated outcry, White concludes with a quotation from *Isaiah* I.30: 'Nevertheless at Thy Word I will let down the net.' The text comes from 'Select Remains of the Rev. E. White, of Potterspury, Northamptonshire', an Ms. in Northamptonshire Record Office. (See *NP&P*, VI, 131.)

F. W. FABER

(1814–63)

We could almost, but not quite, claim the great hymn-writer and Catholic apologist, Frederick William Faber, for our anthology, for he was Rector of Elton, just over the Huntingdonshire border, from 1842 until his conversion to the Catholic faith in 1845. In his poem, *The Cherwell*, he makes this fine tribute to our county in verse:

O silent Cherwell! once wert thou
A minstrel river; thou didst flow
Gently as now, but all along
Was heard that sweet itinerant song,
Which thou hadst learnt in coming down
From the rich slope of Hellidon,
The green-capped hill that overlooks
Fair Warwick's deep and shady brooks,
And blithe Northampton's meadow nooks,
Tamest of Counties! with a dower
Of humblest beauty rich, a power

Only by quiet minds obeyed,
And by the restless spurned,—scant shade,
And ruddy fallow, and mid these
Rare meadows, foliage-framed, which please
The leisure-loving heart, and line
Where the slow-footed rivers shine,
Upon whose reedy waters swim
The roving sea-birds, on the brim
Of flooded Nenna, in a fleet
With a golden lustre lit,
What time the short Autumnal day
Sets o'er the tower of Fotheringay.

The Cherwell

Finally, a poem by a schoolboy visitor who signed himself 'P. M. Leigh Fermor (aged 15)' in a 1930 number of *The Northampton County Magazine*. He later travelled for four years in Central Europe, the Balkans and Greece, enlisted in the Irish Guards in 1939 and had a distinguished wartime career, winning the O.B.E. (1943) and D.S.O. (1944). After the war, he wrote a series of travel books which have become classics of their kind. Patrick Leigh Fermor has moved a long way from those Dodford Fields of 1930.

Northamptonshire Fields

Northamptonshire, Northamptonshire,
Where all the fields are green,
I love to lie beneath a hedge
Of creeping eglantine.

I love to hear the bumble bees
Beneath the summer sky:
To listen to the birds' sweet song,
And see the clouds float by.

And by the winding river's bank.
With willows all entwined;
The lair of coot and kingfisher,
A shady bower I find.

The placid depths with shadows daubed,
The flowers upon the brink,
Where long-legged baby lambs come down
Among the reeds to drink.

On the summit of yon grassy slope,
The spinney sits on high,
A bosky lair, whose feathery elms
Are blending with the sky.

The meadows and the pasture land
Are heaven enough for me.
The hours I spend in Dodford Fields
Do dwarf Eternity.

ANON
(15th century)

The Northampton Play of *Abraham and Isaac*

The Mystery Plays, biblical dramas set out in 'cycles' and enacting events of the Bible from the Creation to the Ascension, were popular in England from the thirteenth to the sixteenth century. Only four complete cycles have come down to us: from York, Chester, Wakefield and Coventry, but it is clear from archives that many other towns had them and fragments of some of these survive. Though Chambers (*Medieval Stage*) observed that there is no record of medieval dramatic performance at Northampton, one play with strong local connections does exist. The Northampton *'Abraham'* survives in a manuscript copy at Trinity College, Dublin (TCD MS 432 fols 75v–81). The last entries date the scribe's work to the year 1461. Nothing in the play connects it with Dublin but the Northampton connection is strong, for interpolated in the manuscript are several pages listing mayors and bailiffs of the town from the reign of Richard II to Henry VI as well as names of some of the people killed at the Battle of Northampton, 1460. Norman Davis, in his edition of the play, writes: 'Seven pages of particulars of the officials of Northampton could surely be of interest only to a Northampton man. . . . It does not, of course, follow that the play was either composed or acted there, though the character of the language would not exclude this.' The extract I print is the conclusion of the play, where Sara welcomes home her husband Abraham and reprieved son Isaac. (The text is given in full in Norman Davis' *Non-Cycle Plays and Fragments*, Early English Text Society, 1970, 32-42.)

from Abraham and Isaac

SARA. A, welcom souereigne, withouten doute;
How haue ye fared whils ye haue ben oute?
And, Isaac, son, in all this rowte?
    Hertly welcome home be ye!
HABRAHAM. Gramercy, wif, fayre most you befalle.
Com thens, wif, out of youre halle,
And let us go walke and I wol telle you alle,
    How God hathe sped this day with me.

Wif, I went for to sacrifye;
But how trowe you, telle me verylye?
SARA. Forsothe, souereigne, I wot not I,
    Parauenture som quyk best?
HABRAHAM. Quyk? Ye forsothe, quyk it was!
As wel I may tel you al the case
As another that was in the same place,
    For I wote wel it wol be wist.

Almighty God, that sitteth on hye,
Bad me take Isaac, thi son, therbye
And smyte of his hed and bren hym veralye,
    Aboue upon yondre hille.
And when I had made fyre and smoke,
And drowe my knyf to yeve hym a stroke,
An aungel cam and my wille broke,
    And seid oure Lord alowed my wylle.

SARA. Alas, all then had gon to wrake!
Wold ye haue slayne my son Isaac?
Nay, than al my ioy had me forsake!
    Alas, where was your mynde?
HABRAHAM. My mynde? Upon the goode Lorde
        on hy!

Nay, and he bid me, trust it verayly,
Though it had be thiself and I,
It shuld not haue ben left behynde.

God gave hym betwix us tweyne,
And now he asked hym of us ageyne.
Shuld I say nay? Nay, in certeyne,
Not for al the world wide.
Now he knoweth my hert verayly;
Isaac hathe his blessing and also I,
And have blessid also all oure progeny,
For euer to abide.

SARA. Now blessid be that Lorde souereigne
That so liketh to say to you tweyne;
And what that euer he lust, I say not theragayne,
But his wille be fulfilled.
HABRAHAM. Isaac hathe no harme, but in maner
I was sory;
And yit I haue wonne his love truly.
And euermore, goode Lord, gramercy
That my childe is not kylled.

Now ye that haue sene this aray,
I warne you all, bothe nyght and day,
What God comaundeth say not nay,
For ye shal not lese therby.

Abraham and Isaac, 15th c.

3. rowte. company 10. trowe. think 12. quyk. live, living
25. wrake. ruin 49. aray. event, happening

MARK AKENSIDE
(1721–70)

Mark Akenside's brief residence in Northampton (1744–5) only just qualifies him as a Northamptonshire poet. There is no evidence that the town had any effect upon his poetry, but, as a Doctor of Physic, he almost certainly had an effect upon the town.

He was born in Newcastle-upon-Tyne, the son of a butcher, and was educated in the City. He began writing poetry at an early age and at fifteen contributed to *The Gentleman's Magazine*. At eighteen he went to Edinburgh with the intention of studying to become a dissenting minister, but changed his mind and entered the university as a medical student. In 1743 he moved to London where his poem, *The Pleasures of Imagination,* was published (1744). He then studied for a short time at Leyden in Holland where he was awarded the degree of Doctor of Physic and then set up practice in Northampton as a rival to the 'sitting tenant', Dr. John

Stonhouse (see Doddridge). He knew Philip Doddridge, who was working with Stonhouse at the time to set up an infirmary in the town. Cole states (*Pop. Biog.*) that 'Dr. Kippis has remarked that "he well remembered hearing Dr. Doddridge and Dr. Akenside carry on an amicable debate at Northampton".' After a residence of only eighteen months he moved on to Hampstead. In 1759 he became Principal Physician at St. Thomas' Hospital and in 1781 was appointed one of the Physicians to the Queen. He died in London of a fever on 23 June 1770.

As well as *The Pleasures of Imagination* (revised and expanded as *The Pleasures of the Imagination* in 1772) he wrote several odes and shorter poems. His success as a physician was never great because of his haughty and pedantic manner, which Smollett satirised in *Peregrine Pickle*, and his poetry suffers from a similar flaw. The ode, *To the Muse*, is one of his more readable pieces.

Ode to the Muse*

Queen of my songs, harmonious maid,
Ah, why hast thou withdrawn thy aid?
Ah, why forsaken thus my breast,
With inauspicious damps oppressed?
Where is the dread prophetic heat,
With which my bosom wont to beat?
Where all the bright mysterious dreams
Of haunted groves and tuneful streams,
That wooed my genius to divinest themes?

Say, goddess, can the festal board,
Or young Olympia's form adored;
Say, can the pomp of promised fame
Relume thy faint, thy dying flame?
Or have melodious airs the power
To give one free poetic hour?
Or, from amid the Elysian train,
The soul of Milton shall I gain,
To win thee back with some celestial strain?

O powerful strain! O sacred soul!
His numbers every sense control:
And now again my bosom burns;
The Muse, the Muse herself returns,
Such on the banks of Tyne, confessed,
I hailed the fair, immortal guest,
When first she sealed me for her own,
Made all her blissful treasures known,
And bade me swear to follow Her alone.

Odes on Several Subjects, 1745

*Akenside's original title was *On the Absence of the Poetic Inclination.*

23. Akenside was born at Newcastle-upon-Tyne.

MARK AKENSIDE, the Newcastle-born poet who worked as a physician in Northampton from 1744 to 1745

JOHN ASKHAM, the Wellingborough-born poet who published five volumes of poetry between 1863 and 1893

MARY ALCOCK

(1741?–98)

Mary Alcock was born into a family with notable ecclesiastical and scholarly connections. Her paternal great-grandfather was Richard Cumberland (1631–1718), Rector of Brampton Ash (1658) and later Bishop of Peterborough (1691); her paternal grandfather, another Richard Cumberland, was Rector of Peakirk and Archdeacon of Northampton and her maternal grandfather was Dr. Richard Bentley, the great classical scholar and Master of Trinity College, Cambridge; whilst her father was Rev. Dr. Dennison Cumberland, Rector of Stanwick (1731–57) and later Bishop of Clonfert (1763–72) and Kilmore (1772–74) in Ireland. Her brother was Richard Cumberland the playwright (1732–1811) whom Sheridan lampooned as 'Sir Fretful Plagiary' in *The Critic*. He published two volumes of rambling *Memoirs* (1807) which make several references to the family home at Stanwick but, unfortunately, few to his sister. There is no record of her baptism at Stanwick, so it is likely that she was born and baptised at her maternal grandparents' home, the Master's Lodge, Cambridge, as was her brother. She moved with her parents to Ireland where she married the Rev. Archdeacon Alcock of Kilmore and after her parents' death resided in Bath. She died at Haselbech, at the home of her relatives, the Ashby family, on 28 May 1798, and there is a monument to her just inside the church door.

Her poems, edited by her niece Joanna Hughes, were published in 1799. Amongst the subscribers was 'His Royal Highness George Prince of Wales'. Many of them seem to have been written in the 1780s during her residence in Bath; at least one was 'Written in Ireland' (it is included in the *New Oxford Book of Eighteenth Century Verse*, No. 548). *The Chimney Sweeper's Complaint*, if lacking the biting moral indignation and pungent brevity of Blake's *The Chimney Sweep*, vividly portrays the 'wretched fate' of sweepers' boys. *The Air-Balloon; or Flying Mortal*, first published in 1784, was inspired by the aerial excursions of the Montgolfier brothers, which aroused great interest at the time.

The Chimney-Sweeper's Complaint

A chimney sweeper's boy am I;
    Pity my wretched fate!
Ah, turn your eyes; 'twould draw a tear,
    Knew you my helpless state.

Far from my home, no parents I
    Am ever doom'd to see;
My master, should I sue to him,
    He'd flog the skin from me.

Ah, dearest Madam, dearest Sir,
    Have pity on my youth;
Tho' black, and cover'd o'er with rags,
    I tell you nought but truth.

My feeble limbs, benumb'd with cold,
Totter beneath the sack,
Which ere the morning dawn appears
Is loaded on my back.

My legs you see are burnt and bruis'd,
My feet are gall'd by stones,
My flesh for lack of food is gone,
I'm little else but bones.

Yet still my master makes me work.
Nor spares me day or night;
His 'prentice boy he says I am,
And he will have his right.

'Up to the highest top,' he cries,
'There call out chimney-sweep!'
With panting heart and weeping eyes
Trembling I upward creep.

But stop! no more–I see him come;
Kind Sir, remember me!
Oh, could I hide me underground,
How thankful should I be!

Poems, 1799

The Air Balloon

No more of Phaeton let poets tell,
I care not where he drove nor where he fell;
No more I'll wish for fam'd Aurora's car,
To drive me forth, high as the morning star;
In Air Balloon to distant realms I go,
'And leave the gazing multitude below.'

No more I'll hear of Venus and her doves,
Nor Cupid flying with the little loves;
Nor would I now in Juno's chariot ride
In princely pomp, with peacock by my side;
In higher state, in Air Balloon I go,
I'd have the gods and goddesses to know.

No more in oriental language fair
I'll read of Genii wafting through the air;
Nor longer will I seek (by Persian wrought)
A carpet, to transport me by a thought;

Enough for me in Air Balloon to go,
And leave th'enquiring multitude below.

No more of Pegasus (unruly steed)
To reach Parnassus' Mount, shall I have need;
Nor will I now the Muses favour court,
To shew me Pindus' Hill, their chief resort;
To these fair realms in Air Balloon I go,
And leave the grov'ling multitude below.

No more shall Fancy now (betwitching fair!)
Erect me castles, floating in the air;
Such vague, such feeble structures I despise,
I'll kick them down as I ascend the skies;
For higher far in Air Balloon I go,
And leave the wond'ring multitude below.

No longer, now, at distance need I try
To trace each planet with perspective eye;
Nor longer wish, with fairies from afar,
To slide me gently down on falling star;
For up or down with equal ease I steer,
And view with naked eye the splendid sphere.

Alas poor Newton! late for learning fam'd,
No more shall thy researches e'er be nam'd;
For greater Newtons now each day shall soar,
High up to Heaven, and new world explore;
Since swift, in Air Balloons, aloft we go,
And leave the stupid multitude below.

No more the terrors of the deep I fear;
Alike to me, if friend be far or near;
This sea-girt isle I distant leave behind,
Visit each kingdom and survey mankind;
For now with ease in Air Balloon I ride,
No more compell'd to wait for wind or tide.

Hail, happy lovers! late by distance curst,
(Of all the worldly tortures sure the worst)
No more condemn'd an absence to deplore,
And, sighing, breathe your vows from shore to shore;
For through the air, swift in Balloons ye roll,
'And waft yourselves from India to the pole.'

In vain may party rage assail mine ear;
If war or peace, alike I'm free from care;
Should plague or pestilence infect the land,
The purest regions are at my command;
Where safe from harm, in Air Balloon I go,
And leave the sickly multitude below.

No more of judge or jury will I hear,
The laws of land extend not to the air;
Nor bailiff now my spirits can affright,
For up I mount, and soon am out of sight;
Thus, screen'd from justice, in Balloon I go,
And leave th'insolvent multitude below.

How few the worldly evils now I dread,
No more confin'd this narrow earth to tread:
Should fire, or water, spread destruction drear,
Or earthquake shake this sublunary sphere,
In Air Balloon to distant realms I fly,
And leave the creeping world to sink and die.

Poems, 1799 (1st publ. 1784)*

*The Montgolfier brothers made their first ascent by balloon 5 June 1783.

1. Phaeton. Son of Phoebus (the sun) who drove his father's chariot with dire results. 3. Aurora. Goddess who set out before the sun rose. 10. Juno. Wife of Jupiter, and Queen of Heaven. 19. Pegasus. Winged horse ridden by Bellerophon in his attempt to fly to heaven.

T. S. ALLEN

(f. 1826–48)

I have found very little information about this particular author. From comments made in his poem *The Weathercock* he resided at, or was a frequent visitor to, indeed may well have been born at, Easton Maudit:

> Hornwood, that sweet retreat where oft I've stray'd . . .

In his Preface to the poem he states:

> *The Weathercock* was composed at the rebuilding of the spire of Easton Maudit, Northamptonshire. The circumjacent scenery is familiar to the author and gives rise to the most pleasant recollection of early and happy days.

He must have been related to one of the many Allens living in the village at the time, though his name does not appear in the parish records. He seems to have been a well-travelled man. His first volume of poems, *Original Rhymes* (1826) was published at Bampton; *The Weathercock and other poems* (1833) was published when he was living at Stourbridge; and *The Parrot and other poems* (1848) when he was living at Daventry. The last is dedicated to the Marquis of Northampton (see Spencer Compton). In 1831 he published *A Trip to Paris in verse* and seems to have been fluent in the French language, as most of the poems in *The Weathercock* and all those in *The Parrot* are translations from the French.

The Weathercock commemorates the repair and restoration of Easton Maudit spire and the 'unveiling' of the new weathercock on 13 November 1832, which event is related in the second extract. The first part of the poem describes, in fascinating detail, the fir-tree grove where Easton Maudit manor-house (the home of the Yelvertons) once stood, 'The changes affected by agricultural improvements', the church, its inscriptions and monuments, the village and the famous people, such as Bishop Morton, Bishop Percy and Dr. Samuel Johnson, associated with it. Our first extract is the opening invocation to the muse and address to the weathercock.

from The Weathercock

(i) Assist, ye Nine, assist me while I sing,
Of Chanticleer, if so he can be call'd,
Whose brazen throat ne'er issu'd forth a sound
To rouse the milkmaid from her flocky couch,
Or call the ploughboy to his wonted toil;
But perch'd aloft on yonder village spire,
A mute spectator of the rural scene,
He turn'd and turn'd to mark the whistling winds,
Or tell them whence the softer breezes blow,
An ever-changing thing–the Weathercock.

Ages have pass'd since first in gilded coat,
Which Time has tarnish'd with his busy hand,
Thou wast enthron'd upon thy lofty perch,
And neighb'ring nymphs and swains came
    flocking round
To gaze upon thee, when the glitt'ring sun
Had reach'd his mid-day height, while bells
Beneath thee, with their iron tongues, proclaim'd
Thy installation. How the welkin rang
With such new music, here ne'er heard before.

Oh, could'st thou say what changes thou hast seen
In all around thee! Yon broad oak, with arms
Of rare gigantic bulk and knotty sides,
Thou saw'st an acorn, or at best a twig.
Hornwood, that sweet retreat where oft I've stray'd,
Was then of humble growth; its sturdy sons
Were then but saplings; and its ridings green,
Through which thy pointed pedestal appears,
Had not been cut by man's reforming hand . . .

(ii) But hark! the wintry winds begin to blow,
And yonder weathercock (which in his turn,
Like other lofty ones, has had his fall)
Points to the frozen regions, and portends
A cold and cheerless night. The blazing hearth
I'll seek, and with my friends, a party small,
Gladly again his history I'll resume.

Time was when he (as I've already told)
Maintain'd a loftier post, and from that spire,
Where now his bright successor boldly stands,
Nicely survey'd the scene beneath his ken,
E'en to the vast horizon's utmost bounds.
Long was his reign, and happy too forsooth,
As any earthly chief could haply boast;
Though warring winds from hyperborean realms
Sent forth their icy show'rs, and forked fires
Flash'd round his sacred head–he firmly stood.

But on a day (that day I need not name,
Which prov'd so fatal to his sov'reign sway)
A reckless stranger, from Helvetia's vales,
With sacrilegious hand, levell'd the tube
And shook the harmless hero to his base.
He fell not, but he droop'd and hung his head,
As though some wound had touch'd him to
the heart–
For he was not invulnerable there:–
No mortal marks were seen, though in his tail
A perforation sore had erst been made
By one not less expert–a gunner too–
(And strange to tell!) the humble village clerk.

Long time elaps'd or e'er the crested bird
From his high perch was hurl'd. Storm after storm
Assail'd with direful strokes: he weaker grew,
And each revolving season serv'd to shew
How much he felt their force: his fate was fix'd;
Each passing peasant view'd him with affright,
While wiser heads, the guardians of the place,
Deem'd him unfit to stand–and doom'd his fall.

Alas! how frail are all terrestial things;
Exalted stations cannot save from harm,
Or shield their proud possessors from the storm.

The humble blade escapes the wintry blast,
While the tall tree beneath the tempest lies:
Or if the storm assail not, some foul worm,
Like that fell tube which wounded Chanticleer,
Preys on the vital part–it droops and dies.
Not so the once exalted bird I sing,
He lives to fill an humbler, happier sphere,
And guards the granary–a precious store.

See how he sits, how well he acts his part,
Moving obedient to the changeful wind.
No circling daws are seen about him now,
As when in regal state; but chirping birds,
An interested race, come hopping round,
And court him mainly for the grain he keeps.

At length arriv'd the long expected day,
And Chanticleer's successor took the throne:
Bells rang, boys shouted, strangers flock'd around,
And all was high festivity and joy.
All parties met–some din'd, some took their tea,
And Herbert was the founder of the feast.

Thus ends my song–or rather tedious tale;
Accept it, O ye friends, to whom 'tis due,
Ye keen-eyed critics be not too severe,
But spare me for my subject's sake–
the Weathercock.

The Weathercock and other poems, 1833

24. Hornwood. The wood still stands, though not the one that Allen knew. It was replanted by the Forestry Commission earlier this century. 48. A reckless stranger. A Swiss, in the service of Lady Frances Compton. (Author's note.) 83. Nov. 13, 1832. (Author's note.) 88. The architect. (Author's note.)

FERDINANDO ARCHER

(1608–1705)

Ferdinando Archer was educated at Christ's College, Cambridge, where he received his B.A. in 1637 and his M.A. (from Queen's) in 1640. In 1646 he was appointed Master of the Free School in Northampton. In 1696, after forty-nine years service, he decided to retire, 'because of his great age which renders him not soe capable in all respects to manage the saide Schoole as he hath formerly done.' He died nine years later and was buried at All Saints on 23 January 1705. In 1677 he translated into rhyming couplets a Latin poem, *Carmen Funebre; ex Occasione Northamptoniae*

Conflagratae Compositum, by Dr. Simon Ford, Vicar of All Saints, 1659–70, under the title *The Fall and Funeral of Northampton*. He also brought out a new edition of *The True Christians Daily Delight* by his predecessor as Master of the Free School, Simon Wastell (q.v.). The following extract from *The Fall and Funeral of Northampton* gives a graphic account of Northampton's Great Fire (1675) by one who was 'a sad spectator of that frightful scene'. It describes how the fire started in a cottage at the upper end of St. Mary's Street near the Castle, and the confusion which followed its rapid spread.

from The Fall and Funeral of Northampton

A Cottage poor there stood, at farthest West
 To poor a Covert, and a Nest;
Thatch'd over head, and Thatch'd o'th floor,
 With Straw and Litter, to the door;
A Barn, a Stable, or a Hog-stye, whether?
 Barn, Stable, Hog-stye, all-together.
A Whisp with Embers, from a Neighbour fetch'd,
 Blazing in hand, the Litter catch'd.
The Wind impetuous, at West-Nor-West;
 The Door stood to the Wind, full breast . . .

Thatch'd Houses, to the Flames are now a Sport,
 Of Pow'r to scale the strongest Fort!
The underlings, of Covert all made bare;
 The loftier, next, assayled are.
Nor Arch, nor Buttress, for Stone-wall can fence
 The Structure from its insolence!
Here, tumbles down a Chimney; there, a Wall;
 Then, the whole Fabric, Roof and all.
The spattering Stones, in flakes, about the place,
 And Slats, spit Wild-fire in the face.
Beams, Tracings, Rafters tumble in, and Floor;
 Flames vomiting through every Door.
Each House of Stone a burning Oven, red,
 With its own Furniture is fed.
Who with devouring Fire can longer dwell?
 There to abide, would be an Hell.

Confusion such: the Eye not onely, here
 Is fill'd with Horrour, but the Ear!
Noise from one quarter, accented with Moans:
 Re-Echoes to another's Groans;
An Howling from a second; from a third
 Heart-piercing Cryes, and Shrieks are heard!
All Ears, the ratling Desolation fills,

As a great Crashing from the Hills!
The Foe the Field has won:–No Place for Fight
Is left us now;–nor yet for Flight.
By Ambuscade of Fire upon the Ground,
And Ruins, quite Beleaguer'd round.
Some weak Efforts, howe're; Before we'll yield;
He shall, by Inches, win the Field.

Help here:–a Ladder quickly:–yonders Hook:–
O:–quickly, quickly:–Sirs, for God-sake look:
The Fire has here but new now took.
Some Buckets there:–What are you Stocks,
or Stone!–
Some Water, quickly.–or the House is gone!
What!–the Pumps burnt!–No Water any where!–
Go stave the Hogs-heads;–fetch up Pails of
Beer!

Dash,–dash;–O quickly;–more yet;–one here!–
(I charge you stand your Ground)–another
there!
Five Pounds (good fellows) here, as a Reward,
To stand your Centry sure, and keep strict Guard.

The Fall and Funeral of Northampton, 1677

51. Centry. Sentry

JOHN ASKHAM
(1825–94)

John Askham, shoemaker and poet, lived in Wellingborough all his life. He was born on 25 July 1825, the youngest of a family of seven, only two of whom survived to adulthood. His father, also a shoemaker, was a native of Raunds; his mother of Kimbolton. He was educated at a Dame School and for a short time at Freeman's School before becoming apprenticed as a shoemaker. His work first appeared in print in the *Wellingborough Independent.* His contributions much impressed the editor of the *Northampton Mercury,* G. J. de Wilde (q.v.) who installed him as correspondent on the Wellingborough paper and became a firm friend. Later he became the Wellingborough correspondent to the *Northampton Herald* and other papers as well as holding a variety of posts in his native town. He co-founded the Wellingborough Literary Institute and became Librarian and Hall-Keeper when the institute was established in the newly-built Corn Exchange, whilst still continuing his trade as a shoemaker. In 1871, when the School Board was formed, he became a member and, in 1874, Attendance Officer. Between 1875 and 1887 he was the town's Sanitary Inspector. Illness forced him to retire from these occupations in 1887. After his first wife died in 1860 he married again, but suffered the deaths of two of his children in childhood. He died in 1894 and is buried in London Road Cemetery.

Askham published five volumes of poetry between 1863 and 1893 which show a wide range of interests. He has often been compared to John Clare, a poet whom he greatly admired, as his fine sonnet shows. The splendour of his poetry about nature and the countryside is all the more remarkable when it is realised that, unlike Clare, he had few opportunities to leave the town for truant wanderings in the field. Though no Chartist himself, he fervently believed in the rights of the working-man and was ever a champion of the labouring classes. One of his best 'social' poems is *The Singers*, whose ironic title refers, not to a group of vocalists, but to the firm of I. M. Singer and Co., the sewing-machine manufacturers.

To John Clare

Son of the Muses, Nature's favourite child,
Hushed are thy numbers, silent is thy song;
The sun of Poesy that on thee smiled
Is set in gloomy night: thy harp, unstrung,
Neglected hangs–its wonted music flown;
Reason, dethroned, hath fled her fair domain;
Thine eye hath lost its light, thy voice its tone;
Thy fire is quenched, thy mantle rent in twain;
Nature shall woo thee to her haunts no more –
The whispering woods, the softly-singing winds,
The brooklet's song, and all thou loved'st of yore,
In thy lorn breast no voice responsive finds.
Alas! we mourn thy fate, poor hapless Clare,
That such a night should follow morn so fair.

Sonnets on the Months, 1863

'The Singers'

The firm of I. M. Singers & Co. is a celebrated Establishment for the Manufacture of Sewing Machines, extensively used in the Shoe Uppers trade. (Author's note.)

Round and round, with monotonous sound,
Till rattle the windows, and shakes the ground,
Till the roof resounds, and the rafters ring
With the noisy chorus the 'Singers' sing.

With the opening day their songs begin–
Clatter, and clamour, and toil, and din–
You can scarcely hear your fellow speak–
From day to day, and from week to week.

By the mid-day sun and the evening lamp,
Reel and bobbin, and treadle and clamp,
Clamp and treadle, and bobbin and reel,
Of iron or brass, or polished steel,

Revolving round in their hempen bands,
Doing the work of a hundred hands;
While each shuttle is running its lightning race,
Like a prisoned slave, in its iron case.

To the foot responds each ready wheel,
As bounds the steed 'neath its rider's heel;
Only a touch, they are still again,
As a horse obeys the bridle rein.

Nought comes amiss to the 'Singers' brave:
They will toil for lordling, serf, or slave;
Stitching with needles sharp and fleet,
The bridal dress or the winding sheet;

The broadcloth coat of the wealthy 'Squire,
The peasant's garb, or the king's attire,
The raiment worn at the festival,
The pall of the pauper's funeral;

The judge's robe, and the felon's dress,
The garments of youth and loveliness,
The parson's vestments, the scholar's gown,
The homely smock of the rustic clown;

The shoon on the maiden's pretty feet,
As she daintily trippeth along the street,
By the merry slaves were deftly wrought;
And a thousand things beyond my thought.

A hasty meal, and once more to toil;
Brief halt, and again the wild turmoil:
A machine like them, though not of steel,
But with brain to think, and a heart to feel,

Perhaps your heart may no music own
In their rustling, restless monotone;
To your ear their voices may sweetness want,
And the songs they sing seem dissonant.

But to me there is harmony in their song,
As they clatter, and spin, and speed along:
You may deem them harsh, but their notes to me
Are sweet as the softest minstrelsy;

For why? Because in their every turn
Is a little of the bread we earn;
And the loaf would be small, and the hearthstone chill,
If the lays of the 'Singers' were hushed and still.

Round and round, with monotonous sound,
Till rattle the windows, and shakes the ground,
Till the roof resounds, and the rafters ring
With the noisy chorus the 'Singers' sing.

Descriptive Poems, 1866

The Mowers

When the farm-yard cock begins to crow,
Ere the red sun kisses the morning's brow,
The sturdy mowers go forth to mow.

The stalwart man and the stripling lithe,
Each bearing aloft his shining scythe,
Trudging along to a ditty blythe.

'Tis a sight to see them strip to their task,
And pass to each other the wooden flask,
Well filled last night from the master's cask.

The ring of their scythes is a sound to hear,
As they sharpen their blades so bright and clear,
Falling in harmony on the ear.

From end to end of the mead they pass,
And drops at their feet the yielding grass,
As falls to the sword an unarmed mass.

Toe to heel in the distance seen,
Cutting a road through the meadow green,
Moving as moves a true machine.

Far off you may see their figures white
As they wield with a will their weapons bright,
Slowly swaying from left to right.

From right to left, and the yielding swathe
Resistless falls in their onward path
As the foemen fall in the battle's wrath.

Over the nest where the callow young
Of the skylark lies the grass among
In regular file they sweep along,

Frighting the partridge away from its lair;
From its cosy form the timid hare;
Laying the nest of the corncrake bare;

Cutting the flags by the river side
As they wave to the gale in their summer
    pride,
And the flowers that lave in its silver tide.

As morning to the meridian grows
They wipe the sweat from their ruddy brows,
And seek in the shadow a brief repose.

Then, baring their brawny arms once more,
Traverse the meadow's velvet floor,
Sweating like rain at every pore.

When the evening shadows begin to grow,
Then with returning footsteps slow,
Homeward the weary mowers go.

Judith, 1868

WILLIAM BASSE
(1583–1653)

Basse presents a poser: was he Northampton-born or not? H. J. Massingham (*Seventeenth Century English Verse*, 317–8) says he was; *DNB* suggests Oxfordshire as his probable birthplace; his editor, Warwick Bond (*The Poetical Works of William Basse*, 1893) is non-committal. Bond gives the relevant facts. In Basse's Fourth Eclogue there is a passage which clearly refers to Northampton. Moreover it suggests that Basse himself was born and went to school there. Anthony à Wood, writing in 1636 (i.e. during Basse's lifetime) describes him as 'of Moreton, near Thame in Oxfordshire, sometime a retainer to the Lord Wenman of Thame Park.' (*Athen. Oxon.* ed. Bliss, IV.222.) Now the first Lady Wenman was daughter of Sir George Fermor of Easton Neston, a lady of much learning and some literary achievement. 'It is possible,' says Bond, 'that her attention had at some time been drawn to William Basse as a promising young scholar at the Northampton Free Grammar School and that on the occasion of her marriage with Sir Richard Wenman (c1596) the boy accompanied her to Thame Park in the capacity of a page.' Let us, for the sake of argument, agree. I for one detect a Northamptonian inflection of speech in *The Angler's Song*. The nature of his end remains shrouded in the same obscurity as his birth. He died, almost certainly, in 1653. He had prepared a collection of his pastorals for publication, marked 'Oxford 1653', but because of his death they did not reach the printed page until 1870.

Basse belongs to the Arcadian school of poets with William Brown, George Wither and the Fletchers, Giles and Phineas, whose 'pastor-figure' was Edmund Spenser. The fine economic sonnet on Shakespeare is untypical. *The Angler's Song* is more characteristic, delightfully combining sententiousness and naivety. It appears as one of the lyrics which intersperse Izaak Walton's *The Compleat Angler* (1653). In Chapter Five, Piscator says:

> 'I'll promise you I'll sing a song that was lately made at my request by Mr. William Basse . . . in praise of angling.'

Afterwards Coridon comments:

> 'Well sung, brother . . . We anglers are all beholden to the good man that made this song.'

Elegy on Mr. William Shakespeare

Renownëd Spenser, lie a thought more nigh
To learnëd Chaucer, and rare Beaumont lie
A little nearer Spenser, to make room
For Shakespeare in your threefold, fourfold tomb.
To lodge all four in one bed, make a shift
Until Doomsday, for hardly will a fift
Betwixt this day and that by Fate be slain,
For whom your curtains may be drawn again.
If your precedency in death doth bar
A fourth place in your sacred sepulchre,
Under this carvëd marble of thine own,
Sleep, rare tragedian, Shakespeare, sleep alone:
Thy unmolested peace, unsharëd cave
Possess as lord, not tenant of thy grave,
  That unto us and others it may be
  Honour hereafter to be laid by thee.

in Donne's Poems, 1633 (written c1620)

The Angler's Song

As inward love breeds outward talk,
The hounds some praise, and some the hawk,
Some, better pleased with private sport,
Use tennis, some a mistress court:
  But these delights I neither wish,
  Nor envy, while I freely fish.

Who hunts, doth oft in danger ride;
Who hawks, lures oft both far and wide;

Who uses games shall often prove
A loser; but who falls in love
Is fettered in fond Cupid's snare:
My angle breeds me no such care.

Of recreation there is none
So free as fishing is alone;
All other pastimes do no less
Than mind and body both possess:
My hand alone my work can do.
So I can fish and study too.

I care not, I, to fish in seas,
Fresh rivers best my mind do please,
Whose sweet calm course I contemplate,
And seek in life to imitate;
In civil bounds I fain would keep,
And for my past offences weep.

And when the timorous trout I wait
To take, and he devours my bait,
How poor a thing, sometimes I find,
Will captivate a greedy mind:
And when none bite, I praise the wise
Whom vain allurements ne'er surprise.

But yet, though while I fish, I fast,
I make good fortune my repast:
And thereunto my friend invite,
In whom I more than that, delight:
Who is more wellcome to my dish
Than to my angle was my fish.

As well content no prize to take,
As use of taken prize to make:
For so our Lord was pleasëd, when
He fishers made fishers of men;
Where, which is in no other game,
A man may fish and praise His name.

The first men that our Saviour dear
Did choose to wait upon Him here,
Blest fishers were, and fish the last
Food that He on earth did taste:
I therefore strive to follow those
Whom He to follow Him hath chose.

The Compleat Angler, 1653

DAUBRIDGCOURT BELCHIER

(1580?–1621)

Belchier was born at Guilsborough Hall, the eldest son of William Belchier and his wife Christian (nee Daubridgcourt). He was a fellow-commoner of Corpus Christi College, Oxford, 1597, and after that a student at Christ Church where he took his B.A. in 1600. He married Elizabeth, daughter of Richard Fisher of Warwick. Later he settled in the Low Countries and in 1617, when residing in Utrecht, wrote *Hans Beer-Pot, his Invisible Comedy of See me and See me not* (published London, 1618). This is thought to be a translation from the Dutch, but no original has been found and in the dedication it is distinctly described as an original production, that cost the author 'not above sixteen days' labour'. The title-page states that it was 'acted in the Low Countries by an honest Company of health-drinkers'. As the extract shows, Belchier possessed a quaint sense of humour as well as a mastery of versification. He died in Utrecht in 1621.

(The Confession)

Walking in a shady grove,
Near silver streams fair gliding,
Where trees in ranks did grace the banks,
And nymphs had their abiding;
Here as I stayed I saw a maid,
A beauteous lovely creature,
With angel's face and goddess grace,
Of such exceeding feature.

Her looks did so astonish me,
And set my heart a-quaking,
Like stag that gazed was I amazed,
And in a stranger taking.
Yet roused myself to see this elf,
And lo a tree did hide me;
Where I unseen beheld this queen
Awhile, ere she espied me.

Her voice was sweet melodiously,
She sung in perfect measure;
And thus she said with trickling tears;
'Alas, my joy, my treasure,
I'll be thy wife, or lose my life,
There's no man else shall have me;
If God so, I will say no,
Although a thousand crave me.

'Oh! stay not long, but come, my dear,
And knit our marriage knot;
Each hour a day, each month a year,
Thou knowest, I think, God wot.

THOMAS BELL. Bell's tombstone in Barnwell
St Andrew churchyard
[photo: Trevor Hold]

WILLIAM BOWLES, cleric-poet born at King's Sutton, posed for an excursion. (Note the rolled umbrella!) [National Portrait Gallery]

Delay not then, like worldly maiden,
Good works till withered age;
'Bove other things, the King of Kings
Blessed a lawful marriage.

'Thou art my choice, I constant am,
I mean to die unspotted;
With thee I'll live, for thee I love,
And keep my name unblotted.
A virtuous life in maid and wife,
The Spirit of God commends it;
Accursèd he for ever be,
That seeks with shame to offend it.'

With that she rose like nimble roe,
The tender grass scarce bending,
And left me then perplexed with fear
At this her sonnet's ending.
I thought to move this dame of love,
But she was gone already;
Wherefore I pray that those that stay
May find their loves as steady.

Hans Beer-Pot, his Invisible Comedy of
See me and See me not, 1618

THOMAS BELL
(1783?–1862)

Thomas Bell, schoolmaster, historian and poet, was born at Lynn in Norfolk but lived at Barnwell for most of his life, and Barnwell seems to have been the family home:

> 'In a village of this description, and in a cottage, endeared to his heart by family associations of more than a century and a half . . . the Author has spent the greater part of his life . . .'

Preface, The Rural Album

If his poem, *The Cadet*, is autobiographical, as it appears to be, the author joined the army (as a 'cadet') and sailed to India ('On distant plains, where duty led/By Ganges' sacred shore . . .'). Here he stayed for 'twice seven years and more . . .' On his return he married a local girl, Martha, seven years his junior, and ran a school in the village which he describes as 'a gentleman's boarding school' (*Whellan*, 1849), spending what spare time and energy he had left pursuing the Muses Clio and Terpsichore. The two were neatly brought together in his first, handsomely-produced publication, *The Ruins of Liveden* (1847). It is a valuable, pioneering work of historical scholarship, describing Sir Thomas Tresham's 'New Building', with chapters on the Manor and Tresham history, the Gunpowder Plot,

Rushton Papers, and Pilton Manor House. The book concludes with *Ruins of Lyveden*, 'a legendary poem' in twenty-five nine-line stanzas. In his introduction to the poem he refers to his book of verse, *The Rural Album*, which was ready to print, though 'prudence' (i.e. lack of money) prevented publication 'at least for the present'. It eventually appeared in 1853. It contains poems supplemented characteristically by historical notes, on Barnwell and its castle, Wadenhoe, Lilford, Fotheringhay and other places in the neighbourhood, as well as several personal poems. In 1856 he published his third and final book, *Winter Evenings at Home*, a kind of update of Cowper's *The Sofa:*

> 'I sing the Cottage now, and Cottage Scenes,
> And War and Victory on battle plains;
> Of Home, and Rural Walks, and Hunting Fields . . .'

As well as topical references, such as the Crimea War (lately fought), it includes some vivid rural descriptions: of the Milton Hunt (Book 3) and of Christmas celebrations (Book 10). He also wrote accounts of village histories for local directories, including Whellan's *History, Gazetteer and Directory of Northamptonshire* (1849) in which he himself is described as a 'local worthy'. He died on 30 January 1862, aged 79 years, and his tombstone stands in the churchyard of Barnwell St. Andrew. His house, a large eighteenth-century building, can still be seen: No. 8 Barnwell.

Bell's poetry shows that melancholic strain so typical of the post-Gray's *Elegy* generation of local poets. Life was hard: 'Hapless man was made to mourn.' It was the poet's job to do the mourning. But it rises above the average through its tangible subject-matter and Bell's skill in versifying. His moping owls and entangled ivy are 'real'; and in some poems, notably *The Village Schoolmaster*, he writes with passion and feeling engendered by bitter personal experience.

The Village Schoolmaster

Who is he, that pacing slowly
    Up and down the village green,
Folding arms, and thinking deeply,
    On a summer's eve is seen?
Winter's cold will find him seated,
    Musing by the glimm'ring light,
That, from half extinguish'd candle,
    Darker makes the gloom of night.
        With broken heart, and aching head,
        Toiling for his daily bread.

Bright the sun shone on his childhood,
    On his manhood fortune smil'd;
Friends abounded, honours courted,
    While the muse his hopes beguil'd.

Ere his harvest had been gather'd,
Storms arose to cloud the sky,
Leaving him with prospects blighted,
Here to weep and here to die.
Truly has the poet shown,
Hapless man was made to mourn.

Bent by age, by sorrows wasted,
Worn his frame, and dim his eye;
Threadbare garments plainly showing
What his frugal means supply.
Coarse his fare, and that but scanty;
From his fate too proud to shrink,
Bread his food, with little added,
Water from the spring his drink.
Hope extinguish'd in his breast,
Longing for eternal rest.

Such the luckless lot of many,
Doom'd to teach, and doom'd to toil;
Working harder, earlier, later,
Than the clown, that tills the soil.
'Tis not want that breaks the spirit;
'Tis not toil that sinks the heart;
But, to find his name forgotten,
Wings the shaft, and points the dart.
Is this true? the reader cries;
Too true, alas! the muse replies.

The Rural Album, 1853

SUSAN BOSTOCK

(1862–1948)

Susan Bostock was born in Northampton, the daughter of Frederick Bostock, the founder of one of Northampton's earliest shoe-manufacturing firms (1835). She contributed poems to the *Northampton and County Independent* and the *Northampton County Magazine* and published three volumes of verse: *Spring Notes and other poems* (1912), *The Call of the Uplands* (1913) and *The World of Heart's Delight* (1930). She was also a gifted artist and musician. She died at her home, 77 Knight's Lane, Kingsthorpe, in August 1948. Her poem, *A Yorkshire Mill Girl*, from her first collection, is reminiscent of similar 'social' poems of the period by Wilfrid Gibson and others.

A Yorkshire Mill Girl

You say she has a rugged face? Perhaps.
Too hard, scarce feminine enough? Ah, well,
Hers is a rugged life. Look at those hills,
A lurid darkening smoke for aye enwraps
Their barren sides, and may be (who can tell!)
Such cheerless gloom for aye her spirit fills.

God made this place a garden. Man has toiled
And turned it to a wilderness. I know
These quarries are a miracle of skill
And struggling labour. Nature has not foiled
A single effort. Every sturdy blow
Leaves here the impress of a human will.

Dost see those many mouths, all belching smoke?
They are the Mills. 'Tis here she spends her days
From early morn to evening's closing light.
Light, did I say! Alas, the sun scarce broke
Each dawn's fair cloud, ere quick the stifling haze
Descended like a dim eternal night.

It is an earnest face. Her shawl, close drawn
O'er head and shoulders, frames it like a hood
And shapes her upright figure. Stalwart, tall,
She walks with swinging stride. No timid fawn
My Mill girl. Still, I'll wager she is good
By that pure honest glance she turns on all.

Yet o'er her stern young life I fain would throw
One softening gleam of beauty. Bid her gaze
On Heaven's blue arch all glorious, undefiled;
On Earth, asmile with flowers, trees that grow
To all their bowery fulness. By sweet ways
I'd lead her on to know she is God's child.

What hidden tragedy within her eyes
Makes silent protest! Death will draw, some day,
His curtain o'er them. Will she wake at last
To welcome with a new and glad surprise
That other Life, that great eternal Day
Which fears no future, and which mourns no past?

Spring Notes, 1912

WILLIAM LISLE BOWLES

(1762–1850)

William Bowles ('Billy' to his family) was born at King's Sutton, where his father was vicar, in September 1762 and spent his early childhood there. In 1769 the family moved to Uphill, near Weston-super-Mare. He was educated at Westminster School (1776–81) and Trinity College, Oxford (1781), though he did not take his B.A. until 1792. In 1783 he won the Chancellor's Prize for Latin Verse with a poem *The Siege of Gibraltar.* After leaving Oxford he travelled much in the north of England and Scotland and abroad. He took holy orders, becoming first curate of Donhead St. Andrews, Wiltshire, and, from 1804 till his death, Vicar of Bremhill in Wiltshire. In 1804 he was appointed Honorary Canon of Salisbury Cathedral and in 1818 Chaplain to the Prince Regent. He lived for most of his later life at Salisbury. He married Magdalene Wake in 1797; she died early and there was no family. He himself died on 7 April 1850, aged 88.

As a writer he is best known for two publications. His *Fourteen Sonnets, written chiefly on Picturesque Spots during a Journey* (1789) is considered to be the forerunner of the romantic movement in English literature. It became very popular–nine editions by 1805 – and was much admired by Wordsworth, Coleridge and Southey. In 1807 he published a highly 'critical' edition of Pope's poetry which caused great controversy and angered Byron who defended Pope against Bowles' strictures. He was extremely prolific, publishing fourteen volumes of poetry between 1789 and 1837, which show an extraordinary range of subject-matter, historical and geographical. These include: *Banwell Hill* (1806); *The Missionary* (1815); *The Grave of the Last Saxon* (1822); and *The Villager's Verse-Book* (1829)–a selection of simple poetry 'to be learned by heart by poor children in my own parish'. He also published various antiquarian works and an autobiography, *Scenes and Shadows of Days Departed* (1837) which gives interesting particulars of his early life, though, disappointingly, nothing about his life at King's Sutton. His *Poetical Works* were edited in two volumes by Gilfillan in 1855.

The poems given below show different facets of Bowles' talent. *At Ostend* shows the romantic poet admired by Wordsworth and Coleridge. The bells referred to are those of Redcliff, Bristol. In a footnote in his autobiography he states:

> 'This [is] the first peal I remember to have heard in my life, (though the parish in which I drew breath, King's Sutton, in Northamptonshire, was distinguished for its musical peal) . . .'
>
> Scenes and Shadows (1837), xxv.

The extract from *Banwell Hill,* a wryly-humorous, Crabbe-like peep through the window of a villager's home, harks back to an earlier Augustan tradition.

At Ostend
July 22, 1787

How sweet the tuneful bells' responsive peal!
As when, at opening morn, the fragrant breeze
Breathes on the trembling sense of wan disease,
So piercing to my heart their force I feel!
And hark! with lessening cadence now they fall,
And now, along the white and level tide,
They fling their melancholy music wide;
Bidding me many a tender thought recall
Of summer days, and those delightful years
When by my native streams, in life's fair prime,
The mournful magic of their mingling chime
First wak'd my wond'ring childhood into tears
But seeming now, when all those days are o'er,
The sounds of joy once heard, and heard no more.

Fourteen Sonnets . . ., 1789

(A Villager's Home)

Enter: within see everything how neat!
One Book lies open on the window-seat,–
The spectacles are on a leaf of Job;
There, mark a map of the terrestrial globe;
And opposite, with its prolific stem,
The Christian's tree, and New Jerusalem;
Here, see a printed paper, to record
A veritable 'Letter from our Lord';
Two books are on the window-ledge beneath,–
The Book of Prayer, and Drelincourt on Death;
Some cowslips, in a cup of china placed,
A painted shelf above the chimney graced;
Grown, like its mistress, old, with half-shut eyes,
Save when, at times, awakened by wand'ring flies,
Tib in the sunshine of the casement lies . . .

from Banwell Hill, 1806;
Part 3, 'The Maiden's Curse'.

10. Drelincourt. Charles Drelincourt (1595-1669), French divine. The English translation of his *Consolations against the Fear of Death* (1651) was very popular in this country.

ANNE BRADSTREET

(1612?–72)

Anne Bradstreet was born in or near Northampton in 1612 or 1613, the daughter of Thomas Dudley of Yardley Hastings and Dorothy Yorke of Hardingstone. Her father was steward to the Earl of Lincoln. She married Simon Bradstreet, a nonconformist minister's son, in 1618 and in 1630 the two families, the Bradstreets and the Dudleys, emigrated with other leading Puritans to America. Her father and then her husband were Governors of the Massachusetts Bay Colony. They later moved to Ipswich and, in 1645, to Andover. Anne suffered much from ill-health in her girlhood and the move from 'civilised' England to primitive colonial America greatly upset her. The emotional stresses of emigration and settlement may well have been a contributory factor in her career as a writer. Her first volume of verse, *Several Poems*, was published in Boston in 1640 and reprinted in London (evidently without her consent) in 1650 under the title, *The Tenth Muse, Lately Sprung up in America*. She can therefore justly claim to be America's first English poet–and the first writer of any significance to come out of New England: always bearing in mind that she was born in Northampton, Old England.

Her poems are pious, often witty, but sometimes flawed in diction and poetic judgement. She is, as one critic has suggested, 'every other inch a poet'. She brought up eight children–'eight birds hatcht in one nest'–whilst her husband, whom she deeply loved, was away on public and private business. She battled with pregnancies, ill-health and misfortune, but continued to find time to write her poetry. When the family's house at Andover was burnt down on 10 July 1666, she wrote a poem *Upon the burning of our house*. She died at Andover in 1672. 'To my Dear and Loving Husband' is one of her finest and most anthologised poems. It was set to music by Leonard Bernstein in his *Songfest* (1976).

To My Dear and Loving Husband

If ever two were one, then surely we.
If ever man were loved by wife, then thee;
If ever wife were happy in a man,
Compare with me, ye women, if you can.
I prize thy love more than whole mines of gold,
Or all the riches that the East doth hold.
My love is such that rivers cannot quench,
Nor ought but love from thee, give recompense.
Thy love is such I can no way repay;
The heavens reward thee manifold I pray.
Then while we live, in love let's persever,
That when we live no more, we may live ever.

Inserted posthumously in 1678 edition of *Poems*.

In Memory of my Dear Grandchild Elizabeth Bradstreet, who deceased August, 1665, being a year and a half old

Farewell dear babe, my heart's too much content,
Farewell sweet babe, the pleasure of mine eye,
Farewell fair flower that for a space was lent,
Then ta'en away unto eternity.
Blest babe, why should I once bewail thy fate,
Or sigh thy days so soon were terminate,
Sith thou art settled in an everlasting state?

By nature trees do rot when they are grown,
And plums and apples thoroughly ripe do fall,
And corn and grass are in their season mown,
And time brings down what is both strong and tall.
But plants new set to be eradicate,
And buds new blown to have so short a date,
Is by His hand alone that guides nature and fate.

The Tenth Muse, 1678 edition

ANNE AND MARIA BROWN

(1837–58) (183?–1922)

Anne and Maria Brown were born at Pytchley, the daughters of Rev. Abner William Brown (1800–72). Brown, born in Jamaica of Scottish parents, was Vicar of Pytchley, 1832–51, and of Gretton, from 1851 until his death. He published several books, pamphlets and tracts on ecclesiastical and village matters, including *The History and Rules of a Village Horticultural Society at Pytchley, Northamptonshire* (1844) and *Village Provident Societies, Rules, tables, and history of the Provident Society established . . . for Pytchley, Isham, and Broughton . . .* (1850). In 1859 he printed, for private circulation, *Home Lyrics: Secular and Sacred. From a Country Parsonage.* It contained 241 poems, all anonymous. Ten years later he published an expanded edition (255 poems) illustrated with his own vignette tail-pieces and extensive notes, retitled *Lyrical Pieces Secular and Sacred. From the Home Circle of a Country Parsonage.* This time he revealed his editorship, but again left the poems anonymous, though he states in the Preface that the contents were written by not only himself but other members of his family. The greater number of the pieces 'are the work of a beloved daughter of the editor, cut off by epidemic fever in the prime of youth'. Fortunately the copy of *Home Lyrics* in the Northamptonshire Studies Collection at Northampton Central Library is extensively revised and annotated by A. W. Brown himself–probably incorporating revisions for the 1869 edition. It also identifies the authors of the poems by initials, revealing that Annie wrote 134, Maria 34 and Abner 70. Annie and Maria are jointly credited with *The Humble Petition.* Anne died in 1858 from typhus fever, aged twenty-one. Maria survived her parents, dying on 7 June 1922. She married Serocold Clarke Skeels (1840–1916) on 6 October 1863. He was her father's curate at Gretton (1869–72) and later Vicar of Abthorpe (1872–93).

A Humble Petition for Life from the Great Lime-Tree at the end of the Pytchley Avenues

Ah, ruthless lord of my unhappy fate!
How may I move thy hand to stay the steel?
How win thy heart to pause, ere yet too late,
And hear my woodland groans,–my anguish feel?

Once, long ago, when the wild thunders rolled,
And hurled their bolt against my stately head,
The guileless sheep that made my roots their fold
Were numbered in an instant with the dead.

Unscathed I braved that fierce, unheeding blast,
While fiery flashes hung on every bough;
Oh, must I die by cold, cold steel at last?
The lightnings spared my life–and wilt not thou?

Pause! Art thou sterner than the unpitying storm
Which scarred my stem, yet suffered me to live?
Turn thy death-glance from my majestic form,
And though my warrant's stamped, the respite give.

Beneath my widespread arms in childhood played
The patriarchs of the village, old and grey;
And now their children's children seek my shade,
And shake their golden ringlets as they play.

Much is my shade beloved, my beauties dear
To all the happy, peaceful, joyous flock,
Who from the quiet parsonage run here;–
O spare them, spare them, this all-dreaded shock!

Time was when some–now turned to churchyard
 clay–
Around my trunk, in innocent delight,
Would guileless sport, like lambkins at their play,
Or sing their hymns with infant faces bright.

Mourn, elder wanderer, often wont to stray
Under my branches, seeking cooler air;
And 'neath the fragrance of my honied spray,
Sit listening to the bees that murmur there.

The nightingale of summer sang its lay,
The cuckoo plumed its wing upon my bough;
When they return from bright climes far away,
Will they not ask, Where, where's our shelter now?

Howl, east wind, and exult in boisterous glee,
No longer shall my giant bulk avail
To check thy blasts which scowl across the lee,
Or guard the vista from thy withering gale.

Lord of my fate, come see me when in flower,
And from the burning sun thy head I'll shade;
Come, own the beauties of my scented bower:
Hast thou the heart to see me prostrate laid?

Dread of my fall with terror overwhelms
Those groves whose finish I was made to be;
That long-sequestered avenue of elms,
Whose leafy grandeur leads to nought but me.

The lordly sycamores, all, all are gone;
And must the lime-tree really, really fall?
Is its bright life for ever o'er and done?
The relic last of barons' ancient hall!

Come, even now, and let thine heart relent,
A tear-drop hangs upon my every bough;
My leafless branches droop, mine arms are bent,
The winds are sadly moaning o'er my brow.

O change thy mind! avert the threatened blow!
My leaves shall rustle thanks in every breeze;
Thy pity every bird of air shall know,
And grateful through my flowers shall hum the
bees.

Lyrical Pieces, 1869

Abner Brown, who edited *Lyrical Pieces*, supplied the following note: 'Pytchley Hall, in Northamptonshire, situated about 200 yards east-south-east of the church, was built in the early part of Elizabeth's reign, by Sir Eusebius Isham, who employed the same architect for it as Sir Christopher

Hatton had employed for Holdenby House. The house and estate passed successively through the families of Isham, Lane, Washbourne, and Knightley, until it became the property of Mr. Payne, of Sulby, by whom it was pulled down in 1829, the beautiful gateways, being, however, left standing. These last relics of its ancient beauty were removed (1843) by the late proprietor, Mr. Lloyd, to his park at Overstone, and a new-made line of village road now runs directly over the site of the old hall. The hall had ceased, since the middle of last century, to be a family residence, but was the club-house of the hunt. The magnificent and venerable lime-tree was kindly spared in compliance with the petition.'

ELIZABETH BROWN

(1809?–post 1842)

English literature has a long tradition of 'peasant' and 'cottage' poets, beginning with Stephen Duck (1705–56) and reaching its apogee with John Clare (1793–1864) (q.v.). Northamptonshire had its share of such 'primitives'. Clare and Mary Leapor (q.v.) rose above the condescending appelations, but to read many of them has an effect similar to watching circus-animals walking on their hind-legs: they do it, but very badly. One's attitude would be straightforward except that the poets exploited were themselves often convinced, beyond hope, that they possessed genius, which their published effusions sharply contradict. Whether they wrote for money or fame, the results are invariably awful or plain dull. Occasionally, however, one of these village bards is so excruciatingly bad that the results sink beyond the realms of bathos into the kingdom of McGonagall. Elizabeth Brown has been described as 'Northamptonshire's female McGonagall' and bids fair to be crowned the world's second best worst poet. Little is known of her life beyond the few fascinating hints she drops in her published poems. On the title-page she describes herself as a 'cottage girl of Woodend Northamptonshire'. The poems 'were wrote merely to chase away a dreary hour in my secluded cottage'. In the 1841 Census return she is aged thirty-two, residing at Southfields with George Brown (aged fifty-three, agricultural labourer: presumably her father). There is no record of either in the 1851 Census return. Her *Original Poetry* went into three editions (1839, 1841 and 1842). The first edition sold 2,500 copies in less than two years! The poem on Queen Victoria's Coronation is a fair sample of her versifying and typical of her subject-matter: royal events, odes to local worthies (including one to 'the County Historian', George Baker) and elegies on local demises.

from Lines on The Coronation of Her Most Gracious Majesty Queen Victoria

O Lovely Victoria, now in her bloom,
And was crown'd on the twenty-eighth day of June;
Rejoice, happy England! we truly may say,
For we're bless'd with a flower both blooming and gay.

Our true British Sceptre, oh, long may she sway,
And so bear the honor to her dying day,
Our Royal Elizabeth cherish'd no fears,
She govern'd the nation full forty-four years;
Her glory and triumph it was not in vain,
And she died in the forty-fifth year of her reign.
I hope long the sceptre she may bear in hand,
And govern in glory like eminent Anne,
And long may she live and prosper, and reign,
Then English rejoicing will not be in vain.
Oh! happy true Britons, how happy are we
To crown a young queen in her virginity!
From Buckingham Palace on that royal day,
The young royal virgin so blooming and gay,
To Westminster Abbey was shouted away.
They greeted the fair one, in love without fear,
And joyfully crown'd her–Victoria, dear:
The holy Archbishop devoutly then prayed;
The sword, orb, and sceptre, they gave her sway,
And blessed her sincerely on that royal day.
It was an affecting and true royal scene
To witness the gracious and virgin-crown'd Queen,
'Midst the blowing of trumpets and beating of drums,
The ringing of bells and the rattle of guns;
But true British voices were louder than all,
And blessed their Sovereign and loudly did call;
God save the Queen, with the English cry,
And many a tear drop fell from the eye.
I hope the dear maiden will reign without fear,
And long be the mistress of King Edward's chair;
True mercy and justice oh, may she extend,
And her true royal subjects justly defend! . . .

Original Poetry, 1839

GEORGE SPENCER CAUTLEY

(fl. 1829–69)

G. S. Cautley was educated at Pembroke College, Cambridge, where he took his B.A. in 1829 and later his M.A. After the death of the 2nd Marchioness of Northampton in 1830 (see Margaret Compton) he became the tutor to the Marquis' sons. In 1836 he was instituted Rector of Castle Ashby, a post he held on the understanding that he would relinquish it in favour of his erstwhile pupil, Alwyne Compton, when the latter qualified for the living (1852). Subsequently he was Vicar of Nettleden near Ashridge. In *A History of the Comptons* (1930), the 6th Marquis gives the following pen-portait of Cautley:

In outward appearance he was insignificant, almost a dwarf in stature, so that he had to stand on a stool to be able to see out of the pulpit, and he was slightly deformed and spoke with a voice harsh and unpleasant. But his face was beautiful, and all who met him soon forgot his voice and appearance in the presence of a personality of such strength and charm.

A History of the Comptons, 263

Two of his sonnets appeared in *The Tribute* (1837) (see Spencer Compton): *Grendon Church* and *Castle Ashby* (printed below). He also published two volumes of poetry: *The After-Glow* (1867) and *The Three Fountains* (1869).

Castle Ashby, Northamptonshire

Upon a green and sunny eminence
    Stands a fair castle, rear'd in those old days
    Which foster'd England with the stedfast blaze
Of her Elizabeth's magnificence.
No hanging bartizan proclaims defence,
    Nor thunder-throated cannon hath a place
    On flanking turret, or the curtain's space
Arcaded with Italia's elegance.
But, where grim battlements are wont to frown,
    The pious architect, with sculpture rare,
A psalm hath letter'd in the massive stone:
    The graven Scripture peoples the blest air
With holiest thoughts; these the eye calleth down
    To teach the heart security thro' prayer.

The Tribute, 1837

5. bartizan. Battlemented parapet.
11. The lettered parapet is dated 1624 and its inscription, from the 127th Psalm, runs as follows: NISI DOMINUS CUSTOS CUSTODIVERIT DOMUM FRUSTRA VIGILAT QUI CUSTODIT EAM: NISI DOMINUS AEDIFICAVERIT DOMUM IN VANUM LABORAVERUNT QUI AEDIFICANT EAM: 1624 ('Except the Lord build the house they but labour in vain that built it . . .')

HESTER CHAPONE
(1727–1801)

Hester Chapone was born at Twywell on 27 October 1727, the daughter of Thomas Mulso. Her maternal uncle, Rev. Dr. John Thomas, held successively the bishoprics of Peterborough, Salisbury and Winchester, and was Preceptor to George III. She was a precocious child; though given little encouragement in her education by her parents, she taught herself French, Italian, Latin, music and drawing to a high standard. She 'could sing exquisitely, and was skilful enough to sketch Miss Carter for

Richardson' (*DNB*). She began writing at an early age, and in 1750, at the age of twenty-three, embarked on a correspondence with the celebrated novelist, Samuel Richardson, whose friend and confidante she quickly became. Richardson called her his 'little spit-fire' and some of his friends considered that he might have used her as a model for female characters in *Sir Charles Grandison* (1754). In the same year that she formed her friendship with Richardson, Dr. Johnson published four contributions of hers in *The Rambler* (21 April 1750). During the next few years she became a prominent figure in London literary society and with Elizabeth Carter, Mary Delaney and Elizabeth Montagu was a leading member of the celebrated Blue Stocking Circle. In 1754 she met and fell in love with a London attorney named Chapone. For several years her father withheld his consent to their marriage and also that of his eldest son and heir, Thomas. Eventually he relented and the two couples were married on the same day, 30 December 1760. Hester's marriage, however, was short-lived – and some say 'not very happy'–for the shadowy Mr. Chapone died from a fever in the following September.

After her father's death in 1762, she continued to reside in lodgings in London but spent much of her time visiting friends and staying with relatives, particularly her second brother, John. It was to her niece, John's eldest daughter, that she addressed the work which brought her fame – *Letters on the Improvement of the Mind.* Encouraged by her friend Mrs. Montagu, she published this in 1773, at first anonymously. Within a year it had run to its third edition and was to remain a popular book for several decades. 'Fling *Peregrine Pickle* under the toilet – throw *Roderick Random* into the closet... Now lay *Mrs. Chapone* in sight,' says Lydia to her maid as Mrs. Malaprop and Sir Anthony Absolute are heard approaching, in Sheridan's *The Rivals* (1775). Her later years were overshadowed by illness, and the deaths in quick succession of her brother Thomas (1799) and youngest niece affected her deeply. In the last year of her life she moved with friends to Hadley where she died on Christmas Day 1801, aged 74.

As well as *Letters on the Improvement of the Mind,* she also published *Miscellanies in Prose and Verse* (1775). Her collected works, including a life and correspondence, were published in four volumes in 1807. Though poetry was the least of her literary accomplishments, *Miscellanies* contains several fine poems, including the following charming sonnet.

To a Robin-Redbreast

Dear social bird! that giv'st with fearless love
    Thy tender form to man's protecting care,
    Pleas'd, when rude tempests vex the ruffled air,
For the warm roof to leave the naked grove;

Kindest and last of Summer's tuneful train!
    Ah! do not yet give o'er thy Plaintive lay;
    But charm soft Zephyr to a longer stay,
And oft renew thy sweetly parting strain.

So when rough Winter frowns with brow severe,
And chilling blasts shall strip the shelt'ring trees,
When meagre Want thy shiv'ring frame shall seize,
And Death, with dart uplifted, hover near,
My grateful hand the lib'ral crumbs shall give,
My bosom warm thee, and my kiss revive.

Miscellanies in Prose and Verse, 1775

JOHN CLARE
(1793–1864)

John Dryden is the only Northamptonshire poet to have become Poet-Laureate; John Clare *is* Northamptonshire's Poet-Laureate. No writer before or since has managed to capture the *genius loci* of the county better than he. Yet, in his lifetime, he was branded 'The Northamptonshire Peasant-Poet', as though he were some kind of literary leper. He was at best condescended to, at worst sneered at (see *Memorials of Old Northamptonshire*, 1903, 228–9). Today the pendulum has adjusted itself and Clare takes his rightful place as one of the freshest, most original poets of the nineteenth century and one of the finest 'nature poets' ever.

He himself tells us that he was born 'on July 13, 1793, at Helpstone, a gloomy village in Northamptonshire, on the brink of the Lincolnshire fens'. He was the son of an impoverished farm-labourer, Parker, and his wife Ann (nee Stimson). His brief formal education took place locally and from the age of twelve he was variously employed as flail-thresher, horse-boy, plough-boy, under-gardener and limekiln-worker. He even enlisted in the Oundle Militia. From his early teens he began writing poetry on whatever scraps of paper were to hand: newspapers, magazines, discarded sugar-bags. His first surviving poem, *Helpstone*, is dated 1809. In his early twenties he was 'taken up' by the London publisher John Taylor and his partner Hessey and his first collection, *Poems Descriptive of Rural Life and Scenery* was published to great acclaim in 1820. Clare went to London where he met Charles Lamb and other well-known literary and artistic figures and was lionised by London literary society. This popular success did not last long. Subsequent publications, though containing better poetry, were commercial failures. He married Martha Turner ('Patty'), the daughter of a smallholder from Bridge Casterton, in March 1820 and she bore him eight children. Until 1832 they lived in his family's cottage at Helpston. In that year they moved to Northborough: only four miles from Helpston, but to Clare a world away. The move affected him badly. Already subject to intense moods of melancholy, his mind gave way and in 1837 he was admitted as insane to an asylum at High Beech, Essex. In 1841 he escaped, walking all the way home to Northamptonshire, but was once more certified as insane and spent the remaining twenty-two years of his life at Northampton General Asylum. Here he was well cared-for and given much freedom and wrote some of his finest poetry. He died at

Northampton on 20 May 1864, in the very week that the town was celebrating the opening of its new Town Hall, and was buried at Helpston.

A large number of poets, particularly 'local' poets, write about nature and the countryside. How does Clare differ from them? Firstly, in superior observation: he has a better eye; secondly, in superior poetic technique: he transmutes his observations into vivid language and memorable images. It is impossible to do Clare justice in an anthology such as this. I have therefore made a very personal choice of poems to give as wide an indication of his genius as possible. I have retained, or added, punctuation to the texts. The current practice of printing his poetry 'raw' seems to me to be an insult, in its way as condescending as his nineteenth-century critics. All poets are edited in some way by their publishers; why should Clare be excepted from this sensible service?

Remembrances

Summer's pleasures they are gone like to visions every one,
And the cloudy days of autumn and of winter cometh on.
I tried to call them back, but unbidden they are gone
Far away from heart and eye and forever far away.
Dear heart, and can it be that such raptures meet decay?
I thought them all eternal when by Langley Bush I lay,
I thought them joys eternal when I used to shout and play
On its bank at clink and bandy chock and taw and ducking stone,
Where silence sitteth now on the wild heath as her own
Like a ruin of the past all alone.

When I used to lie and sing by old Eastwell's boiling spring,
When I used to tie the willow boughs together for a swing,
And fish with crooked pins and thread and never catch a thing,
With heart just like a feather—now as heavy as a stone;
When beneath old Lea Close Oak I the bottom branches broke
To make our harvest cart like so many working folk,
And then to cut a straw at the brook to have a soak.
O I never dreamed of parting or that trouble had a sting,
Or that pleasures like a flock of birds would ever take to wing,
Leaving nothing but a little naked spring.

When jumping time away on old Crossberry way,
And eating awes like sugarplums ere they had lost the may,
And skipping like a leveret before the peep of day
On the roly poly up and down of pleasant Swordy Well,
When in Round Oak's narrow lane as the south got black again

We sought the hollow ash that was shelter from the rain,
With our pockets full of peas we had stolen from the grain;
How delicious was the dinner time on such a showery day!
O words are poor receipts for what time hath stole away,
The ancient pulpit trees and the play.

When for school o'er little field with its brook and wooden brig,
Where I swaggered like a man though I was not half so big,
While I held my little plough though 'twas but a willow twig,
And rove my team along made of nothing but a name,
'Gee hep' and 'hoit' and 'woi'–O I never call to mind
Those pleasant names of places but I leave a sigh behind,
While I see the little mouldiwarps hang sweeing to the wind
On the only aged willow that in all the field remains,
And nature hides her face while they're sweeing in their chains
And in a silent murmuring complains.

Here was commons for their hills where they seek for freedom still,
Though every common's gone and though traps are set to kill
The little homeless miners–O it turns my bosom chill
When I think of old Sneap Green, Puddock's Nook and Hilly Snow,
Where bramble bushes grew and the daisy gemmed in dew
And the hills of silken grass like to cushions to the view,
Where we threw the pismire crumbs when we'd nothing else to do,
And levelled like a desert by the never weary plough,
All banished like the sun where that cloud is passing now
And settled here for ever on its brow.

O I never thought that joys would run away from boys,
Or that boys should change their minds and forsake such summer joys;
But alack I never dreamed that the world had other toys
To petrify first feelings like the fable into stone,
Till I found the pleasure past and a winter come at last,
Then the fields were sudden bare and the sky got overcast
And boyhood's pleasing haunt like a blossom in the blast
Was shrivelled to a withered weed and trampled down and done,
Till vanished was the morning spring and set the summer sun
And winter fought her battle strife and won.

By Langley Bush I roam but the bush hath left its hill,
On Cowper Green I stray, 'tis a desert strange and chill,
And spreading Lea Close Oak, ere decay had penned its will,
To the axe of the spoiler and self-interest fell a prey,
And Crossberry Way and old Round Oak's narrow lane
With its hollow trees like pulpits I shall never see again.
Enclosure like a Buonaparte let not a thing remain,
It levelled every bush and tree and levelled every hill
And hung the moles for traitors; though the brook is running still
It runs a naked stream cold and chill.

O had I known as then joy had left the paths of men,
I had watched her night and day, be sure, and never slept again,
And when she turned to go, O I'd caught her mantle then,
And wooed her like a lover by my lonely side to stay;
Ay, knelt and worshipped on, as love in beauty's bower,
And clung upon her smiles as a bee upon a flower,
And gave her heart my poesies all cropt in a sunny hour,
As keepsakes and pledges all to never fade away;
But love never heeded to treasure up the may,
So it went the common road to decay.

Poems by John Clare, ed. Arthur Symons, 1908

6. Langley Bush. This, with the litany of other locations in the poem, was to be found in the vicinity of Clare's native Helpston. 8. clink, bandy chock, taw and ducking stone. Children's games played with marbles and stones. 22. awes. Haws. 37. mouldiwarps. Moles. 47. pismire. Ant.

Evening Schoolboys

Hark to that happy shout!—the school-house door
Is open thrown and out the younkers teem.
Some run to leapfrog on the rushy moor
And others dabble in the shallow stream,
Catching young fish and turning pebbles o'er
For mussel clams. Look, in that mellow gleam
Where the retiring sun that rests the while
Streams through the broken hedge! How happy seem
Those schoolboy friendships leaning o'er the stile,
Both reading in one book! Anon a dream,
Rich with new joys, doth their young hearts beguile,
And the book's pocketed most hastily.
Ah, happy boys, well may ye turn and smile
When joys are yours that never cost a sigh!

The Rural Muse, 1835

The Skylark

The rolls and harrows lie at rest beside
The battered road; and spreading far and wide
Above the russet clods, the corn is seen
Sprouting its spiry points of tender green,
Where squats the hare, to terrors wide awake,
Like some brown clod the harrows failed to break.
While 'neath the warm hedge, boys stray far from
home
To crop the early blossoms as they come,
Where buttercups will make them eager run,
Opening their golden caskets to the sun,
To see who shall be first to pluck the prize–
And from their hurry, up the skylark flies
And o'er her half-formed nest with happy wings
Winnows the air till in the clouds she sings,
Then hangs a dust spot in the sunny skies
And drops and drops till in her nest she lies,
Where boys unheeding pass–Ne'er dreaming then
That birds which flew so high would drop agen
To nests upon the ground where anything
May come at to destroy. Had they the wing
Like such a bird, themselves would be too proud
And build on nothing but a passing cloud.
As free from danger as the heavens are free
From pain and toil–there would they build and be,
And sail about the world to scenes unheard
Of and unseen–O, were they but a bird!
So think they while they listen to its song
And smile and fancy and so pass along;
While its low nest, moist with the dews of morn,
Lies safely with the leveret in the corn.

The Rural Muse, 1835

Clock-a-Clay*

In the cowslip peeps I lie,
Hidden from the buzzing fly,
While green grass beneath me lies
Pearled with dew like fishes' eyes.
Here I lie, a clock-a-clay,
Waiting for the time o' day.

While grassy forests quake surprise
And the wild wind sobs and sighs,
My gold home rocks as like to fall
On its pillar green and tall.
When the pattering rain drives by
Clock-a-clay keeps warm and dry.

Day by day and night by night
All the week I hide from sight;
In the cowslip peeps I lie,
In rain and dew still warm and dry,
Day and night and night and day,
Red, black-spotted clock-a-clay.

My home it shakes in wind and showers,
Pale green pillar topped withe flowers,
Bending at the wild wind's breath
Till I touch the grass beneath.
Here still I live, lone clock-a-clay,
Watching for the time of day.

Life and Remains of John Clare,
ed. J. L. Cherry, 1873

* Clock-a-Clay. Ladybird 1. peeps. Flower-heads

I Am

I am – yet what I am, none cares or knows;
My friends forsake me like a memory lost;
I am the self-consumer of my woes –
They rise and vanish in oblivious host,
Like shadows in love, frenzied stifled throes,
And yet I am, and live like vapours tost.

Into the nothingness of scorn and noise,
Into the living sea of waking dreams,
Where there is neither sense of life or joys,
But the vast shipwreck of my life's esteems;
Even the dearest that I love the best
Are strange–nay, rather, stranger than the rest.

I long for scenes where man hath never trod,
A place where woman never smiled or wept,
There to abide with my Creator, God,
And sleep as I in childhood sweetly slept,
Untroubling and untroubled where I lie,
The grass below–above, the vaulted sky.

The Life of John Clare, by F. Martin, 1865

JOHN COLES and JOSEPH FURNISS, Snr.

(1775–post 1841) (1783–post 1841)

John Coles and Joseph Furniss were members of that small but extensive brotherhood of 'peasant poets' that flourished in Northamptonshire during the eighteenth and nineteenth centuries, of whom Mary Leapor (q.v.) and John Clare (q.v.) were the outstanding figures. They usually published, locally, one slim volume of verse, invariably prefaced with a degradingly humble *apologia*. Little is known of their lives and they quickly faded into oblivion. The facts known about John Coles and Joseph Furniss can quickly be stated. Both were born at Weedon Lois, Coles in 1775 (baptised 19 November), the son of John and Hannah; Furniss in 1783 (baptised 18 April), the son of Richard and Jane. In 1811 they jointly published *Poems Moral and Religious*, dedicated to 'Lieutenant-Colonel Commandant Clarke and the officers of the West Northamptonshire Local Militia'; Clarke himself subscribed for six copies. In their preface they state:

> 'We are plain unlettered men; having never received the advantages of an education . . . from our childhood to the present time we have been under the necessity of labouring hard for our daily support . . .'

It is evident from Coles' *Address to the Readers* (see below) that they were shoemakers by trade. They signed their poems respectively 'C' and 'F'.

In a dedicatory poem 'To Mr. John Coles', William Chown, a schoolmaster-poet from Moulton (see Appendix A) writes:

> 'Shall Weedon once again uplift its head,
> Since WEST, the musical sweet bard is dead?'

The allusion was to the late Benjamin West (q.v.) For a schoolmaster, Chown's knowledge of local geography was hazy: West lived and died at Weedon Beck; Weedon Lois is eight miles and several villages away. The connection with West, however, is by no means fortuitous. *Poems Moral and Religious* contains an elegy on the death of Benjamin's son (also Benjamin) who died on 30 June 1809 aged thirty. Moreover Joseph Furniss subsequently married a daughter of Benjamin West senior and *their* son, Joseph Furniss junior (b. 1821) produced a slim volume of verse, *Miscellaneous Poems*, in 1841, to which Coles supplied a prefatory poem. Thus we have a dynasty of rural poets:

Benjamin West, Snr. (Weedon Beck)
|
Joseph Furniss, Snr. (Weedon Lois) = daughter
co-author with John
Coles (Weedon Lois) who
contributed a poem to
Miscellaneous Poems by — Joseph Furniss. Jnr. (Weedon Lois)

I have found no further references to the careers of these two men. Both were alive in 1841 — Coles' prefatory poem to *Miscellaneous Poems* states that Joseph Snr. 'is now living'. The 1841 Census returns for Weedon Lois records 'John Coles, aged 64, agricultural labourer and Hannah, his wife, aged 61'. This could be our John with a changed job. Joseph Jnr. 'aged 20, agricultural labourer' is also there, but there is no mention of his father.

Address to the Readers

Ye sons of learning and of taste,
To whom this work may fall,
Pardon my leaving this my Last,
My Hammer, Knife, and Awl.

Unknown I am to public schools,
Where science takes its seat;
Nor understand their forms and rules,
Which lead to learning sweet.

In narrow cell confin'd I spend
My days in joy and peace;
I new Shoes make and old ones mend,
My customers to please.

Yet when I from my Thread and Wax
Can spare an hour or two;
And from all cares my mind relax,
The Muses still I woo.

With Crispin's sons thus let me join,
Who have before my time
Invoked the sacred tuneful nine
To aid the flowing rhyme.

No florid language I impart,
No sparkling wit here shines,
No charms to captivate the heart
In these our humble lines.

But in our work I hope you'll find,
Tho' like a mended Shoe,
Some thoughts that may amuse your mind,
And thus 'tis left to you.

Poems, Moral and Religious, 1811

24. Coles is addressing the reader on behalf of himself and his co-author, Joseph Furniss.

MARGARET COMPTON

(1791–1830)

Margaret Compton, the eldest daughter of Major-General Douglas-Maclean-Clephane and god-daughter of Sir Walter Scott, was born at Kirkness on 13 December 1791. From the age of eight she lived at Torloisk on the Isle of Mull. She married Spencer Compton, later 2nd Marquis of Northampton (q.v.), on 24 June 1815 and bore him six children: four sons and two daughters. The eldest, Charles became 3rd Marquis on the death of his father in 1851. The youngest son, Alwyne, was Rector of Castle Ashby, 1852-79. For many years the Comptons lived in Italy and Margaret died in Rome on 2 April 1830, a few weeks after the premature birth of her daughter Margaret. She is buried at Castle Ashby.

Margaret Compton was a remarkable lady – 'one of the most amiable and distinguished of women', as *The Times* obituary of Spencer Compton observed. She spoke French, Italian and Portuguese as well as English and her native Gaelic, was a good musician – Raeburn's portrait (1813) hanging at Castle Ashby shows her singing and accompanying herself at the harp – and an accomplished artist – Tenerani's monument (1836) in Castle Ashby church incorporates an artist's palette and brushes in its design as well as music manuscript and books. She held highly liberal ideas and was a supporter of Wilberforce. *Irene, a poem, in six cantos,* edited by her husband, was privately printed in London in 1833. As well as the title poem (written June 1814) it contains lyrics and several translations from the Gaelic, German (Goethe and Uhland) and Italian (Petrarch). Wordsworth, acknowledging the present of a copy, wrote: 'They are written with simplicity, pathos and energy.' Three further poems were included by the Marquis in his anthology *The Tribute* (1837).

The two stanzas from *Irene* give us a rare glimpse of her personal feelings. She must have met that 'civil county neighbour' in the wilds of Mull before her marriage. The translation of the Gaelic song, 'Ge Fada Mo Choiseachd', reminds us that she would delight family and friends by singing her native folksongs to the harp in her Castle Ashby home.

from Irene

(A County Neighbour)

Parting is ill to bear–ev'n when we leave
Some town or city on a distant shore,
The heart flies back a moment's space to grieve,
And sighs to hear the knell of Never more!
And those indifferent and ne'er priz'd before
Excite the wish on earth again to meet,
With one exception only;–that fell bore
Who seizes on you in your last retreat–
A civil county neighbour, in your country seat.

Who stuns you with the talk of bullocks, till
You wish with all your soul that he were one,
That you might turn him out to graze his fill,
And leave you with your thoughts, in peace alone;
Or preaches upon turnpikes, one by one
Thrumming them o'er, till from his mouth you'd swear
Fly bushels of dry dust and lumps of stone,
While in your heart you curse them in despair,
And, chief of all, the one which serv'd to bring him there.

From Canto IV,
Irene, 1833

Translation of the Gaelic Song

'Ge Fada Mo Choiseachd'

Now sinks the wild combat to silence and rest,
And the field by the dead and the dying is prest,
Where, mid the sad relics of slaughter I lie,
And the corpse of my friend and companion is nigh.

O love of the fair, and delight of the wise,
Hast thou fall'n in thy vigour, no more to arise?–
Loud, loud, the lament that thy people will spread
When they hear their young chieftain in battle is dead.

And mine will lament when their leader they see
With a crutch in that hand where a broad-sword
should be.
When Slàtan's high steep I gaze wistfully o'er,
And sigh for the strength that shall aid me no more.

The spoiler came past, and no mercy had he,
And the night-breeze is cold on the wound in my knee,
But though smarting and chill,–and so dark the nightfall,
To see thee lie slaughtered, is keener than all.

ibid.

SPENCER COMPTON
2nd Marquis of Northampton
(1790–1851)

Spencer Compton was born 2 January 1790 at Erle Stoke, Wiltshire (the maternal home), the second and eldest surviving son of Charles and Maria Compton. He married Margaret Douglas-Maclean-Clephane (see

ANNE BRADSTREET, 'America's first English poet', who was born in Northampton in 1612. Detail from a window in St Botolph's church, Boston, Lincolnshire

JOHN CLARE'S birthplace at Helpston

(No. 14.)

Northamptonshire

Local Militia.

County of Northampton, } TO WIT. *To* John Clare —
Subdivision of Peterboro. } *of the* Parish *of* ~~Maxey~~ Helpstone *in the said County and Subdivision.*

IN pursuance of an Act of Parliament passed in the 52d year of his present Majesty's reign, intituled, "An Act for amending the Laws "relating to the Local Militia in England;" and of all and every other Act and Acts of Parliament now in force and relating to the said Militia, and also in pursuance of a warrant to me for that purpose directed, I do hereby give you notice, that you are required to appear personally on the Market-place, in the town of Oundle — in the said county, on Friday. - - - the twenty eighth — day of May — by nine of the clock in the forenoon, in order to be trained and exercised under the directions and regulations of the said first-mentioned Act, for the space of fourteen entire days, exclusive of the days of arriving at and departure from, and marching to and from the place appointed for exercise. And I do further give you notice, that if (not labouring under any infirmity incapacitating you) you shall not appear at the time and place aforesaid, you will be deemed a deserter, and if not taken until after the time of such exercise, you will be liable to forfeit and pay the sum of £20. And if after having joined your regiment, or any company or companies, or detachment or division thereof, you shall desert or absent yourself during the time of exercise, and shall not be taken until after the time of such exercise, you will be liable to forfeit and pay the sum of £20. And if such penalty shall not be immediately paid, the Justice of the Peace before whom you shall be convicted of such offence, will commit you to the house of correction to hard labour, or to the common gaol of the county, there to remain without bail or mainprise for any space not exceeding three months, and not less than fourteen days, or until you shall have paid the said penalty. And I do further give you notice, that no person will have leave of absence during the period of assembly, except in cases of the most urgent necessity.

Given under my hand the 15 — day of May in the year of our Lord one thousand eight hundred and 13

Thos. Sherritt } *Constable of the* parish *of* Maxey *aforesaid.*

Notice from the Maxey parish constable requiring Clare to appear personally at the Market-place, Oundle, on Friday, 28 May 1813, to be trained for the Northamptonshire Local Militia.

JOHN CLARE. The solitary figure of John Clare, Northamptonshire's 'Peasant Poet', in the portico of All Saints Church, Northampton, 1848. In 1841 Clare had become an inmate, though free to visit Northampton, of the 'General Lunatic Hospital and Asylum' off Billing Road, Northampton. (Water-colour by George Maine)

Margaret Compton) in 1815. He was Independent Tory M.P. for Northampton, 1812–20, losing his seat 'through neglect to show proper gratitude after the 1812 Election to those who had voted for him' (*History of the Comptons*). When he succeeded his father as 2nd Marquis of Northampton in 1828, he sat in the House of Lords as a Whig peer. He was a distinguished scientist, President of the Royal Society (1838–48) and of many other learned and cultural bodies. He was also a poet of no mean ability. In 1837 he edited *The Tribute: a collection of Miscellaneous Unpublished Poems, by Various Authors* in aid of the family of the late Rev. Edward Smedley. The Marquis managed to persuade a remarkable group of people to contribute, including Southey (then Poet-Laurate), Wordsworth and Tennyson (both future Poets-Laureate), Bowles (q.v.), Darley, Landor, Moore and Spring Rice (the then Chancellor of the Exchequer). Of the contributions, Tennyson's is possibly the most important. His lyric, *O that 'twere possible,* was to form the basis, eighteen years later, of *Maud.* Compton included three unpublished poems by his late wife and ten poems of his own, of which the following fable, with its strong local connections, is a lively example.

Cowper's Oak and the Emperor Butterfly

A FABLE

A Butterfly one summer's day
Sat on an old oak's topmost spray–
A Butterfly that but of late
Had left the chrysalis's state:
Emerging from that narrow room
Of sloop, imprisonment, and gloom,
For a brief space he flutters round,
Then settles on the verdant ground:
About impertinently stares,
And gives himself most mighty airs.
Ungrateful to his foster oak,
At length contemptuously he spoke:

'Huge mass of dingy brown and green,
Thou ugliest tree that e'er was seen!
With those gaunt arms that white and bare
Thou raisest to the ambient air,
Like mendicant whose shrivell'd limb
Brings many a pity's dole to him:
Thy trunk as hollow to my eye
As pride combined with Poverty:

Thy foliage thin and poor, and then
Upon thy side that frightful wen!
I wonder what could make my mother
Prefer thy oakship to another?
When round and near is to be seen
So many a tree, young, straight and green,
I cannot think the reason why–
I do not need a foil–not I–
The peacock's plumage bright may shine,
Yet it might serve as foil to mine!
My wings are form'd to soar on high
And emulate the azure sky!'

Though oaks are not thin-skinn'd, we know,
A proper feeling yet they show,
As much as any other tree,
When treated with indignity–
So gravely thus our oak replied:–
'Gay insect, full of idle pride,
Ungrateful dost thou scoff at me
Whose leaves have fed thine infancy?
Whose boughs protected thy weak form
From piercing wind and angry storm?
Ugly thou say'st I am, and old–
And yet, if truth is to be told,
Art here has spent full many a day
To bear my lineaments away.
Thou art an Emperor–idle name!
Thy purple robes thy rank proclaim–
Alone proclaim!–Thine empire, where?
In earth, in ocean, or in air?
The eagle rules the liquid sky;
Wilt *thou* dispute his sovereignty?
The lion reigns through Afric's groves,
Where panther, leopard, tiger roves.
The whale, whose power no fish can brave,
Is autocrat in every wave;
While aged oaks with giant stem,
Upraise their leafy diadem:
Oaks that for centuries have stood
The mighty monarchs of the wood:
Then give–no idle boast and vain–
To man his empire o'er the main.

Poor insect, though thy hue be gay,
Perhaps a week, perhaps a day,
Thou'lt live–a few miles round to soar,
Then fall, thy little being o'er–
While aged oaks, as ships, shall ride
In triumph o'er the bounding tide,
And, wing'd with sails, shall treasure bear,
To distant ports from regions fair,
Where'er the foaming billows roll,
From East to West, from Pole to Pole!
Thy mother–dost thou ask why she
Did not as cradle choose for thee,
Some younger, straighter, greener tree?
Alas! I speak with ruth and sorrow,
They all may be cut down tomorrow.
A mighty bard has giv'n to me
From woodman's axe immunity;
A Poet, of far different school,
Has turn'd thee into ridicule,
As making a wise man a fool!
To boast of Cowper's praise is mine–
To wince at Wolcot's lash is thine!
Go!–I forgive thee–off–away–
Enjoy thy very little day;
Ere yet thy fleeting course be run,
Show thy bright colours to the sun,
Sport in his beam from flower to flower–
Soon o'er thine eyes death's cloud shall
lour–
An age is but to me as is to thee an hour!'

The Tribute, 1837

78. The 'mighty bard' is William Cowper (1731–1800) whose oak-tree, commemorated in his poem, *Yardley Oak* (1791; publ. 1804), is speaking.
84. Wolcot. John Wolcot (1738–1819) was a satirist who wrote under the pseudonym 'Peter Pindar'. His sixty or seventy verse pamphlets (1778–1818) include *The Lousiad, Whitebread's Brewery visited by their Majesties* and *Lyrical Odes* on the Royal Academy Exhibitions.

EDWARD DANIELL
(c1790–post 1860)

It is not often that a person gaoled and tried for murder appears in a poetry anthology. Indeed the facts we have of Edward Daniell's life would supply a good plot for a Victorian melodramatic novel.

Daniell was born in or near Uppingham in about 1790. He was residing in London as a medical student during the winter of 1812–13. By 1817 he was living in Weldon and signing himself 'Edward Daniell, Surgeon'. It was in this year that he was gaoled for ten weeks at Northampton Assizes for murder. In his poem, *The Gaol*, 'written in confinement' and published in the same year, he explains the events leading to this drastic situation. He had made one of his maidservants pregnant. He tried unsuccessfully to persuade her to leave his house and go to London. She gave birth prematurely to a daughter who lived for only a few hours, despite 'every requisite and facility being supplied'. Afterwards the girl continued a month at his house before at last being prevailed upon to leave. In order to clear his name of ill-natured gossip, Daniell applied to a neighbouring magistrate who at first appeared sufficiently satisfied of his innocence, but at the same time advised Daniell to leave the country to avoid recriminations. Daniell refused. A year-and-a-half later, the ex-maid and her friends began blackmailing him, threatening a prosecution for murder upon non-compliance. Daniell refused their demand and they carried out their threats. Ironically the very magistrate to whom he had made his previous application was the person who committed him to prison, where he languished for ten weeks. He was subsequently arraigned and honourably acquitted. (The *Northampton Mercury* briefly reports the proceedings in its issues of 12 and 19 July 1817.) He expressed his gratitude 'to the gentlemen composing the grand and petty jury at Northampton Assizes, July 1817' by dedicating *The Gaol* to them:

> 'Believe me, Gentlemen, I shall ever associate with your names the most profound sentiments of gratitude, as being the means of Providence to rescue me from the designs of the most cruel conspirators that ever disgraced the human form.'

He showed great courage by returning to his practice at Weldon and was still there in 1824 when he published *The Woodland Muse*. His subscribers included several Rutland and Leicestershire people and Rev. Talbot Keene of Brigstock (q.v.) to whom he addressed a *Poetical Epistle*. By 1842 he appears to be living in or near Newport Pagnell where he was active with the local Lodge of the Oddfellows Friendly Society. He was still alive in 1860 when he published a 'monody' on the death of a Newport Pagnell vicar; but I have no further information on this fascinating man.

That he was fairly headstrong by temperament is evident from the provocative preface he wrote for *The Woodland Muse*. He is explaining why he has not supplied the usual 'dedication':

> '. . . it generally happens that the Author stumbles upon that 'rara avis in terris' – a noble, generous, and enlightened patron' . . . Now, though we have examined the country round, and even ransacked the County Calendar, we really have not ourselves been able to meet with any, answering to the description above stated . . .'

As well as poetry, *The Woodland Muse* contains several prose works, including two autobiographical pieces (*Early Recollections* tantalisingly gives no hint as to *where* he was born, though the village now (1824) has a 'Greyhound' inn-sign in place of a 'Malt Shovel') and concludes with *The Club-Night: or Master Anthony Snipe's Last Visit in London: a series of Comic*

Tales, Songs, Bon Mots, and Pieces of Humor . . .' very much in the style of Tom Hood. Of the poems, the finest is the first: *Woodland Scenes*, in two parts: *A Morning's Ramble* and *The Fox Chase*. I quote from the latter, a fine, early example of an anti-foxhunting poem.

from Woodland Scenes

PART II. THE FOX CHASE

See where yon verdant coppice blooming smiles,
And matted furze impedes the cautious tread,
There in his secret haunt the cunning fox
In hidden ambush lies. But hark! the horn
Thrills through the air and vibrates far and wide;
While dale and thicket echo back the sound
In many a hollow strain, that fearful strikes
Upon the watchful reynard, who, appall'd,
Sneaks from the shade, and rushes from pursuit.
And now the dreaded tempest hath begun:
For lo! the treacherous foot betrays the prey;
And loud and long the boisterous shout resounds,
While the hoarse barking of the hostile foe
Joins in the huntsman's bawl.

The prancing steed
Elated by the sound, now snorts along,
Bearing his joyous rider with a pride
And pleasure equal to his own—proud beast!
Nor gate nor ditch impede his bounding pace.
Up flies the loosen'd turf, nor bogs arrest
The breathless courser in his ample flight;
Now see the vaulter leaps the towering hedge;
Nor heeds the foaming rivulet that rolls
Its swelling stream along the winding vale.
Deep in its bosom boldly doth he plunge,
Nor fears to buffet with the rapid stream:
The bank he gains, and as the arrow flies
Shot by the archer's strong and nervous arm,
Through the vast trackless region of the air—
So bounds the willing steed in hot pursuit.
Meantime, the skulking object of this rage
Seeks every hidden hole for safe retreat;
Fear nerves his strength, and terror fleets his limbs,
High o'er the hill and down the dale he flies!

But still the knell of death pursues him on,
Till panting and exhausted by the chase,
He dares the dreaded phalanx for awhile–
Contends–and sinks a victim in their jaws!
And where, ye sporting heroes of the age,
Ye friends of Dian, vot'ries of the chase–
Where is the mighty triumph of the deed?
There lies your arrant foe, a bleeding corse;
And all the raving uproar of the day,
The noise and tumult of contending lungs,
Was to obtain the mean ignoble death
Of a defenceless victim such as this!
To him the chance of combat you deny,
Since an unequal legion you produce
Of hardy veterans, 'gainst an ill-train'd foe.
Vain waste of time! too useless the pursuit,
Such soul-absorb'd attention to employ,
Such breathless speed, and energy untold,
Thus lost and wasted on a worthless cause.
Much nobler would it be for gifted man
To choose a path more suited to his powers,
More fitting for his high exalted state
Of intellectual supremacy,
The lord and monarch of created things . . .

The Woodland Muse, 1824

GEORGE JAMES DE WILDE
(1804–71)

G. J. De Wilde, though not born in the town, became one of Northampton's most honoured and respected inhabitants. (See the poetic tribute to De Wilde, *Est Qui*, by Christopher Hughes on p. 91.) He was born in London 19 January 1804 into a family of Dutch origin. His father was a very talented painter specialising in theatre scenes and personalities, and G.J. was himself destined for the same profession. Whilst living in London he became acquainted with literary society of the day. For a short time he was employed in the Colonial Office but in 1830 (at the precocious age of twenty-six) he was appointed editor of the *Northampton Mercury*. He held this position to the day of his death, 16 September 1871, a remarkable tenure of forty-one years. A few hours before his death, he corrected the proof-sheets of the forthcoming number of the *Mercury*. His liberal and humane outlook is nowhere more evident than in his long and detailed appreciations of the life and achievements of John Clare, both in *Rambles Roundabout* and the *Northampton Mercury* obituary. He married twice: in 1825 to Mary Butterworth who died in 1841 leaving him a widower with five children, and again in 1845 to Miss Packer by whom he had one daughter, Edith, who married the architect Matthew Holding.

Except for short holiday rambles in the summer—the inspiration for *Rambles Roundabout*—he never left Northampton for any length of time. The contents of *Rambles Roundabout and Poems* had been published in the *Northampton Mercury* over many years and were edited with a prefatory memoir by Edward Dicey after De Wilde's death. There are twenty-five poems amongst the prose pieces, of which the following sonnet on *Eydon Hall* is a fine and characteristic example.

Eydon Hall*

Vert alleys with trim trees arching o'erhead,
And ending in a vista of blue hills,
Statue, or vase, or nook where grottoes' rills,
Trickling from stone to stone, clear coolness shed;
Elsewhere a pleasance, with quaint patterns spread
Of rarest flowers; an orangery that fills
The air with that sweet odour which distils
From Lisbon or the Azores, seaward led.
There needs but laughter from the shrubberies
coming,
Ladies and rustling silks, a gorgeous show,
And mantled cavaliers chitarras strumming
Of whispered love in willing ears;—and lo!
A picture by Lancret or by Watteau,
Or tale recorded by Boccaccio.

Rambles Roundabout, 1872

*The seat of the Rev. C. F. Annesley when this Sonnet was written; now occupied by Colonel Henry Cartwright. (Author's note.)

PHILIP DODDRIDGE
(1702–51)

Philip Doddridge, minister, teacher and hymn-writer, was born in London on 26 June 1702, of Devonshire gentry stock. His father was a trader in oils and pickles, which gives the opening line of his son's epigram on the family arms, 'Dum Vivimus Vivamus' (considered by Dr. Johnson to be 'one of the finest epigrams in the English language') an ironic ring for pickle-eaters today:

'Live while you live,' the Epicure would say,
'And seize the pleasures of the present day.'
'Live while you live,' the sacred Preacher cries,
'And give to God each moment as it flies.'
Lord, in my views let both united be;
I live in pleasure, when I live to Thee.

Miscellaneous Pieces of Poetry (Edinburgh, 1765)

He lost both parents in childhood and of his nineteen brothers and sisters–all older–only one, Elizabeth, survived into adult life. After schooling in St. Albans, he moved in 1719 to Kibworth Harcourt, Leicestershire, to train for the dissenting ministry with a local minister, John Jennings. When Jennings left three years later, Doddridge succeeded him. In 1729 he moved to Northampton where he was minister at Castle Hill Congregational Chapel (the oldest nonconformist chapel in the town, built in 1695) till his death. He married Mercy Maris in December 1730 and in the same year moved his dissenting academy from Kibworth, first to Marefair and then to the Earl of Halifax's town house in Sheep Street, where part of the building (marked by a plaque) still stands. In addition he was co-founder with Dr. John Stonhouse (see Mark Akenside) of the town's first Infirmary (now the General Hospital) in 1744 and was an active member of the Northampton Philosophical Society, founded in 1743. In 1736 he was awarded an Honorary D.D. by University College, Aberdeen. He died in Lisbon where he had gone for his health, in October 1751, and is buried in the Protestant cemetery there.

Doddridge's contributions to spiritual, educational, cultural and welfare activities in his adopted town were incalculable, but it is as a hymn-writer that he is universally remembered today. With Isaac Watts (1674–1748) he is one of the two great hymn-(text)-writers of the older dissent. Hymn-singing was only just beginning to be accepted by dissenting churches at the time. Doddridge's technique was to summarise his sermons in hymn-form in order to drive home their message. He wrote nearly 400 hymns, several of them still sung in churches today, including *Hark the glad sound, Awake my Soul* and *O God of Jacob.* The first edition of these hymns appeared after his death, collected and published by his friend Job Orton in 1755. It ran into several editions. The example chosen, *Hark the glad sound,* is familiarly sung to the tune 'Bristol' (*Ravenscroft Psalter,* 1621). Doddridge was by no means the solemn-sides that his 'official' publications would suggest and his letters show a quite different side to his personality. The charming piece of doggerel is taken from a letter to his wife, dated 26 January 1742/3. He had been to Creaton to see her newly-married cousin, Benjamin Perkins.

Christ's Message

LUKE IV. 18,19

Hark the glad sound! the Saviour comes!
The Saviour promis'd long!
Let ev'ry heart prepare a throne,
And ev'ry voice a song.

On Him the Spirit largely pour'd
Exerts its sacred fire;
Wisdom and Might, and Zeal and Love
His holy breast inspire.

SPENCER COMPTON,
2nd Marquis of Northampton, Tory MP, Whig Peer, President of the Royal Society, editor of *The Tribute* (1837). [Marquis of Northampton]

Inset. Spencer Compton's monument (by Tenerani) in Castle Ashby church [Marquis of Northampton].

GEORGE DE WILDE, influential nineteenth-century editor of *The Northampton Mercury* from 1830 till the day of his death in September 1871

He comes the pris'ners to release,
In Satan's bondage held;
The Gates of Brass before him burst,
The iron fetters yield.

He comes, from thickest films of vice
To clear the mental ray,
And on the eye-balls of the blind
To pour celestial day.

He comes the broken heart to bind,
The bleeding soul to cure,
And with the treasures of his grace
T'enrich the humble poor.

His silver trumpets publish loud
The Jub'lee of the Lord;
Our debts are all remitted now,
Our heritage restor'd.

Our glad hosannas, Prince of Peace,
Thy welcome shall proclaim;
And Heaven's eternal arches ring
With thy beloved name.

Hymns, No. CCIII, 1755

(A Letter Home)

Resolved I will but little write
I take but half a sheet to-night,
Which is two quarters more than you
Would me by this night's post allow,
Though I'm but one, and you are two;
Yet I'd excuse it, could you tell
In your next letter, that you're well:
You may conclude that I am so
When this day's busy train you know.
At Little Creaton I have been
And happy cousin Perkins seen;
Married two months ago at least,
To his first mistress, and the best
Which he in twenty might have found;
He seems in all his wishes crown'd.
She's modest, courteous, young, and fair,
And not above domestic care,
Though worth three hundred pounds a year.

Correspondence and Diary of Philip Doddridge D.D.
ed. J. D. Humphreys (1829–31), IV, 186–7

DIGBY MACKWORTH DOLBEN
(1848–67)

Digby Augustus Stewart Mackworth Dolben, the third and youngest son of William Mackworth and Frances Dolben, was born 8 February 1848 in Guernsey but brought up at the family home, Finedon Hall. His father was the builder of those mock-Gothic structures, including the *Bell Inn*, which still catch your eye as you pass through Finedon. He was educated at Eton where he was a contemporary of the future Poet-Laureate, Robert Bridges. Bridges edited his *Collected Poems* with a memoir in 1911. Dolben had strong leanings to Roman Catholicism from his early teens, joined the High Anglican religious Order of St. Benedict (signing himself 'Brother Dominic') and talked of converting Finedon Hall into a monastery. Before his death he had more or less decided to become a Roman Catholic. In the summer of 1867 he spent a few months at the home of Rev. Constantine Pritchard, Rector of Luffenham, to receive private tuition before going to Oxford. On 28 June he was drowned whilst bathing in the River Welland with Pritchard's son, Walter; it is thought that he fainted whilst swimming. He was buried under the altar at Finedon on 6 July.

That he was highly regarded and loved by those who knew him can be gauged from the letter that Gerard Manley Hopkins wrote to Bridges in August 1867 after he had heard of Dolben's tragic death:

> You know there can very seldom have happened the loss of so much beauty (in body and mind and life) and of the promise of still more as there has been in his case.

His poetry, like that of Hopkins, is an expression of his faith in all its glory and despair:

> Poetry, the hand that wrings
> (Bruised albeit at the strings)
> Music from the soul of things.

('Core')

The Northampton-born composer, Edmund Rubbra, set the poem *Requests* (see below) in his *Advent Cantata*, Opus 136.

Requests

I asked for Peace—
    My sins arose,
    And bound me close,
I could not find release.

I asked for Truth—
    My doubts came in,
    And with their din
They wearied all my youth.

I asked for Love–
My lovers failed,
And griefs assailed
Around, beneath, above.

I asked for Thee–
And Thou didst come
To take me home
Within Thy Heart to be.

Poems, 1911

A Prayer

From falsehood and error,
From darkness and terror,
From all that is evil,
From the power of the devil,
From the fire and the doom,
From the judgement to come–
Sweet JESU, deliver
Thy servants for ever.

ibid

JOHN DRYDEN
(1631–1700)

The Poet-Laureate, John Dryden, was born 9 August 1631 at his maternal grandfather's rectory, All Saints Aldwincle, the eldest son of Erasmus Dryden and Mary Pickering. Both parents were from old county families with strong Puritan tendencies in politics and religion. He lived during his boyhood at Titchmarsh and was educated locally, at Westminster School and at Trinity College, Cambridge. After he left Cambridge in 1657 he lived for the rest of his life in London, though he frequently returned for 'holidays' to the Nene valley of his childhood, staying sometimes at Titchmarsh, sometimes with relatives or friends at Chesterton, Cotterstock and Lilford. In 1663 he married Lady Elizabeth Howard, daughter of the Earl of Berkshire. He became Poet-Laureate in 1668 and Historiographer Royal in 1670. Dryden is Literature's 'Vicar of Bray'. His first poem of importance, *Heroic Stanzas*, was an elegy on the death of Cromwell; *Astra Redux* (1660) welcomed King Charles II. Beginning life as a Puritan, he was by the time he wrote *Religio Laici* (1682) defending Anglicanism, whilst *The Hind and the Panther* (1687) marks his conversion to Rome. Needless to say, in 1688, on the accession of Protestants, William and Mary, he lost both his court offices and had to earn his living writing plays and translations. Poet, playwright, critic and translator, he is rightly regarded as England's greatest literary figure in the latter half of the seventeenth century. He died at his Gerard Street home in Soho, 1 May 1700.

As with Clare, it is impossible to do justice to a major poet like Dryden in such an anthology. What I have endeavoured to do is to represent him in as many genres as possible (which means, with a long poem such as *Absalom and Achitophel*, giving a representative extract). Quite unlike Clare, who is the 'local' poet *par excellence*, Dryden could have been born practically anywhere. It is almost impossible to find a poem which has a local connection. The *Harvest Song* from *King Arthur* is perhaps the closest. The image of the tithe-happy parson, 'prating so long like a book-learn'd sot', seems to be based on personal experience, whilst the reference to 'pudding and dumpling burnt to pot' is strangely reminiscent of the cottage cooking described by another Aldwincle poet, Nathaniel Whiting (q.v.). Henry Purcell (1659–95), the subject of Dryden's noble elegy, was of course Dryden's collaborator in *King Arthur*.

from Absalom and Achitophel*

Some, by their Monarch's fatal mercy grown,
From pardon'd rebels, kinsmen to the throne
Were raised in pow'r and public office high;
Strong bands, if bands ungrateful men could tie.
Of these the false Achitophel was first,
A name to all succeeding ages curst.
For close designs and crooked counsels fit,
Sagacious, bold, and turbulent of wit,
Restless, unfixt in principles and place,
In pow'r unpleased, impatient of disgrace;
A fiery soul, which working out its way,
Fretted the pigmy body to decay;
And o'r informed the tenement of clay.
A daring pilot in extremity;
Pleas'd with the danger, when the waves
    went high
He sought the storms; but, for a calm unfit,
Would steer too nigh the sands to boast his wit.
Great wits are sure to madness near alli'd
And thin partitions do their bounds divide;
Else, why should he, with wealth and honour
    blest,
Refuse his age the needful hours of rest?
Punish a body which he could not please,
Bankrupt of life, yet prodigal of ease?
And all to leave what with his toil he won
To that unfeather'd two-legg'd thing, a son:
Got, while his soul did huddled notions try;
And born a shapeless lump, like Anarchy.

In friendship false, implacable in hate,
Resolv'd to ruin or to rule the state;
To compass this the triple bond he broke;
The pillars of the public safety shook,
And fitted Israel for a foreign yoke;
Then, seiz'd with fear, yet still affecting fame,
Usurp'd a patriot's all-atoning name.
So easy still it proves in factious times
With public zeal to cancel private crimes:
How safe is treason and how sacred ill,
Where none can sin against the people's will,
Where crowds can wink; and no offence be known,
Since in another's guilt they find their own.
Yet, fame deserv'd, no enemy can grudge;
The statesman we abhor, but praise the judge.
In Israel's courts ne'er sat an Abbethdin
With more discerning eyes or hands more clean,
Unbrib'd, unsought, the wretched to redress;
Swift of dispatch and easy of access.
Oh, had he been content to serve the crown
With virtues only proper to the gown,
Or had the rankness of the soil been freed
From cockle that opprest the noble seed,
David for him his tuneful harp had strung,
And heav'n had wanted one immortal song.
But wild ambition loves to slide, not stand,
And Fortune's ice prefers to Virtue's land . . .

Absalom and Achitophel, 1681

* an allegory based on 2 Sam. 13-19. It deals with the ambitions of the Duke of Monmouth (Absalom) and the intrigues of the Earl of Shaftsbury (Achitophel).

(Harvest Song)*

Comus. Your hay it is mow'd, and your corn is reap'd;
Your barns will be full, and your hovels heap'd:
Come, my boys, come;
Come, my boys, come;
And merrily roar out Harvest Home.
Chorus. Come, my boys, come, &c.

1 *Man.* We ha' cheated the parson, we'll cheat him agen,
For why shou'd a blockhead ha' one in ten?
One in ten,
One in ten,
For why shou'd a blockhead ha' one in ten?

2 *Man.* For prating so long like a book-learn'd sot,
Till pudding and dumplin burn to pot;
Burn to pot,
Burn to pot,
Till pudding and dumplin burn to pot.

3 *Man.* We'll toss off our ale till we canno' stand,
And hoigh for the honour of old England:
Old England,
Old England,
And hoigh for the honour of old England.
Chorus. Old England, &c.

King Arthur, 1691

* 'Enter COMUS with three Peasants, who sing the following Song in Parts.' (Author's stage-direction.)

On the Death of Mr. Purcell

Mark how the lark and linnet sing,
With rival notes
They strain their warbling throats
To welcome in the spring.
But in the close of night,
When philomel begins her heav'nly lay
They cease their mutual spite,
Drink in her music with delight,
And list'ning and silent, and silent and list'ning,
and list'ning and silent obey.
So ceas'd the rival crew when Purcell came,
They sung no more, or only sung his fame.
Struck dumb they all admir'd
The godlike man,
Alas, too soon retir'd,
As he too late began.
We beg not Hell our Orpheus to restore;
Had he been there,
Their sovereign's fear
Had sent him back before.

The pow'r of Harmony too well they knew;
He long e'er this had tun'd their jarring sphere,
And left no Hell below.

The Heav'nly quire, who heard his notes from high,
Let down the Scale of Music from the sky:
They handed him along,
And all the way he taught, and all the way they sung.
Ye brethren of the lyre and tuneful voice,
Lament his lot: but at your own rejoice.
Now live secure, and linger out your days,
The gods are pleas'd alone with Purcell's lays,
Nor know to mend their choice.

An Ode, on the Death of Mr. Henry Purcell;
Late Servant to his Majesty, and
Organist of the Chapel Royal, 1696

6. philomel. The nightingale.

from The Secular Masque

MARS. Sound the trumpet, beat the drum;
Through all the world around,
Sound a reveille, sound, sound,
The warrior god is come.

Cho. of all. Sound the trumpet, &c.

MOMUS. Thy sword within the scabbard keep,
And let mankind agree;
Better the world were fast asleep,
Than kept awake by thee.
The fools are only thinner,
With all our cost and care;
But neither side a winner,
For things are as they were.

Cho. of all. The fools are only, &c.

enter VENUS

VENUS. Calms appear, when storms are past;
Love will have his hour at last:
Nature is my kindly care;
Mars destroys, and I repair;
Take me, take me, while you may,
Venus comes not ev'ry day.

Cho. of all. Take her, take her, &c.

CHRONOS. The world was then so light,
  I scarcely felt the weight;
  Joy rul'd the day, and Love the night.
But since the Queen of Pleasure left the ground,
    I faint, I lag,
    And feebly drag
  The pond'rous orb around.

MOMUS. All, all of a piece throughout:
Pointing
to DIANA. Thy chase had a beast in view;
to MARS. Thy wars brought nothing about;
to VENUS. Thy lovers were all untrue.

JANUS. 'Tis well an old age is out.

CHRONOS. And time to begin anew.

Cho. of all. All, all of a piece throughout:
  Thy chase has a beast in view;
Thy wars brought nothing about;
  Thy lovers were all untrue.
'Tis well an old age is out,
  And time to begin anew.

Dance of huntsmen, nymphs, warriors and lovers

The Pilgrim, 1700

JEFFREY EKINS
(1731–91)

Jeffrey Ekins was born on 10 June 1731 at Barton Seagrave where his father (also Jeffrey) was rector, 1723–73. He was educated at Eton and King's College, Cambridge, where he obtained a fellowship (1753), B.A. (1755), M.A. (1758) and D.D. (1781). He was a contemporary and friend of the playwright Richard Cumberland (see under Mary Alcock) who mentions him in friendly terms in his *Memoirs* (1807). On graduating, he became assistant master at Eton and subsequently chaplain to the Earl of Carlisle. Later he was rector of various livings, in Quainton (Buckinghamshire), Morpeth (Northumberland), Sedgefield (Durham) and in 1782 was appointed Dean of Carlisle. His younger brother, John (d. 1808), became Dean of Salisbury in 1786 and both he and Jeffrey married daughters of Philip Baker of Colston, Wiltshire. Jeffrey died at Parson's Green on 20 November 1791 and was buried in Fulham church. His *Poems* were published posthumously in 1810.

His affection for his birthplace is evident from the poem addressed to the Rev. Joshua Stephenson who took over the living of Barton Seagrave on the death of Jeffrey Snr. in 1773.

To the Rev. Mr. Stephenson upon the family of his predecessor removing from Barton*

. . . Nos dulcia linquimus arva!

You, happier friend, in Barton's rural seat
With sweet contentment fix your calm retreat;
In the late pastor's honour'd steps you tread,
And lead a flock which once my father led:
While we, forsakers of our native plain,
One aged parent's feeble steps sustain;
Content, tho' sad, if yet our pious care
Might mitigate the loss we can't repair!
Farewell! lov'd plains, where first our childhood stray'd,
Dear scenes, more dear by fond reflection made,
Farewell!–in vain your verdant landscapes rise,
Fair lawns in vain salute our parting eyes;
Set is that sun, whose all-enlivening ray
Cheer'd every scene, and gilt each smiling day!

Taste thou, my friend, what joy those scenes afford,
Peace guide thy steps, and Plenty crown thy board!
What tho' with pain I fly my natal home,
My soul repines not at thy happier doom,
And tho' the tear of genuine grief will flow,
Regret, not envy, points the sting of woe.
Wouldst thou the paths of virtuous fame pursue,
Still keep my sire's example in thy view;
Still open wide thine hospitable door
To a meek, honest, and a grateful poor;
Spread true religion's pure, unsullied beam,
Thyself the bright example of thy theme;
Cherish the seeds a pious hand had sown,
And make my parent's blessings all thine own!
When thou at length his portion must resign,
When what was his, shall be no longer thine,
May'st thou, like him, life's last sad load sustain,
With mind unshaken in the hour of pain!
Death's call, like him, undaunted may'st thou hear,
And want no son to mourn thy sacred bier!

Poems, 1810

* The living of Barton-Seagrave, near Kettering in Northamptonshire, had

been long in the possession of the Rev. JEFFREY EKINS, father to the Dean of Carlisle: on his death, it was given by the patron, the late Duke of Montagu, to the Rev. JOSHUA STEPHENSON, to whom these lines are address'd. (Author's note.)

JULIAN FANE
(1827–70)

Julian Fane, diplomat and poet, was the younger son of John Fane, 11th Earl of Westmorland, and Priscilla Wellesley, daughter of the 3rd Earl of Mornington. He was born on 2 October 1827 in Florence where his father was British Minister to the Grand Duke of Tuscany; the family returned to their English home, Apethorpe Hall, in 1830. Julian Fane was educated privately at Thames Ditton and for a short time at Harrow which he left because of ill-health. He then joined his parents in Berlin where his father had been appointed British Minister, and in 1844 was attached to his father's Mission. He returned to England in 1846 and went up to Cambridge, where he was awarded the Chancellor's Medal (1847) for a poem on the death of the Queen Dowager, Queen Adelaide. In 1852 he published a selection of early poems, influenced *inter alia* by Heine and Tennyson, and in 1854 *Translations of Heine.* From 1851-55 he was reattached to his father, now British Minister at Vienna. From here his diplomatic career took him to Paris (1856), St. Petersburgh (1856–8) and finally back to Vienna (1858–65) where he was Secretary of Legation and Embassy. It was here that he met Robert Lytton ('Owen Meredith' the poet, later 1st Earl of Lytton) who published a memoir of Fane in 1871. He also met the composer, Richard Wagner and in 1861 he and Lytton published *Tannhäuser and other Poems,* Fane writing under the pseudonym 'Neville Temple' (= family motto, 'Ne vile fano'...). From 1865–8 he was Secretary to the Embassy in Paris and in 1866 married Lady Adine Cowper, who bore him a son and a daughter. In 1868 they took a long lease of a small house in Fotheringhay, but she died soon afterwards. In January 1870 Fane developed a throat infection from which he died on 19 April at his mother's house in London.

Julian Fane was an accomplished musician. Whilst living in Vienna he even taught himself to play the zither! and Lytton includes two examples of his compositions–a setting of Waller's *Go, lovely Rose* and a Waltz for piano–in the appendix to his memoir. The memoir contains a large selection of Fane's poetry, including the poem on *Apethorpe* printed here. John Betjeman considered it to be one of the finest poems ever written on Northamptonshire.

Apethorpe

The moss-grey mansion of my father stands
Park'd in an English pasturage as fair
As any that the grass-green isle can show.

Above it rise deep-wooded lawns; below
A brook runs riot thro' the pleasant lands,
And blabs its secret to the merry air.
The village peeps from out deep poplars, where
A grey bridge spans the stream; and all beyond,
In sloping vales and sweet acclivities,
The many-dimpled, laughing landscape lies.
Four-square, and double-courted. and grey-stoned,
Two quaint quadrangles of deep-latticed walls,
Grass-grown, and moaned about by troops of doves,
The ancient House! Collegiate in name,
As in its aspect, like the famous Halls
Whose hoary fronts make reverend the groves
Of Isis, or the banks of classic Cam.

Julian Fane: a Memoir, by Robert Lytton, 1871

MILDMAY FANE
2nd Earl of Westmorland
(1602–66)

Mildmay Fane was born on 24 January 1601/2, probably at the family home, Apethorpe Hall. His father, Sir Francis Fane, had married Mary, daughter of Sir Anthony Mildmay (d. 1617) and became 1st Earl of Westmorland in 1624. Mildmay was educated at Emmanuel College, Cambridge (M.A. 1619) and represented Peterborough in the Short Parliament of 1620–1. He was created Knight of the Bath at the coronation of Charles I (1625) and Charles acted as godfather to his son and heir, Charles (b. 1634). He succeeded to the earldom on the death of his father in 1629. At the outbreak of the Civil Wars, he fought for the King, was lodged in the Tower (1642), took the Covenant, having been compounded in £2,000, was released (1643) and returned to Apethorpe to cultivate his estate and poetry. He was appointed Lord-Lieutenant of Northamptonshire in 1660. On the death of his first wife, Grace (1636), he married Mary, daughter of Sir Roger Townsend, and a letter written from Apethorpe to his stepson, Lord Townsend (23 March 166?) gives a touching picture of the elderly couple:

> 'Your mother . . . is much after the old manner never perfectly well. So like Bausis and Philemon we two owld acquaintances set cherishing one the other in the chimney corner hawking [spitting] and coughing like mad . . .'

He died on 12 February 1665/6.

Mildmay Fane was one of those influential courtiers and amateur poets who acted, in H. J. Massingham's words, as 'an ornamental bridge between literature and fashionable society'. He was a friend and patron of Herrick, who dedicated his poem *The Hock Cart* to Mildmay and encouraged him to go into print himself:

'You are a Lord, an Earle, nay more, a Man,
Who writes sweet Numbers well as any can.'

In 1648 he took Herrick's advice and printed for private circulation a volume of verse, *Otia Sacra*. He left among his papers a volume of *Fugitive Poetry* consisting of epigrams, acrostics and anagrams, in English and Latin, suggested by events of the Interregnum and was also author of seven plays, six still extant (BM Add. MS. 34,221) which were enacted at his private theatre at Apethorpe (see *NP&P*, VII, 397–408). One of his most attractive poems is *My Happy Life*, an account of the joys of rural living at his home at Apethorpe. It is virtually a verse-catalogue of birds, fish, flowers – and other rural 'beauties' – and for the naturalist a treasure-trove of Northamptonshire records. For years it was assumed that John Clare was the first person to record in the county such birds as the jay, magpie, cuckoo, buzzard, kite, moorhen, dabchick, pied wagtail and kingfisher. But Fane had anticipated him by nearly 200 years. The following is an extract from this 170-line poem.

My Happy Life

First, my God serv'd; I doe commend
The rest to some choice Book or Friend,
Wherein I may such Treasure finde
T'inrich my nobler part, the Minde.
And that my Body Health comprise,
Use too some moderate Exercise;
Whether invited to the field,
To see what Pastime that can yield,
With horse, or hound, or hawk, or t'bee
More taken with a well-grown Tree;
Under whose Shades I may reherse
The holy Layes of Sacred Verse;
Whilst in the Branches pearched higher,
The wing'd Crew sit as in a quier:
This seems to me a better noise
Than Organs, or the dear-bought voice
From Pleaders breath in Court and Hall
At any time is stockt withall:
For her one may (if marking well)
Observe the Plaintive Philomel
Bemoan her sorrows; and the Thrush
Plead safety through Defendant Bush:
The Popingay in various die
Performes the Sergeant; and the Pie
Chatters, as if she would revive
The Old Levite prerogative,

And bring new Rotchets in again:
Till Crowes and Jackdaws in disdain
Of her Pide-feathers, chase her thence,
To yeeld to their preeminence:
For you must know't observ'd of late,
That Reformation in the State,
Begets no less by imitation,
Amidst this chirping feather'd Nation;
Cuckoes Ingrate, and Woodcocks some
Here are, which cause they't seasons come,
May be compar'd to such as stand
At Terms, and their returns command;
And lest Authority take cold,
Here's th' Ivyes guest of wonder, th' Owl,
Rufft like a Judge, and with a Beak,
As it would give the charge and speak:
Then 'tis the Goose and Buzzards art
Alone, t'perform the Clients part;
For neither Dove nor Pigeon shall,
Whilst they are both exempt from gall.
The Augur Hern, and soaring Kite,
Kalendar weather in their flight;
As doe the Cleanlier Ducks, when they
Dive voluntary, wash, prune, play;
With the fair Cygnet, whose delight
Is to out-vie the snow in white.
And therefore alwayes seeks to hide
Her feet, lest they allay her pride.
The Moor-hen, Dobchick, Water rail,
With little Washdish or Wagtail;
The Finch, the Sparrow, Jenny Wren,
With Robin that's so kinde to men;
The Whitetail, and Tom Tit obey
Their seasons, bill and tread, then lay;
The Lyrick Lark doth early rise,
And mounting, payes her sacrifice;
Whilst from some hedg, or close of furrs,
The Partridge calls its Mate, and churrs;
And that the Countrey seem more pleasant,
Each heath hath Powt, and wood yeelds Phesant;
Juno's delight with Cock and Hens
Turkies, are my Domestick friends:
Nor doe I bird of Prey inlist,
But what I carry on my Fist:

Now not to want a Court, a King-
Fisher is here with Purple wing,
Who brings me to the spring-head, where
Crystall is Lymbeckt all the yeere, . . .

Otia Sacra, 1648

20. Philomel. Nightingale. 23. Popingay. Jay. 24. Pie. Magpie.
27. Rotchets. Bishop's cloak or mantle. 47. Hern. Heron.
50. prune. Preen. 51. Cygnet. Swan.
55. Dobchick. Dabchick, or Little Grebe.
59. Whitetail/?Wheatear. Tom Tit/Bluetit. 63. furrs. Furze.

'MARIANNE FARNINGHAM' (MARY ANNE HEARNE)

(1834–1909)

Mary Anne Hearne was born at Farningham, Kent, on 17 December 1834, the eldest daughter of Joseph Hearne, a small tradesman and village postmaster, and Rebecca Bowes, daughter of a working papermaker from Eynsford. She adopted the pen-names 'Marianne Farningham' (a mixture of forenames and birthplace) for her poetry and religious writings and 'Eva Hope' for biographical and edited works. She was educated at the local dame school and the Lancasterian school at Eynsford. On her mother's death (December 1846) she looked after the family home and helped in her father's business. She first published poetry in the *Gospel Magazine* and so successful were her early efforts that she was taken onto the staff of a weekly paper, *The Christian World.* Concurrently she continued a career as a school-teacher, in Bristol and later in Kent. In 1859 she moved to Northampton as headmistress of the British School's infant department and resided in the town until her death. After eight years she resigned her teaching-post to concentrate on writing, though between 1867 and 1901 she conducted the Girls' Bible Class at College Street Baptist Chapel. In 1885 she became editor of the influential *Sunday School Times.* She died at Barmouth on 16 March 1909.

Marianne Farningham was one of the most prolific and influential 'religious' writers of her day. As well as stories, religious commentaries and biographies, she published several volumes of poetry and hymns and a fascinating autobiography, *A Working Woman's Life* (1907). *Just as I am*–one of several 'imitations' of Charlotte Elliott's famous hymn-text with the same opening line–is probably her most popular hymn and is still to be found in current hymnals. *Geve thanks to God Alwaies,* one of her more successful 'serious' poems, was published in *Harvest Gleanings* in 1903.

'Geve Thanks to God Alwaies'

(An Inscription on a Church Bell)

For more than thrice a hundred years
Of dark or sunny days
This bell has pealed its message forth,
'Geve thanks to God alwaies';
And village folk from age to age
The legend held for heritage.

The old church tower has drawn all eyes,
Young eyes with glad hopes bright,
And eyes of old men dull with toil,
And faces turned t'ward night;
And the great bell through all the days
Has called, 'Geve thanks to God alwaies'.

In fruitful seasons when the trees
With crimson fruits were crowned,
When golden corn enriched the fields
And harvest wreathed the ground;
And in the days of drought or rain,
'Geve thanks to God' was the refrain.

Some heard, gave heed, and understood
The message of the bell,
And they have lived their lives of joy
By valley, field, and fell.
For light has shone on all their days
Who have given thanks to God always.

Today the bell peals as of yore,
Day breaks, and evening glooms,
And birds sing out their songs of joy
Above the orchard blooms,
And happy are those sons of men
Who heed the legend once again.

Harvest Gleanings, 1903

THOMAS FULLER

(1608–61)

'Genial Tom Fuller,' one of the most lovable writers this county has produced, was born at the vicarage of Aldwincle St. Peter's in 1608, twenty-three years before and half-a-mile from John Dryden (q.v.). He was educated at Queen's and Sidney Sussex Colleges, Cambridge, and afterwards held various clerical posts: Prebendary of Salisbury (1631–4), Rector of Broadwindsor, Dorset (1634–42), Perpetual Curate of Waltham Abbey (1647) and Rector of Cranford in Middlesex (1658). Shortly before the Civil War, he was appointed preacher at the Savoy. During the war he was chaplain to Sir Ralph Hopton. A 'stout Church- and King-man', Fuller nevertheless was allowed on his return to London to preach on sufferance. After the Restoration, he resumed his canonry and lectureship at the Savoy and became 'chaplain-in-extraordinary' to the new king for the brief period to his death, of a fever, on 16 August 1661.

Fuller's peculiar humour and wit made him a popular preacher in the 'voiced pulpits' of London, though Pepys, when he heard him, found his sermon poor and dry. It was as a writer on theological and antiquarian matters that he made his reputation. His books include: *History of the Holy Warre* (viz. the Crusades), 1639; *The Holy State and the Profane State*, 1642; *Good Thoughts in Bad Times*, 1645; and *Church History of Britain*, 1655. But his best-loved, best-known work is *The Worthies of England*, left unfinished and published by his son in 1662. Fuller collected most of the material for this work during his itinerance with Hopton during the Civil War. *Worthies* is a miscellany about the counties of England and their notable men. England, he said, might be compared to a house and the counties to the rooms; as others (e.g. Drayton) had described the rooms, he proposed to describe the furniture and the people in them. He speaks with special affection of his own county: 'If that county esteem me no *disgrace* to it, I esteem it an *honour* to me.' 'There is a secret loadstone in every man's native soil, effectually attracting them home again to their country, their centre.' His writings, highly regarded by Southey, Coleridge and Lamb, are marked by humour, quaint wit and wisdom, out-of-the-way anecdotes and information, all expressed with epigrammatic brevity. His 'quaint learning' and erudite digressions are worthy of *Tristam Shandy*. 'Who, for example, while reading about dotterels in Lincolnshire, would expect to be told a tale about apes in India?' (Addison: *Worthy Doctor Fuller*). One has the strong feeling that the famous epitaph written for him was not anonymous but his own work, it is so very characteristic:

HERE LIES FULLER'S
EARTH

Though the first and last books published during his lifetime were poems—*David's Heinous Sin* (1631) and *A Panegyric to His Majesty* (1600)—Fuller cannot, even with the widest allowances, be called a poet. The verse translations and epigrams which punctuate his prose, like witty asides or private jokes, are hardly more than engaging doggerel, but it would be a great pity not to include him in an anthology of his county's poetry. Here are four brief examples.

(Epigram on Sir Thomas Wyatt)

Let Florence fair her Dante's justly boast
And royal Rome her Petrarch's numbered feet:
In English Wiat both of them doth coast
In whom all graceful eloquence doth meet.

Worthies of England, 1662

PHILIP DODDRIDGE, who was minister of Castle Hill Congregational Chapel, Northampton, and ran a dissenting academy in the town. This engraving was made in 1750, the year before his death

DIGBY DOLBEN, the promising young poet from Finedon Hall, who was tragically drowned whilst swimming in the River Welland in 1867, aged 19.

JOHN DRYDEN, Poet-Laureate and leading man-of-letters of his day, who was born in Aldwincle All Saints in 1631.

(On Thomas Bannister, and his wife who died the day after her husband)

He first deceasëd: she for few hours try'd
To live without him, lik'd it not, and dy'd.

ibid

(On Henry II)

He whom alive the world would scarce suffice,
When dead, in eight foot earth contented lies.

Church History of Britain, 1655

(Inscriptions for a Peal of Six Bells)

1. Funera plango	Men's deaths I tell By doleful knell
2. Fulgara Fulmina frango	Lightning and thunder I break asunder
3. Sabbata frango	On Sabbath, all To Church I call
4. Excito lentos	The sleepy head I raise from bed
5. Dissipo ventos	The winds so fierce I doe disperse
6. Paco cruentes	Men's cruel rage I doe assuage

ibid

HENRY GARDNER

(fl. 1893–1910)

Beyond the facts that he was a farmer, lived at Guilsborough and published a volume of poetry, I have little information about Henry Gardner. He is mentioned in *Stevens' Directory* (1893) as 'Henry P. Gardner, farmer', though there is no mention of him in Whellan (1874). *Poems* was printed by Arlidge and Son, Northampton. There is no publication date, but internal evidence—one poem marks the death of Gladstone and another is entitled

The Harvest, 1898—would suggest 1898 or soon after. *The Pytchley Huntsmen* is included as one of the best examples of a genre popular with local poets (see Whyte-Melville). It is a veritable litany of names of famous personalities connected with the Pytchley Hunt during the nineteenth century. If, as the poem suggests, he saw Squire Osbaldeston in action, Gardner must have been in his eighties by 1898, for Osbaldeston relinquished Mastership of the Pytchley Hunt in 1834.

The Pytchley Huntsmen

Tally Ho! Tally Ho! let us cheer up the hounds,
They meet at eleven you know;
There's plenty of foxes, and on a good horse
We are ready and willing to go.

Osbaldeston, the squire, as he went to the meet
Was a figure one never forgets,
His stable of horses the pick of the land,
On which he won many big bets.

He would cheer up his hounds with cap in
his hand,
Not a man in the field for a match;
He would jump a big fence, a gate, or a brook,
The fox quite determined to catch.

Charley Payne was a man–I remember him
well–
Not a sign of a funk on his face;
He would strike out a line for himself in the field,
Sit down on the saddle and race.

Get the hounds on the line of a stout-hearted fox,
And a run to remember again
Was sure to come off, without any doubt
In the front you would see Charley Payne.

Captain Thomson, both master and huntsman
was he,
A better man could not be found,
At a bullfinch or double or post and rail fence,
He'd get over and never went round.

The run of the day was from Waterloo Gorse,
What a stinger! what fences to clear!
Few horses could stand it, but Thomson was there,
We'll remember it many a year.

Will Goodall, a jolly and good-tempered man,
Had a cheery 'Good morning' for all,
He could ride like the best in any hard run,
And seldom that he had a fall.

He would cheer on his bitches from North Kilworth Sticks,
With a hot burning scent what a go,
And many hard riders have been on their backs,
Through their horses not having a blow.

After twenty years' hunting, our genial Will–
We tremble to mention, it's hard–
Was laid to his rest by old hunting friends
In a corner of Brington Churchyard.

There's lots of good fellows who follow the hounds
Who don't care a straw what they jump:
And plenty of ladies well in at the death,
They shine in the old Pytchley Hunt.

A word for old Reynard, he's crafty and sly–
We miss a few fowls it is true–
Don't he run for his life with tongue hanging out,
When the huntsman and hounds are in view!

Poems (?1898)

5. Osbaldeston. George Osbaldeston (1787–1866), known universally as 'The Squire', was Master and Huntsman of the Pytchley Hunt 1827–34. Yorkshire-born, he was a remarkable sportsman–one of the few to find a place in *DNB*. He lived at Pitsford Hall.
13. Charley Payne (1815–95). The most famous of all Pytchley huntsmen (1848–64), Charley Payne, 'the inimitable', was 1st Whip to George Payne (Master 1835–38 and 1844–48) and Earl Spencer (Master 1868–78). He appears as a character in Whyte-Melville's *Holmby House* (1860).
21. Captain Thomson. Colonel Anstruther ('Jack') Thomson was Master of the PH 1864–9, doubling with Huntsman 1865–69.
23. Bullfinch. See note under *Whyte-Melville*.
25. Waterloo Gorse. The famous Waterloo Run took place on February 2nd 1866 (see Nethercote: *The Pytchley Hunt*, 1888, 171–6).
29. Will Goodall. Goodall was successor as 1st Whip to Charley Payne and was Huntsman 1874–95, serving under Lord Spencer and Herbert Langham. A portrait of 'genial Will' by W. B. Shoosmith appears in *Our County* (1893).

GEORGE HARRISON

(1876–1950)

George Harrison was one of the most popular local poets of the inter-war years and contributed to several local newspapers, including the *Kettering Leader, Wellingborough News, Rushden Argus* and *Northampton and County Independent.* He was born in 1876 in Workhouse Lane, Kettering, the third son of Joseph and Rose Harrison. He was educated in the town, worked there and died there. He followed his father's trade as a hair-dresser, owning at the end of his life two shops in Kettering, in Rockingham Road and Gold Street. His artistic ability was recognised at an early age and a number of Kettering friends combined together to enable him to go to Antwerp to study. His work soon attracted the attention of the eminent Kettering-born artist, Sir Alfred East. During his lifetime Harrison held several successful exhibitions and was a regular contributor to the local art-gallery exhibitions. He died at his home, 'Coniston' in Bath Road, on 31 December 1950.

When Harrison began publishing his poems in book form he made use of his artistic talent by illustrating them with his own paintings and drawings, adding an extra charm and dimension to them. His earliest publication is *Poems* (1921) which was followed by five volumes of *Poems and Sketches,* published between 1927 and 1946. Most of his poetry takes as its subject-matter specific villages and landscapes in the county. *A Wanderer in Northamptonshire* (1948), his last and most substantial publication, is a collection of articles, drawings and verse which he had contributed to Northamptonshire papers between 1925 and 1945. It includes a delightful memoir of his early days in Kettering, *The Wanderer Sets Out. Northamptonshire Lanes,* from the same publication, sums up his abiding love for his native landscape.

Northamptonshire Lanes

With simple beauty born of lovely grace,
Our County lanes a tender welcome give
The thoughtful wanderer, who loves to trace
The open book of nature's narrative.
We have no soaring mountains, on whose crest
The light of morning glows, while far below
The darkness lingers, and earth's creatures rest
In humble homes that line the river's flow.

We have no waterways where great ships ride,
That dip their flags in homage as they pass,
Nor do we hear the murmur of the tide,
Nor see its colours change like painted glass,
But we have deep sunk lanes, by woodlands set,
That hold the scent of larch and lofty pine,
Where blooms the primrose pale and violet,
And wide hedgerows where harebells deftly twine.

I love the rolling glory of the sea,
The breezy moorlands and the quiet hills,
But deeper love my home lanes hold for me,
Near old-world gardens filled with daffodils.
Here I can wander through the Summer noon,
Or rest awhile at tender evening's close,
When softly beams the sickle of the moon,
The moist air fragrant with the scent of rose.

A Wanderer in Northamptonshire, 1948

PETER HAUSTED

(159?–1645)

Peter Hausted (pronounced 'Haw-sted') was born in Oundle and educated at Queen's College, Cambridge (B.A. 1624, M.A. 1627). With the composer George Jeffreys he became a protégé of Sir Christopher Hatton at Kirby Hall. He held two clerical appointments in the county, as Vicar of Gretton, 1639–40, and Rector of Old, 1642–3. In 1642 he was awarded the D.D. from the University of Oxford. At the outbreak of the Civil War, he became chaplain to Spencer, Earl of Northampton, and was besieged with him at Banbury Castle where he died, in 1645.

Though hardly remembered at all today, Hausted was one of the most popular playwrights of his time: 'a wit with an itch for reform, whose sharpest arrows were directed against the church' (Addison: *Worthy Doctor Fuller*). His play, *The Rival Friends*—with music by his friendly rival, George Jeffreys—was performed along with *The Jealous Lovers* by Thomas Randolph (q.v.) in the presence of Charles I and his queen when they visited Cambridge in March 1631/2. It is a satire upon simony. The cast of thirty characters had their qualities 'writ large upon their names': Sacrilege Hooke, Zealous Knowlittle, Hugo Obligation, etc. Though 'cried down by boys, faction, envy, and confident ignorance' it was (according to its author) 'approved by the judicious'. Hausted is said to have composed the inscription on Nicholas Stone's marble memorial to Randolph at Blatherwycke:

Here sleepe thirteene together in one Tombe
And all these greate, yet quarrell not for rome.
The Muses and ye Graces teares did meete
And grav'd these letters on ye churlish sheete
Who having wept, their fountaines drye,
Through the Conduit of the Eye
For their freind who here does lye,
Crept into his grave and dyed,
And soe the Riddle is untyed
For which this Church proudly the Fates bequeath
Unto her ever-honour'd trust
So much and that so precious dust
Hath crown'd her Temples with an Ivye wreath
Which should have Laurell been

But yt the greived plant to se him dead
Tooke pet and withered.

His skill as a lyric poet is well illustrated by the two extracts from *The Rival Friends* given below.

'Have You a Desire . . .'

Have you a desire to see
The glorious Heaven's epitome?
Or an abstract of the spring?
Adonis' garden? or a thing
Fuller of wonder? Nature's shop displayed,
Hung with the choicest pieces she has made?
Here behold it open laid.

Or else would you bless your eyes
With a type of Paradise?
Or behold how poets feign
Jove to sit amidst his train?
Or see (what made Actaeon rue)
Diana 'mongst her virgin crew?
Lift up your eyes and view.

The Rival Friends, 1632

'Have Pity, Grief . . .'

Have pity, Grief; I cannot pay
The tribute which I owe thee, tears.
Alas, those fountains are grown dry,
And 'tis in vain to hope supply
From others' eyes; for each man bears
Enough about him of his own
To spend his stock of tears upon.

Woo then the heavens, gentle Love,
To melt a cloud for my relief,
Or woo the deep, or woo the grave;
Woo what thou wilt, so I may have
Wherewith to pay my debt, for Grief
Has vowed, unless I quickly pay,
To take both life and love away.

ibid

FELICIA DOROTHEA HEMANS

(1793–1835)

Like that of Mark Akenside (q.v.), Felicia Hemans' brief sojourn in Northamptonshire only just qualifies her for inclusion in this anthology. She was born on 25 September 1793 in Liverpool, daughter of George Browne, a merchant, and his wife Felicity. In 1800 the family moved to Abergele in North Wales, where her education was supervised by her mother. She was a precocious and very prolific author. Her first volume of poems was published when she was only fifteen and from 1812 (*Domestic Affections and other Poems*) she published almost a volume a year until her death. In 1812 she married an Irishman, Captain Hemans, a veteran of the Peninsular War, and bore him five sons. Soon after their marriage they moved to Daventry where Captain Hemans had been appointed Adjutant to the Northamptonshire Local Militia. Here they remained for just over a year during which time their eldest son, Arthur, was born. She does not appear to have enjoyed her stay in the county and was no doubt delighted when they returned to Wales:

> 'The transition from her "own mountain land", as she would fondly call it, to a county so tame and uninteresting as the neighbourhood of Daventry, was felt by Mrs. Hemans to a degree almost amounting to the *heimweh* (home sickness) of the Swiss. The only scenery within reach of her new abode, which excited any pleasant associations, was that of Fawsley Park.'
>
> 'Memoir of Mrs. Hemans' by her sister
> in *The Works of Mrs. Hemans*, I (1844)

In 1818 Captain Hemans went abroad and never saw his wife again, though they corresponded amiably. She continued living in North Wales at the home of her eldest brother until her mother died (1827) and in the following year moved to Wavertree, then a village near Liverpool. In 1831 she moved to Dublin, where her second brother lived, and here she died on 16 May 1835.

She met both Wordsworth and Scott. Wordsworth recommended her in his *Epitaphs* (No. xii stanza 10); Scott perspicaciously described her writings as 'too poetical . . . Too many flowers, too little fruit.' She is probably best remembered today for two poems: *Casabianca*, with its notorious opening line, 'The boy stood on the burning deck' (*Forest Sanctuary*, 1829) and *The Homes of England*, wittily parodied by Noel Coward in his song, *The Stately Homes of England*. It may well have been Fawsley House she was thinking of when she wrote this, for it was, after all, 'the only representative of the great English country house we can be positive she knew well when she wrote it'. (Trinder: *Mrs. Hemans*, 1984). The most positive memorial of her stay in the county is the sonnet, *An Old Church in an English Park*, which she herself identifies as Fawsley.

An Old Church in an English Park*

Crowning a flowery slope, it stood alone
In gracious sanctity. A bright rill wound,
Caressingly, about the holy ground;
And warbled with a never-dying tone,
Amidst the tombs. A hue of ages gone
Seem'd, from that ivied porch, that solemn gleam
Of tower and cross, pale-quivering on the stream,
O'er all th'ancestral woodlands to be thrown—
And something yet more deep. The air was fraught
With noble memories, whispering many a
thought
Of England's fathers: loftily serene,
They that had toil'd, watch'd, struggled to secure,
Within such fabrics, worship free and pure,
Reign'd there, the o'ershadowing spirit of the scene.

Sonnets Devotional and Memorial, in
Scenes and Hymns of Life with other
Religious Poems, 1834

* Fawsley Park. (Author's note.)

JOHN HOPE

(fl. 1769–80)

In *Occasional Attempts at Sentimental Poetry* (London, 1769), John Hope describes himself as 'a Man of Business'. Albeit, from 1775 to 1778 he was an officer in the Northamptonshire Militia (see C. A. Markham: *The History of the Northamptonshire & Rutland Militia*, 1924, 37–38) and it was to his fellow officers that he dedicated his second book, *Thoughts in Prose and Verse started in his Walks* (published at Stockton in 1780):

> 'My Lords and Gentlemen,
> I have received infinite pleasure in your company, without making any Return for it. I have frequently enjoy'd your Discourse, without contributing one word to the conversation . . . To many friends, indeed, my natural taciturnity lays me under equal obligation; but, if there be any entertainment in this Book, it ought particularly to be presented to You; for the Thoughts, contained in it, were mostly started in my agreeable Walks in your County. Where the Game is Sprung, some acknowledgement is due to the Lord of the Manour . . .'

His poem in memory of Robert Cox, the Town Crier, is a rare vignette of a character who must have been very familiar in Northampton at the time. The footnotes are the author's own.

MILDMAY FANE, 2nd Earl of Westmorland, of Apethorpe Hall: poet, dramatist and staunch 'King's man'; friend and patron of Robert Herrick

'MARIANNE FARNINGHAM' (Mary Anne Hearne).
This formidable-looking Victorian matron, prolific poet and author, lived and taught in Northampton from 1859 until her death in 1909

THOMAS FULLER: 'Genial Tom Fuller', who was born at Aldwincle St Peter's in 1608

GEORGE HARRISON, the Kettering hairdresser, poet and painter. In this photograph, taken c1920 at the opening of the annual exhibition of the Kettering Art Society, Harrison (clearly the only hairdresser amongst them) stands to the right, next to fellow Kettering artist J. Alfred Gotch, standing centre [Mr Frank Thompson]

In Memory of Robert Cox

Who died on the 26th of March 1777, in the 78th Year of his Age;
Having long and faithfully served, in the Office of Common-Crier, the Town and Corporation of Northampton

Then silenced, by the voice of Death,
Tall *Robin* fell–whose mighty breath
Gave vent to speech, in stronger strain
Than Mortal e'er shall speak again;
Who words, in tidings, never spared,
But freely with his neighbours shared;
Who news of *wanton murder** bore,
With sound of bell, to ev'ry door;
And oft, in honour of the *dead,*
Such fervent praises sang, or said,
Some were (he'd vow with little thinking)
Return'd to *life,*† when they were *stinking;*
Who loud proclaim'd, to foe and friend,
The *losses* which misfortunes send;
Who told of *robberies* and *theft,*
And men of goods, by *fraud,* bereft.–
    Such were the services, of late,
One noisy Man, perform'd the state!
And now *another,* with *his* bell,
Attempts to toll the warning knell;
Attempts the praises of the dead;
O! may ye profit by his trade!
Each time his bell alarms the streets
Remember,–life is short and fleet!
Think on the hours (to your sad cost)
Which time hath *stol'n,* and ye have *lost;*
Reflect how oft ye heedless *stray*
From honour's path, from virtue's way;
O! let *its sound* supply your *sense,*
And think–ye'll soon be *summon'd* hence!

Thoughts in Prose and Verse
started in his Walks, 1780

* Dead rabbits, turkeys, and geese;–fresh salmon, cod, and all kinds of fish.
† eke live lobsters and oysters, are advertised for sale by the town-crier.

CHRISTOPHER HUGHES

(1816–post 1874)

'A most excellent judge of port wine, and a well read, witty man,' said an article in the *Northampton and County Independent* (June 1910) of the late Christopher Hughes, adding: 'Mr. Hughes had a very pretty taste in poetry.' Hughes was a well-known solicitor in Northampton and for many years Clerk of the Peace for the Borough, with an office at 23 Newland. In 1864 he wrote the libretto for the cantata performed at the opening of the new Town Hall, set to music by Charles MacKorkell. He included this text in his *Poems Early and Late* (1871) which contains several witty and topical poems with local subject-matter, such as *A Remonstrance to the Wood Hill* (complaining about live- and (dead-) stock smells wafting onto Wood Hill), *To the Trustees of the Northampton and Newport Pagnell Turnpike Road* and *The Royal Agricultural Show at Northampton In the Year 1847* printed below. Hughes' poem is so topical and specific in subject-matter and so Punch-like in its facetious irony that it requires, for the present-day reader, more words to gloss than to print. The effort required is, I think, worthwhile, for it encapsulates in twenty lines a past age and a past society bathing in an event 'which old Northampton's glory much enhances'. (For a fuller account, see my article, 'The Royal Agricultural Show at Northampton, in the Year 1847', *NP&P*, VII, 434–6.) I also include Hughes' fine tribute to his friend and fellow Northampton poet, G. J. De Wilde (q.v.). Hughes also published a volume of translations, *The Odes, Epodes, Carmen Seculare, and the First Satire of Horace* (1867).

The Royal Agricultural Show at Northampton,

In the Year 1847

Heavy, plethoric, unpoetic bulls,
And mighty horses of the cart description,
Marched on for prizes for pure breeds and mules
Like soldiers, less unwilling, to conscription.

The Horticultural show with grapes and pines,
Its fruits and flowers and everything which nice is,
Where taste with luxury and art combines
The sounds of melody and Nippin's ices.

The Distins, a most talented quartett,
Blowing sweet sounds from sax-horns and
sax-tubas,
With Klitz's 'Mother Earth', I hear it yet,
And Ethiops (modern Syphaxes and Jubas).

The private spreads and the pavilion dinner,
The Mayor's good breakfast and the George's dances,
All seemed to form a show as I'm a sinner,
Which old Northampton's glory much enhances.

And then there were machines for tiles and chaffing,
And noble lords who chaff'd with the machines,
With wit which set the dull bystanders laughing,
And drills which sowed the wheat and went like beans.

Poems, Early and Late, 1871

5. 'Pines' probably refers to the pineapple ('Queen pine': see *OED* sb[2]5).
8. A William Nippin was 'inn-holder' at the *Saracen's Head* in Abington Street, Northampton, during the 1830s.
9/10. The celebrated Distin family performed at Mr. Klitz's concerts at the New Hall, Newland, during the show. They had in 1846 become British agents for the 'sax-horns' newly-patented by Adolph Sax.
11. James Frederick Klitz (1813–70) was one of the leading musicians in Northampton at the time. He owned a Music Repository on the corner of the Market Square. To commemorate the visit of the Royal Agricultural Society, he wrote and published *'The Song of the British Farmer: Hurrah for the Land Mother Earth'*, dedicated to Earl Spencer, which he sold for 2s. 6d a copy. The words of the song were by none other than Christopher Hughes –'I hear it yet'!
12. 'Ethiops' = 'Black-and-white minstrels'. The 'Lantum Ethiopian Serenaders' gave performances in the town during the show week. These minstrel shows were often called 'Ethiopian Opera'. 'Ethiop' means, literally, 'burnt-face'.
14. 'The George's dances.' The *George Hotel* at the top of Bridge Street. Two public balls were held there during the show week: one for the gentry, one for the *hoi polloi.*

'Est Qui' – Horace

I know the Man–who as he lives
Still better proof of manhood gives:
A man the longer I have known
Still dearer to myself hath grown:
Year after year with him gone by
Seem age and labour to defy.
A man so good, so just, so true,
And then, he's so hard-headed too–
But that's the secret (but in part)
Add to it all a warm, kind heart:
In brain a Nestor, heart a child,
Need I declare his name?–DE WILDE?

Poems, Early and Late, 1871

GEORGE JEFFREYS

(1678–1755)

The poet and dramatist George Jeffreys, son of Christopher and grandson of the composer George Jeffreys (1610?–85) (see Peter Hausted), was born at Little Weldon in 1678. He was educated at Westminster School and Trinity College, Cambridge, where he became a fellow and sub-orator of the university. After leaving Cambridge he was for a time secretary to the Bishop of Kerry and later held a post at the Custom House in London. He passed much of his life in the houses of his relations, the Dukes of Chandos, where, as Lord Cork says, 'he moved and spoke the gentleman'. His tragedy, *Edwin* (1724), is said to have brought its author 'above £1,000' before acting. His *Miscellanies in Verse and Prose* (1754) is a collection of songs, riddles, odes, epitaphs, epigrams and translations. It also includes longer poems such as *Chess* as well as *The Triumph of Truth: an Oratorio* and the texts of his plays *Edwin* and *Merope*. He died on 17 August 1755. His poem, *The Peach Stone*, refers to Astrop Spa, a fashionable watering-place of the day near King's Sutton.

The Peach Stone

Where healing Springs, by Astrop plac'd,
Their wat'ry stores supply,
A Peach Stone yields the Wine as fast,
And fills the Glass as high.

Such Magic in that Prize is found
By bright Maria taught
To speed the cheerful Brimmer round,
And consecrate the draught.

Bless'd by those lips, whose touch divine
Might wasting life repair;
To nectar it converts the wine,
To gladness ev'ry care.

Give me that balm to ease my pain,
My Cordial when I faint;
And let the Relique still remain
To witness for the Saint.

Miscellanies in Verse and Prose, 1754

1. Astrop Spa, in the parish of Kings Sutton, was a fashionable watering-place in the early eighteenth century: see 'Thomas Thornton at Astrop Spa', by Christopher Tongue, *NP&P*, IV, 281-5. A drawing of the spa by Thomas Rowlandson, dated 1813, appears in *NP&P*, V, 127.

TALBOT KEENE

(1735–1824)

The son of William Keene of Dublin, Talbot Keene was educated at Westminster School and Trinity College, Cambridge, of which he was a fellow. He was appointed Vicar of Brigstock with Stanion in April 1773 and held the office for fifty-one years until his death at the age of eighty-nine on 26 February 1824. There is a stone tablet to him on the south chancel wall of Brigstock church, which includes the following epitaph (possibly written by himself):

Lie lightly here, O! cold and cheerless dust,
For he was virtuous: he was kind and just.
Death drops the curtain! hides the fleeting scene;
And only mem'ry tells what he has been.
Yet all our sorrows cry, 'Ah! here lies Keene.'

He married Hester–when we do not know–and his eldest son, John Wroe, became his curate at Brigstock in 1795. Edward Daniell *(q.v.)* wrote an epistle to him in *The Woodland Muse* (1824) and two of his sons, John Wroe, and Talbot Jnr., are listed amongst the subscribers to Elizabeth Scot's *Alonzo and Cora* (Northampton, 1801). In 1787 he published anonymously ('by a Clergyman of Northamptonshire') *Miscellaneous Pieces: Original and Collected*, from which I take the witty (and ever-pertinent) *Short Rules to be observ'd by all/who on the B-------k-Vicar call.* The present vicarage was built during Keene's incumbency and the present vicar's study is almost certainly the one alluded to in the poem.

(House Rules)

Short Rules to be observ'd by all
who on the B-------k-Vicar call.

Whoe'er within this roof doth come,
Let him the robe of mirth put on,
For brow austere and looks demure,
The matter of it can't endure.

If he should be in studious fit,
Why! in the study he may sit:
But if inclin'd to laugh and talk,
Then in the parlour let him walk,
And in the wheel of each narration
Put in this spoke of conversation:
Let those who thus shall honour me,
Be as at home, and just as free.

Know then, a flower in ev'ry room
Here grows, in full eternal bloom:
Hearts-ease, tis call'd: and may each guest
Pluck off that leaf he likes the best.

Miscellaneous Pieces: Original and Collected, 1787

CHARLES KINGSLEY

(1819–75)

Charles Kingsley, poet, novelist and cleric, was the eldest surviving son of Charles and Mary Kingsley (nee Lucas) and brother of the travel-writer George and novelist Henry. Though born in Devon (12 June 1819) at Holme vicarage 'under the brow of Dartmoor', he lived from 1824 to 1830 at Barnack where his father was rector. Those crucial boyhood years he never forgot and were to supply him with theme, background and landscape for his novel *Hereward the Wake* (1866) and his essay *The Fens* (*Prose Idylls*, 1873), an evocative recollection of his Northamptonshire childhood at the edge of the fen country. He was living at Barnack at the same time that John Clare (q.v.) was living in the neighbouring village of Helpston. It is not improbable that they crossed each other's path at some time; that they actually met and spoke is one of the might-have-beens of literary history. Kingsley's subsequent career is too well-known to be detailed here. A celebrated and revered figure, albeit always a centre of controversy, he died at Eversley, Hampshire, on 23 January 1875. His *Ode to the North-East Wind* is not only a statement in verse of his philosophy of 'muscular Christianity', but also a vivid portrait of winter by the Whittlesey fens.

Ode to the North-East Wind

Welcome, wild North-easter!
    Shame it is to see
Odes to every zephyr;
    Ne'er a verse to thee.
Welcome, black North-easter!
    O'er the German foam;
O'er the Danish moorlands,
    From thy frozen home.
Tired we are of summer,
    Tired of gaudy glare.
Showers soft and steaming,
    Hot and breathless air.
Tired of listless dreaming,
    Through the lazy day:
Jovial wind of winter
    Turns us out to play!
Sweep the golden reed-beds;
    Crisp the lazy dyke;
Hunger into madness
    Every plunging pike.
Fill the lake with wildfowl;
    Fill the marsh with snipe;

While on dreary moorlands
    Lonely curlew pipe.
Through the black fir-forest
    Thunder harsh and dry,
Shattering down the snow-flakes
    Off the curdled sky.
Hark! The brave North-easter!
    Breast-high lies the scent,
On by holt and headland,
    Over heath and bent.
Chime, ye dappled darlings.
    Down the roaring blast;
You shall see a fox die
    Ere an hour be past.
Go! and rest to-morrow,
    Hunting in your dreams,
While our skates are ringing
    O'er the frozen streams.
Let the luscious South-wind
    Breathe in lovers' sighs,
While the lazy gallants
    Bask in ladies's eyes.
What does he but soften
    Heart alike and pen?
'Tis the hard grey weather
    Breeds hard English men.
What's the soft South-wester?
    'Tis the ladies' breeze,
Bringing home their true-loves
    Out of all the seas.
But the black North-easter,
    Through the snowstorm hurled,
Drives our English hearts of oak
    Seaward round the world.
Come, as came our fathers,
    Heralded by thee,
Conquering from the eastward,
    Lords by land and sea.
Come, and strong within us,
    Stir the Vikings' blood;
Bracing brain and sinew;
    Blow, thou wind of God!

Poems, 1879

HENRY KINGSLEY
(1830–76)

Henry Kingsley was born at Barnack Rectory on 2 January 1830, the fifth and youngest son of Rev. Charles Kingsley, Rector of Barnack 1824–30. His eldest surviving brother was the poet and novelist, Charles (q.v.); the travel-writer George (1827–92) was another brother. In 1830 the family moved to Devon where his father had been appointed Rector of Clovelly. His residence in Northamptonshire therefore lasted for only a few months. In that time, though, he almost came to a fatal end. His sister Charlotte and brother George wheeled the baby Henry in a garden barrow into a pond and abandoned him there–from motives of childhood jealousy, it is thought. Fortunately the gardener, having need of the barrow, found him just in time. The only other impression that the county seems to have had on him was a supernatural one. The ghostly Lady Hillyar in chapter five of his novel, *The Hillyars and the Burtons* (1865), is thought to be based on the genial ghost 'Button Cap' who haunts the medieval Great North Room of Barnack Rectory.

Henry was educated at King's College School, London, and Worcester College, Oxford, which he left after three years without taking a degree. He seems to have devoted most of his time (like his hero, Charles Ravenshoe) to athletics and social pleasures. Edwin (later Sir Edwin) Arnold records that he once wagered Henry that he 'could not "run a mile, row a mile, and trot a mile" within fifteen minutes, yet he accomplished this remarkable feat'. In 1852 he won the Diamond Sculls at Henley. In 1853, at the height of the Gold Rush, he emigrated to Australia to prospect for gold. For a short time he was a trooper in the Sydney Mounted Police. All these experiences he was to use in his first novel, *Geoffry Hamlyn*, which he began writing whilst in Australia. In 1858 he somehow raised money for the passage home to England and lived until his marriage at Eversley, Hampshire, in a cottage next to his brother Charles. Here he completed *Geoffry Hamlyn* (1859) and wrote *Ravenshoe* (1862) and *Austin Elliot* (1863). He married a distant cousin, Sarah Haselwood, in July 1864 and they lived at Wargrave, Berkshire (1864–69). Financial difficulties forced him to accept the editorship of the *Edinburgh Daily Review* (1869–71), not a congenial job for a man of his temperament. At the outbreak of the Franco-Prussian War in 1870, he appointed himself war correspondent and was present at the entry into Sedan after its capitulation: with a colleague from *The Times* he entered the town 'through an open sewer with our bodies bent and our hats off'. In 1871 the Kingsleys moved to London and in 1874 to Cuckfield in Sussex where he died of cancer of the tongue on 24 May 1876, aged forty-six. His wife Sarah survived him by forty-six years. They had no children.

Though he achieved considerable success in his lifetime, Henry Kingsley is today a most under-rated novelist. Many of us find his novels far more readable than those of his more famous brother Charles. *Geoffry Hamlyn* is rightly regarded as the first great Australian novel, and despite some *longeurs*, *Ravenshoe* has a force and drive, bonhomie and ease of manner that the more pompous Charles could never achieve. Henry was also a fine poet when he put his mind to it. His best-known poem–one that has been set to music on several occasions by, *inter alia*, Liza Lehmann and Percy Buck–is incorporated in his allegorical fable, *The Boy in Grey* (1871). Prince Philarete is hunting for the 'Boy in Grey' (a symbol of the working-class poor of the world). He speaks to a blackbird:

'How beautifully you sing!' said the Prince, 'and what a fine golden bill you have!'
'My ancestor, sir, got that bill at Glastonbury, hundreds and hundreds of years ago. Were you ever there?'
'No. Tell me the story,'
'At Glastonbury is the thorn planted by Joseph of Arithmathaea down in the valley, and at the top of the hill called 'Weary All' was the church of St. Michael. And somebody toiled up that hill one wild early spring evening; and my ancestor (who afterwards took the title of Earl of Chysorinchus, not now continued in the family, in consequence of our great lawsuit with the ring-ouzels about their assuming the white collar of the order of St. Agnes, which we have discarded) was on the bush; and we sing the story like this:

Magdalen at Michael's gate
    Tirlëd at the pin;
On Joseph's thorn sang the blackbird,
    'Let her in! Let her in!'

'Hast thou seen the wounds?' said Michael,
    'Knowest thou thy sin?'
'It is evening, evening,' sang the blackbird,
    'Let her in! Let her in!'

'Yes, I have seen the wounds,
    And I know my sin.'
'She knows it well, well, well,' sang the
        blackbird,
    'Let her in! Let her in!'

'Thou bringest no offerings,' said Michael,
    'Nought save sin.'
And the blackbird sang 'She is sorry, sorry,
        sorry.
    Let her in! Let her in!'

When he had sung himself to sleep,
    And night did begin,
One came and opened Michael's gate,
    And Magdalen went in.

The Boy in Grey, 1871

2. To 'tirl at the pin' = 'to rattle the latch'.

MARY LEAPOR

(1722–46)

Mary ('Molly') Leapor was born at Marston St. Lawrence on 26 February 1722, the daughter of Philip and Anne (nee Sharman). Her father was gardener to Judge (Sir John) Blencowe. After the judge's death (1726) the family moved to Brackley where Molly resided for the rest of her short life. Her father continued his work as a jobbing gardener and market gardener and Mary was employed for a time as a cook-maid in a gentleman's family –where, possibly, she obtained details for her poem, *Crumble Hall.* She died of measles on 12 November 1746, aged 24. Her poems were collected together and edited by Isaac Hawkins Browne the elder, with a biographical memoir by her friend 'Artemesia', and published in two volumes as *Poems upon Several Occasions* in 1748 and 1751.

David Powell, in his article, *Five Best Poets of Northamptonshire* (*Northamptonshire and Bedfordshire Life,* April/May 1972) places her amongst the 'Five Best' poets born in the county alongside Thomas Randolph, John Dryden, John Clare and William Bowles, and those who know her poetry will readily agree. She has never been quite forgotten since her death. She was admired by Cowper, has her niche in *DNB* and Southey included her in *Specimens of Later English Poets* (1807), Dyce in *Specimens of British Poetesses* (1827) and Sir John Squire in *A Book of Women's Verse* (1921). Roger Lonsdale includes three of her longer poems –*An Essay on Woman, Mira's Will* and *Epistle to a Lady*–in *The New Oxford Book of Eighteenth Century Verse* (1984). But the person who did most to reveal her worth was the late Edmund Blunden. In 1936 he published a seminal article, 'A Northamptonshire Poetess: Glimpses of an Eighteenth-Century Prodigy', in the *Journal of the Northamptonshire Natural History Society and Field Club;* he also included a number of her poems in *Wayside Poets of the Early Eighteenth Century* (1964). David Powell has written:

> Her poems are mainly concerned with the human comedy, the wisdom and folly of men and women, and she is specially delighted when poking gentle fun at herself.

Crumble Hall, one of her longest poems, must, from its carefully-observed detail, have been based on a local mansion she knew well (see note to the poem). It is wonderful how she manages to give you the impression that you are being taken on a tour of the various rooms of the house–poet and reader like a pair of inquisitive mice. The great Northamptonshire naturalist, James Fisher, once wrote that *The Enquiry* was his favourite Northamptonshire poem. In *To Cloe* she shows that she can handle a short lyric with wit and humour.

Song to Cloe,
playing on her spinet

When Cloe strikes the trembling Strings,
Applauding Cupids round her fly;
Exulting clap their little Wings
Bak'd in the Sunshine of her Eye.
    The Graces too,
    As others do,
In Raptures stand to hear,
Time stays his flagging Wings, and adds,
One Hour to the rolling Year:
    Keep off, ye Beaus,
    For who but knows

That Cloe's Eyes can wound?
If those you miss—yet pray avoid
The Danger of enchanting Sound.

Amphion led the ravish'd Stones
(They say)—and as he'd rise or fall,
Bricks, Pebbles, Slats, and Marrow-Bones
Wou'd form a Steeple or a Wall:
But this, you know,
Is long ago:
We fancy 'tis a Whim:
O had they charming Cloe heard,
They'd surely not have stir'd for him.
The Thracian Bard,
Whose Fate was hard,
(And Proserpine severe)
Had Brought Eurydice back—alas!
But Cloe was not there.

Poems upon Several Occasions (vol. 1), 1748

The Enquiry

In vain, alas! (do lazy Mortals cry)
In vain wou'd Wisdom trace the boundless Sky,
Where doubled Wonders upon Wonders rise,
And Worlds on Worlds confound our dazzl'd Eyes:
Better be still—Let Nature rest, say they,
Than err by Guess and with Opinion stray:
Then tell me, why our Eyes were made to view
Those Orbs that glister in the fluid Blue?
Why in our Sight those shining Wonders roll?
Or why to Man was giv'n a thinking Soul?
May I not ask how moves the radiant Sun?
How the bright Stars their pointed Circuits run?
What warms those Worlds that so remotely shine?
And what can temper Saturn's frozen Clime?
Who that beholds the full-orb'd Moon arise,
That chearful Empress of the nightly Skies;
Who wou'd not ask (cou'd learned Sages tell)
What kind of People on her Surface dwell?
But there we pause—Not Newton's Art can show
A Truth, perhaps, not fit for us to know.
How great the Pow'r, who gave those Worlds to roll;

The Thought strikes inward, and confounds the Soul;
Fall down, O Man–Ah fall before the Rod
Of this Almighty, All-creating God:
But hark–from Heav'n there came a chearing Sound;
Now Man revives, and smile the Worlds around:
'Tis Mercy–lo a golden Ray descends,
And Hope and Comfort in the Lustre blends.
When from the Stars we turn our aching Eyes,
To Earth we bend them where new Wonders rise;
Where Life and Death the equal Scale suspend,
New Beings rising as the former end.
Who not surpris'd can trace each just Degree
From the swift Eagle to the peevish Bee;
From the fierce Lion that will yield to none,
To the weak Mouse that hides her from the Sun!
How near one Species to the next is join'd,
The due Gradations please a thinking Mind;
And there are Creatures which no Eye can see,
That for a Moment live and breathe like me:
Whom a small Fly in bulk as far exceeds,
As yon tall Cedar does the waving Reeds:
These we can reach–and may we not suppose
There still are Creatures more minute than those?
Wou'd Heav'n permit, and might our Organs bear
To pierce where Comets wave their blazing Hair:
Where other Suns alternate set and rise,
And other Moons light up the chearful Skies:
The ravish'd Soul might still her Search pursue,
Still find new Wonders op'ning on her view:
From thence to Worlds in Miniature descend,
And still press forward, but shou'd find no End:
Where little Forests on a Leaf appear,
And Drops of Dew are mighty Oceans there:
These may have Whales that in their Waters play,
And wanton out their Age of half a Day:
In those small Groves the smaller Birds may sing,
And share like us their Winter and their Spring.
Pluck off yon Acorn from its Parent Bough,
Divide that Acorn in the midst–and now
In its firm Kernel a fair Oak is seen
With spreading Branches of a sprightly Green:
From this young Tree a Kernel might we rend,
There wou'd another its small Boughs extend.
All Matter lives, and shews its Maker's Power;

There's not a Seed but what contains a Flower:
Tho' unobserv'd its secret Beauty lies,
Till we are blest with Microscopick Eyes.
When for blue Plumbs our longing Palate calls,
Or scarlet Cherries that adorn the Walls;
With each plump Fruit we swallow down a Tree,
And so destroy whole Groves that else wou'd be
As large and perfect as those Shades we see.
    Behold yon Monster that unwieldly laves
Beneath the Surface of the briny Waves:
Still as he turns, the troubl'd Sea divides,
And rolls in Eddies from his slimy Sides.
    Less huge the Dolphin to the Sun displays
His Scales, and in the smoother Ocean plays:
Still less the Herring and round Mackrel sweep
The shallow Tide, nor trust the roaring Deep:
How far by gradual numberless Degrees,
The senseless Oyster is remov'd from these.
    Who follows Nature through her mazy Way,
From the mute Insect to the Fount of Day,
(Where now she rises, now her Steps decline)
Has need of Judgment better taught than mine:
But on this Subject we have talk'd too long,
Where grave-fac'd Wisdom may itself be wrong.

Poems upon Several Occasions (vol. 1), 1748

from Crumble Hall*

. . . Of this rude Palace might a Poet sing
From cold December to returning Spring;
Tell how the Building spreads on either Hand,
And two grim Giants o'er the Portals stand;
Whose grisled Beards are neither comb'd nor shorn,
But look severe, and horribly adorn.

Then step within—there stands a goodly Row
Of oaken Pillars—where a gallant Show
Of mimic Pears and carv'd Pomgranates twine,
With the plump Clusters of the spreading Vine.
Strange Forms above, present themselves to View;
Some Mouths that grin, some smile, and some
    that spew.

Here a soft Maid or Infant seems to cry:
Here stares a Tyrant, with distorted Eye:
The Roof–no Cyclops e'er could reach so high:
Not Polypheme, tho' form'd for dreadful Harms,
The Top could measure with extended Arms.
Here the pleas'd Spider plants her peaceful Loom:
Here weaves secure, nor dreads the hated Broom.

But at the Head (and furbish'd once a Year)
The Heralds mystic Compliments appear:
Round the fierce Dragon *Honi Soit* twines,
And Royal Edward o'er the Chimney shines.

Safely the Mice through yon dark Passage run,
Where the dim Windows ne'er admit the Sun.
Along each Wall the Stranger blindly feels;
And (trembling) dreads a Spectre at his Heels.

The sav'ry Kitchen much Attention calls:
Westphalia Hams adorn the sable Walls:
The Fires blaze; the greasy Pavements fry;
And streaming Odours from the Kettles fly.

See! yon brown Parlour on the Left appears,
For nothing famous, but its leathern Chairs,
Whose shining Nails like polish'd Armour glow,
And the dull Clock beats audible and slow.

But on the Right we spy a Room more fair:
The Form–'tis neither long, nor round, not square;
The Walls how lofty, and the Floor how wide,
We leave for learned Quadrus to decide.
Gay China Bowls o'er the broad Chimney shine,
Whose long Description would be too sublime:
And much might of the Tapestry be sung:
But we're content to say, The Parlour's hung.

We count the Stairs, and to the Right ascend,
Where on the Walls the gorgeous Colours blend.
There doughty George bestrides the goodly steed;
The Dragon's slaughter'd, and the Virgin freed:
And there (but lately rescu'd from their Fears)
The Nymph and serious Ptolemy appears:
Their awkward Limbs unwieldly are display'd;
And, like a Milk-wench, glares the royal Maid.

From hence we turn to more familiar Rooms;
Whose Hangings ne'er were wrought in Grecian
    Looms:
Yet the soft Stools, and eke the lazy Chair,
To Sleep invite the Weary, and the Fair.

Shall we proceed?–Yes, if you'll break the Wall:
If not, return, and tread once more the hall.
Up ten Stone Steps now please to drag your Toes,
And a brick Passage will succeed to those.
Here the strong Doors were aptly fram'd to hold
Sir Wary's Person, and Sir Wary's Gold.
Here Biron sleeps, with Books encircled round;
And him you'd guess a Student most profound.
Not so – in Form the dusty Volumes stand:
There's few that wear the Mark of Biron's Hand.

Would you go farther?–Stay a little then:
Back thro' the Passage–down the Steps again;
Thro' yon dark Room–Be careful how you tread
Up these steep Stairs–or you may break your Head.
These Rooms are furnish'd amiably, and full:
Old Shoes, and Sheep-ticks bred in Stacks of Wool;
Grey Dobbin's Gears, and Drenching-Horns enow;
Wheel-spokes–the Irons of a tatter'd Plough.

No farther–Yes, a little higher, pray:
At yon small Door you'll find the Beams of Day,
While the hot Leads return the scorching Ray.
Here a gay Prospect meets the ravish'd Eye:
Meads, Fields, and Groves, in beauteous Order lie.
From hence the Muse precipitant is hurl'd,
And drags down Mira to the nether World . . .

Poems upon Several Occasions (vol. 2), 1751

* Crumble Hall is almost certainly Edgecote House, which was extensively rebuilt after Mary Leapor's death. However, drawings of the original building by the topographical artist, Pieter Tillemans (c1684–1734), still exist and show the 'two grim Giants o'er the Portals' described in lines 4–6. I am indebted to Victor A. Hatley for this identification. Further information will be found in Bruce A. Bailey's forthcoming edition of Tillemans' drawings of Northamptonshire buildings for the Northamptonshire Record Society.

80. 'Mira' is the anagrammatic nickname Mary Leapor used in her poetry.

JOHN AYRE LEATHERLAND
(1812–74)

John Ayre Leatherland was born in Kettering on 11 May 1812, the only son of John, a carpenter, and Martha, daughter of the notable Baptist minister, John Ayre. His father died when he was a boy and his mother remarried a foreman silk-weaver of strict Calvinist principles. He was educated at dame school and day-school in Kettering, then apprenticed, first as a shoemaker, then as a ribbon-weaver. In 1836, during a depression in the ribbon-weaving trade, he turned to velvet-weaving. In 1846, with others, he formed a company to manufacture and trade plain and fancy silk goods, he himself acting as the commercial traveller. For five years he was the secretary of the local working men's association and sympathetic to the Chartists' cause, as his popular contribution to the *Chartist Hymn Book, Base Oppressors, leave your slumbers*, shows. His later shift of political allegiance he traced to the study of Burke's writings and his indirect involvement in a local rick-burning incident (see his autobiographical memoir in *Essays and Poems*). In July 1850 a serious injury in a coach accident inflamed a dormant tumour which kept him bedridden for two years. Thereafter he devoted himself to literary work. In 1849 he had been appointed local reporter for the *Northampton Herald*. In 1859 he was appointed Postmaster at Higham Ferrers but was unable to take the position up. Instead he continued his journalistic activities and other literary work. He married and had one daughter, born February 1849. He died at Kettering in December 1874.

It was his maternal grandfather, John Ayre, who instilled in Leatherland his love of literature. He informs us that he had been introduced to poetry by reading Milton at the age of fourteen. His *Essays and Poems*, much of which had appeared previously, was published in 1862 with a dedication to Sir Fitzroy Kelly, Q.C., M.P. Most of the essays had been written for competitions and they show his attempts at 'self-help'. The poems take as their themes familiar Victorian preoccupations: poverty, orphans, cemeteries, honour. There are several topical poems, including the inevitable eulogy on the death of the Duke of Wellington and *Lines to Earl Grey*, written in 1831 just before the passing of the Reform Bill, but the most attractive is one of his lightest efforts, *The Forsaken Maid*, an ingenious 'eye-play' with typographical symbols.

The Forsaken Maid

A Typographical Epistle to a Friend

Dear Friend I take my pen in ☞,
    But write with heavy heart,
Hoping to make you understand
    The secrets I impart.

For not to all would I reveal
    My wrongs and miseries;
Therefore by *points* my griefs conceal,
    And use ' s.

My trembling quill I scarce , nd,
My sorrows are so great;
Nor can Time's renovating hand
Heal my afflicted state.

My hopes are ----d, my lover's fled,
The pole * of my life
Has woo'd another in my stead,
And took her for a wife.

The direful tidings pierced me through,
Like †s in my breast;
Like ‡s strike anew,
And rob my soul of rest.

The .'s past of tranquil joys
And dreams of fancied bliss,
Clos'd from the world and all its noise
In Love's ( ).

My bosom like a : fire
From Cupid's altar burn'd,
For him, my lord, my heart's desire,
Who now my love has spurn'd.

O, how I longed his face to view,
How prized his salutation;
And thought each tender *billet-doux*
A !

His " ever charm'd my ear,
So musical they fell;
In form and worth did none appear
My lover's ||.

But he is false, and I'm undone;
Ah, miserable day!
Each § of my life must run
In sad complaints away.

I ? if I long can bear
My weight of heavy sorrow;
To-day the victim of despair,
The same sad wretch to-morrow.

Pity my woes, my dearest friend,
Beyond all computations;
So now my ¶ I end
In bitter !!!!

Essays and Poems, 1862

Just in case you haven't managed to solve Leatherland's ingenious puzzle, the typographical answers are (give or take a ?) as follows:

1. hand 8. apostrophe 9. comma 13. dash 14. star
18. dagger 19. double-dagger 21. period 24. parenthesis
25. colon (i.e. 'coal on') 32. mark of exclamation
33. (?)speeches 36. parallel 39. section 41. question
47. paragraph 48. exclamations

'Base Oppressors, Leave Your Slumbers'*

Base Oppressors, leave your slumbers,
Listen to a nation's cry;
Hark! united, countless numbers,
Swell the peal of agony!
Lo! from Britain's sons and daughters,
In the depths of misery–
Like the sound of many waters–
Comes the cry 'We will be free!'

Tyrants quail! the dawn is breaking–
Dawn of Freedom's glorious day;
Despots on their thrones are quaking,
Iron bands are giving way;
Kingcraft, priestcraft, black oppression,
Cannot bear our scrutiny;
We have learnt this startling lesson–
'If we will, we may be free!'

By our own, our children's charter;
By the blood that fires our veins;
By each truth-attesting martyr,
By their tears, and groans, and pains;
By our rights, by nature given;
By the voice of Liberty;
We proclaim before high heaven,
That we must, we will be free!

Winds and waves the tidings carry;
Spirits, in your stormy car,
Wing'd with lightnings, do not tarry;–
Bear the news to lands afar!
Tell them–sound the thrilling story,
Louder than the thunder's glee–
That a people, ripe for glory,
Is determined to be free.

The Chartist Hymn-Book, 184?

* This song was later included by Holyoake and Watts in *The Secularist's Manual of Songs and Ceremonies* (c 1872).

ROBERT LUCAS

(1747–1812)

Robert Lucas was born at Northampton in 1747, brother of Martin Lucas, wine-merchant, banker (premises in Bridge Street) and High Sheriff of the County in 1799. He was educated at the Free Grammar School and Trinity College, Cambridge, taking his B.D. in 1787 and D.D. in 1793. He was appointed Curate of Hardingstone (1778) and Vicar of Pattishall (1782). From 1787 he was Vicar of Ripple, Worcestershire, an appointment he held jointly with that of Pattishall until his death, at Ripple, on 1 March 1812. He married a niece of Richard Hurd, Bishop of Worcester, and left a son, Richard (b. 1789) and a daughter, Harriet.

In 1809 Lucas published his *Occasional Sermons* which included a sermon preached at Hardingstone when he was curate there on the establishment of a Sunday School (1786). *Poems on Various Subjects . . . written chiefly in the early part of the author's life* was published at Tewkesbury in the following year and is dedicated to Mrs. Bouverie of Delapre Abbey. Several of the poems are signed 'Delapre Abbey' and 'Hardingston'. The *Ode on Death* was written for the Northampton Bill of Mortality (1773). The major item, however, is *Boughton Green*, describing the annual three-day summer Fair, written in 1775. Lucas allots a canto to each day of the Fair. The following extracts give, I hope, some idea of the vigour, humour and imagination of the poem–in my opinion one of the finest 'Northamptonshire' poems ever written. It deserves to be more widely known.

from Boughton Green

(i) (The Villagers Get Ready for the Fair)

Now, every meaner care each gladly shuns,
And, thro' the house, the preparation runs;
Old Fairfield's blossom coat is brought to light,
And moths and winged worms are put to flight;
The sunshine, too, his damask waistcoat sees,
Whose ample skirts protect his breeches knees:
Whilst dame unlocks, in haste, her hidden store,
And gladly turns the female wardrobe o'er;
Airs the new satin gown she bought in strife,
Ten years ago, to spite the parson's wife.
With ready hand their lovely daughter too
Her fair equestrian habit brings to view:
But, ah! its scanty form, with doubtful eye,
Their lovely daughter views, and heaves a sigh:
Three summers back the favourite dress was made,
Ere budding nature had to ripeness spread;
And much she fears her bolder form will grow
Impatient of so close confinement now:

Her fears are just–the favourite dress is tied,
And feeble seams give way on every side;
Each swelling limb the offered veil denies,
And down an useless spoil the vestment lies.

from Canto I

(ii) (The Gentry Get Ready for the Fair)

Moved by the welcome day that warms the plain,
The restless Fair begins to swarm again;
In dazzling tints the finery spreads around,
And on the ear returns the varying sound;
Pleasure and gain the bustling crowd pursue,
And all the scenes of yesterday renew.
But ah! the bright addition how shall I,
In numbers worthy of the tale, supply!
From humble swains, the vent'rous muse aspires
To sing of lords and ladies, dames and 'squires;
Who, once a year, to this gay spot repair,
To eat their breakfast at a country Fair!

And fitly some, with previous care, engage
The public eye with glittering equipage:
Bright shines the harness for the horses' heads,
And, on the dingy coach the varnish spreads;
But oft the labour of the coachman fails,
The rust to harass from the brazen nails.
Ten days are past, since (thoughtful of the show)
The steeds were ordered from the labouring
    plough;
For prudent folks esteem it no reproach,
If now they draw a dung-cart, now a coach:
What if, they hang their ears and look forlorn,
With too much labour, and too little corn,
The liberal feed, with leisure, never fails
To make them snort, and kick, and cock their tails.

from Canto II

(iii) (The Wrestling Match)

Now, from the center, goes the summons loud,
To call the wrestlers from the circling crowd:
Th'inspiring sound to valourous heroes came,
Who scorn to linger at the call of fame,
Whilst, on a pole, their longing eyes behold
The glossy prize, rimmed round with glittering gold.

With eager stride and fierce demeanour, first,
Into the vacant list a blacksmith burst;
A cindry darkness on his garments hung,
That round him smells of conflagration flung;
Umcombed and ragged, on his rusty skull,
His dinghy locks stuck close, like clotted wool;
About his face his grim employ had thrown
A surly sadness and a lowering frown;
Eternal smokes had striped his brow with black,
And round his features fixt a sable track.
Oft, at the scorching forge, his arm had swung
The ponderous sledge, as loud the anvil rung;
Beneath his blow the mass submissive grew,
The bar now lengthened, and now turned the
shoe,
Whilst round the artist stars of iron flew:
Nor less his potent arm, well-skilled and bold,
With nervous grasp, the restive beast could hold:
Caught by the shank, with many a mighty strain,
The struggling steed for freedom strove in vain.

Such was the champion, first, who took the ground,
And black defiance looked to all around:
But though of threatening aspect, stern and strong,
He stood not there, without a rival, long:
For lo! the glittering prize and fame to win,
A lusty miller from the crowd rushed in . . .

from Canto III

Poems on Various Subjects, 1810

SHAKERLEY MARMION
(1603–39)

Shakerley (or Shackerley or Schackerley) Marmion (or Marmyon or Mermion) was born at Aynho, the son of a father of the same impossible name who was lord of the manor. He went to school at Thame, matriculated at Wadham College, Oxford, in 1617, taking his M.A. seven years later. This 'goodly proper gentleman', as Anthony à Wood calls him, 'had once in his possession seven hundred pounds per annum at least'. This fortune he managed to dissipate. Like his poetical 'father', Ben Jonson, he served in the Low Countries and got into difficulties for stabbing someone at home. Little else is known of his life. He enlisted in Suckling's troop of cavalry for the ill-fated expedition against the Scottish Covenanters, but fell ill at York and was conveyed to London where he died in 1639.

He is mainly remembered as a playwright; his plays include *The Antiquary*, performed c1635 and published in 1641. His one non-dramatic work is an epic poem, *Cupid and Psyche*, published in 1637 with prefatory poems by (*inter alia*) Richard Brome, Thomas Nabbes and Thomas Heywood. It is composed of heroic couplets throughout except for two 'lyrical advertisements', one of which is printed below in (ii).

(i) (Proserpine Tempts Psyche to Remain in the Underworld)*

But Proserpine replied, 'You do not know,
Fair maid, the joys and pleasures are below.
Stay and possess whatever I call mine,
For other lights and other stars do shine
Within our territories; the day's not lost,
As you imagine, in the Elysian coast.
The golden age and progeny is here,
And that famed tree that does in Autumn bear
Clusters of gold, whose apples thou shalt hoard,
Or each meal, if thou please, set on the board.
The matrons of Elysium at thy beck
Shall come and go, and buried queens shall deck
The body in more stately ornaments
Than all earth's feigned majesty presents.
The pale and squalid region shall rejoice,
And Silence shall break forth a pleasant voice:
Stern Pluto shall himself to mirth betake
And crownèd ghosts shall banquet for thy sake;
New lamps shall burn, if thou wilt here abide,
And night's thick darkness shall be rarified;
What'er the winds upon the earth do sweep,
Rivers or fens embrace, or the vast deep,
Shall be thy tribute, and I will deliver
Up for thy servant the Lethèan river:
Besides the Parcae shall thy handmaids be,
And what thou speak'st stand for a destiny.

*Proserpine, Queen of the infernal regions, is addressing Psyche, a beautiful maiden, who is eventually united with Cupid.

17. Pluto. Ruler of the infernal regions in Roman mythology.

24. Lethèan. A river in Hades. 25. Parcae. The fates.

(ii) (The Hue-and-Cry)

When Venus heard how the world stood in awe
Of her son's desperate valour, and no law
Might curb his fierceness, flattery nor force
Prevail, she then resolv'd a course,
With open libels, and with hue and cry,
To publish to the world his infamy:
And therefore caus'd in every town and street,
And in all trivial places where ways meet,
In these words, or the like, upon each post,
A chartel to be fix'd that he was lost:

The wanton Cupid t'other day
Did from his mother Venus stray.
Great pains she took, but all in vain,
How to get her son again:
For since the boy is sometimes blind,
He his own way cannot find.
If any one can fetch him in,
Or take him captive in a gin,
And bring her word, she for this
Will reward him with a kiss.
That you the felon may descry,
These are signs to know him by:
His skin is red with many a stain
Of lovers, which by him were slain;
Or else it is the fatal doom,
Which fortells of storms to come:
Though he seem naked to the eye,
His mind is cloth'd with subtlety;
Sweet speech he uses, and soft smiles,
To entice where he beguiles:
His words are gentle as the air,
But trust him not, though he speak fair,
And confirm it with an oath.
He is fierce and cruel both;
He is bold and careless too,
And will play as wantons do:
But when you think the sport is past,
It turns to earnest at the last.
His evil nature none can tame,
For neither reverence nor shame
Are in his looks: his curlèd hair

Hangs like nets for to ensnare:
His hands, though weak and slender, strike
Age and sexes all alike;
And when he list, will make his nest
In their marrow or their breast:
Those poison'd darts shot from his bow,
Hurt gods above, and men below.
His left hand bears a burning torch,
Whose flame the very same will scorch;
And not hell itself is free
From this imp's impiety.
The wounds he makes no salve can cure;
Then if you catch him, bind him sure:
Take no pity, though he cry,
Or laugh, or smile, or seem to die,
And for his ransom would deliver
His arrows and his painted quiver;
Refuse them all, for they are such
That will burn where'er they touch.

When this edict was openly declar'd,
And Venus' importunity, none dar'd
To be so much of counsel as to hide,
And not reveal where Cupid did abide.

Cupid and Psyche, 1637

GEORGE EDMOND MAUNSELL
(1816–75)

George Edmond Maunsell, the second but eldest surviving son of Thomas Philip Maunsell of Thorpe Malsor, was born at Rushton Hall on 17 April 1816. He was educated at Christ Church, Oxford (B.A. 1838) and succeeded to the family estate at Thorpe Malsor on the death of his father, 4 March 1866. He had been ordained deacon in 1841 and in the following year became Chaplain to the Earl of Westmorland. In 1841 he succeeded to the living of Thorpe Malsor and remained as rector until his death, at St. Leonards-on-Sea, on 29 October 1875. He is buried at Thorpe Malsor. He married twice: in 1846 to Theodosia Mary, third daughter of Sir John Palmer of Carlton, who bore him a son, Cecil (1847–1911: Rector of Thorpe Malsor, 1888–1911). She died in September 1868. In 1869 he remarried, to Matilda the eldest daughter of Hon. Hugh Tollemache, Rector of Harrington and fourth son of William Lord Huntingtower. She died without issue in February 1899.

In a foreword to his *Poems* (1861), Maunsell states that 'these pieces, with the exception of those of later date, were printed for private circulation in the years 1853–56'. The contents include poems on topical

FELICIA HEMANS, whose brief sojourn in Northamptonshire inspired 'The Stately Homes of England' and a sonnet on Fawsley church

CHRISTOPHER HUGHES, Clerk to the Peace for Northampton: ‘a most excellent judge of port wine, and a well read, witty man’

subjects, such as *Scutari Nurses* and *A Legend of Inkermann* (the latter 'set to music by Professor Bernhard Althaus') and poems on local subjects, such as *Rushton Hall* and the *Execution of Mary, Queen of Scots*, from which the following extract is taken.

from Execution of Mary, Queen of Scots

She heard unmoved the fatal message told,
Her cheek blanched not, nor ran the life-blood cold
Back to the sickening heart; but as a queen
She bore her, whilst around her maids were seen
In all the frantic attitudes of woe.
One, bending downwards, rocks her to and fro;
One stands as all aghast: no breath, no moan,
Betrays another's grief, but marble, stone,
She sits, while from the eyes like thunder rain
The tears splash down; one starting up amain,
Shrieks, bans and curses. Near, the Kentish chief
Turns down his wolfish eyes, as when a thief
Gripped in the act stands sullen, or some sprite
Of hated darkness, by the enchanter's might
Forced up to outer day, with evil glance
Glares from his downcast eyelids all askance.

''Tis sudden,' were the words Queen Mary spoke,
'Sudden, but not less welcome comes the stroke
That ends my sorrows; yet I scarcely deemed
That she, my sister–she who surely seemed
Throned to love mercy, justice and defend
The suppliant and the stranger–thus should bend
Her thoughts to slay the stranger, the opprest.
Yet be it so–to me the change is blest,
Nor deem I worthy of eternal bliss,
The shrinking soul that, at such time as this,
Bears not the body up through that short strife
That bars the passage to eternal life.
But mine stands fix'd and firm–although, perchance,
In girlhood's days, in happy, blithesome France,
Some natural dread had been, some tears had passed
To hear to-morrow's sun must be my last.
Now, all is o'er, mine own familiar friends
Against me draw the sword; a dark cloud bends
O'er Scotland's royal race; and all I pray,

Is that from Mary's blood some happier day
May dawn on Stuart's name. For England's Queen
I have unfeign'd forgiveness: none, I ween,
Deem gentlier of her deed. 'Tis sure no wrong
To grant the freedom I have sighed for long.
Weep not! to-morrow all shall see that I,
As Christian and as Queen know how to die;
Nor deem them for myself, if trace of tears
On this wan cheek at early dawn appears;
My spirit joyous stirs, and in this breast
Pants but to flee away and be at rest.'

The fatal hour is come, that morning's red,
Whose eve shall see thee numbered with the dead,
Wronged Mary Stuart! All death's hideous gear–
The axe, the block, the headsman–wait thee near.
Yet still, with heart unstirred, with look serene,
Moves onward to her death fair Scotland's queen.
Calm she unrobes her, calmly bends and prays
For England's queen–success, and length of days
For her who shortens hers. 'Tell each true heart'
(These her last words) 'that firmly I depart
Fixed in the ancient faith: I know no wrong
That I have done to any; but ere long
Before His throne, we, face to face, shall plead,
Who sees the secret thought clear as the deed.
There I repose my trust: His doom shall tell
Mine innocence or guilt–and now, farewell!'

'Tis done! one bigot voice is heard alone,
'Thus die Eliza's foes!' One sullen tone
Singly replies 'Amen!' The heaving breast,
The starting tear-drop, show how feel the rest.
O Mary Stuart! gentlest of thy race,
Unmatched in form and loveliness of face!
How can we deem thee guilty, yet survey
Thy last calm hours, when hope had passed away!
Surely, no sullen apathy of crime
Bore up thy spirit in that awful time;
Not the dull consciousness of hidden guilt,
But, thy firm trust on Jesu's mercy built,
Bade thee, with Faith's strong eye, the future scan,
And hope that mercy here denied by man.
In the dark shadow of that gloomy vale,
Where e'en the mightiest spirits bend and quail,

There wast thou proved, there counted to be pure;
Thence hast thou passed in innocence secure,
Safe from the smiter's hand, the oppressor's rod,
Wafted on seraph wings to meet thy God . . .

Poems, 1861

JOHN MERRY

(1756–1821)

How little is known about the lives of some of our minor local poets! Their names are writ on water, carved in wet sand which the tide of years has washed away. John Merry tells us in his poem *On the Author's Birth-Day* that he was born in 1756. He was a miller by trade and was known as 'The Bard of Moulton Mill' ('Merry the Miller of Moulton'). He later moved mills to Abington Mill about which he wrote a poem. He was a friend of Moulton-born schoolmaster-poet, William Chown, whom he describes, in a poem written on Chown's death, as 'my first, my earliest friend'. However I can find no trace of his being born at Moulton and, significantly, his *Miscellaneous Pieces; in Verse* was published in Bedford. He died on 12 September 1821, aged 65.

Miscellaneous Pieces was published posthumously in 1823. Amongst the subscribers were Thomas Bell (q.v.) and John Coles (q.v.). Several of the poems, with their references to local preachers such as Thomas Jones of Creaton and Legh Richmond of Turvey, suggest that Merry had Evangelical leanings. Cole (*Pop. Biog.*) says he 'possessed no contemptible powers of versification, being particularly apt in displaying his thoughts in rhyme on any occasional subject'. The song, *Marriott and Co.* is a good example – so occasional that today it needs a gloss to explain it. The collection also includes three poems in memory of his wife, Elizabeth, and one to his daughter, Alice, 'on her first Birth Day'. There is also an 'Answer' to the Prize Enigma published in the *Gentleman's Diary* for 1786 by Weedon poet, Benjamin West (q.v.).

Song.–Marriott & Co.

Why neighbours! what ails you? why look ye so sad?
'Tis Christmas you know, and you ought to be glad;
I rejoice in the season–but if you must know,
I cannot help thinking of MARRIOTT & Co.

This MARRIOTT & Co. had establish'd their fame,
And by civil behaviour had got up their name;
In the air they were building fine castles, when lo!
All at once stopp'd the bank of fam'd MARRIOTT & Co.

NORTHAMPTON was never in such consternation,
Since England became a commercial nation;
All faces look sad, both with high and with low,
And join in condemning this MARRIOTT & Co.

Again, if your neighbours you happen to meet,
Abroad, or at home, in the field, or the street;
The first question answer'd of, 'how do you do?'
You're sure to converse about MARRIOTT & Co.

If a man had but got a few guineas to spare,
He would speedily to the said bankers repair;
In their hands he would place them–return on tip-toe,
Well pleas'd he had left them with MARRIOTT & Co.

Or if a man wanted a few hundred pounds,
To build, or to plant, or to follow the hounds;
Thus each speculator would instantly go,
And get a supply from this MARRIOTT & Co.

But now 'tis all over, and some are undone,
Some curse, and some pity, but which 'tis all one;
Time will prove whether bankers are honest or no,
So with patience we'll wait for this MARRIOTT & Co.

But in my opinion, it was very cruel,
To change our hot minc'd pies for cold water gruel;
You might have stay'd longer, a fortnight or so,
For you've quite spoil'd our mirth, Messieurs
MARRIOTT & Co.

Miscellaneous Pieces; in Verse, 1823

Note: Richard Marriott, a Northampton draper, set up a bank in the town in c1800. All went well until 1809; then rumours began to circulate that it was in a bad way financially. By Christmas of that year, Marriott himself announced that 'circumstances have rendered it necessary for him to DISCONTINUE the BANKING BUSINESS entirely'. (See Victor A. Hatley: 'Phoenix in the Drapery', *Northampton Historical Series*, No. 3, 1970.)

CHARLES MONTAGU-DOUGLAS-SCOTT

(1862–1936)

Charles Scott was born in London on 16 June 1862, the second son of Lord Walter Scott and Anna Hartopp and grandson of the 5th Duke of Buccleugh and Queensbury. At the age of three he contracted polio which left him crippled for life: he was never able to walk without crutches. He was educated privately, and though he missed the advantages of a normal classical education he became a man of wide reading and culture. Despite his physical disability, as a young man he travelled widely on the continent. He spent much of his life at Boughton House–'the old place I love to the verge of idolatory'–and, after his father's death, at Geddington Priory, where he became something of a recluse. He died at Geddington Priory on 4 March 1936 and is buried in Weekley churchyard.

Scott published several collections of poetry during his lifetime, including translations from the French and Italian. He had a fine poetic technique: the deprecatory subtitle that he gave to *The Sonnets of Ceccio Angiolieri*–'Done into English Doggerel'–is quite unnecessary. His main poetical work is his monumental collection, *Northamptonshire Songs and Others*, privately printed in three volumes between 1904 and 1906, from which I print two examples. Just before he died he prepared for the press *Tales of Northamptonshire*, 'written at various dates before 1906'. 'His affection for his family home was extended to the shire which forms its setting,' wrote his editor, and his poems are some of the most evocative of the county ever written.

Suggested in Cotterstock Churchyard

Over the old Church-tower
I watch the white clouds go,
And the old clock strikes the hour
With measured beat and slow;
While the Nene sighs ever so slightly
As it wanders away to the sea,
And the sun and shadow go lightly
O'er the graves of the dead and me.

All as the dead looked on it,
The quiet Midland scene;
No change of Time upon it,–
The Church, the Mill, the Nene;
And the willowed isle where nightly
The otters yet gambol free,
As they did when the moon shone brightly,
As it shone last night for me.

So the 'mavis and merle' were singing
In the pollarded elms by the road,
So a boy on the gate was swinging,
So a waggon went by with its load;
So a maiden came tripping as sprightly
As the maiden this morning I see,
And once was the vision as sightly
To him at my feet as to me.

So the spire of Oundle pointed
To heaven of blue or grey,
And the times seemed ever disjointed,
As the wise men cry to-day;

But earth now holds them tightly
Who couldn't on earth agree,
While others yet talk as tritely
To the wilfully deaf like me.

And Dryden he passed along here
To his cousins who lived at the Hall;
Perchance he fashioned a song here,
And leant on this selfsame wall.
Tho' my numbers can never come rightly,
In common this little may be,
That the sun and the shadow went lightly
O'er him as they slip over me.

Northamptonshire Songs, II, 1905

Oundle Bells

Bells of Oundle, bells of Oundle,
Ringing thro' the frosty air,
Like the snatches of some roundel
Heard atop of winding stair,
Borne to the attics of existence
From the drawing-room of dreams–
So your chiming in the distance
To my fancy seems.

Bells of Oundle, bells of Oundle,
Sacred are your songs to me,
For I know that they must sound all
Thro' the year where I would be:
Still I hear your voices singing
O'er the silence of the snow,
In my ears their echoes ringing
Wheresoe'er I go.

Northamptonshire Songs, III, 1906

JOHN PELL

(1790–1862)

The son of strict nonconformist parents, John Pell was born in Guilsborough in 1790 and spent nearly all his life in the county. He studied medicine, firstly at Wellingborough, then Northampton and finally London, before setting up medical practice at Yardley Hastings where he remained until his death in 1862. According to the prefatory memoir to *Over's Hill*, Pell possessed a sensitive shyness of character, under the influence of which, he seemed to go through life contentedly as a village apothecary. To the poor, he was ever most considerate and charitable in the exercise of his profession: the mournful aspect with which he was followed to the grave by a crowd of this class of his patients, evinced their sense of the loss of a benefactor.

Over's Hill, a poem and other poems, edited by Rev. T. C. Haddon, appeared in 1863, dedicated to the Marquis of Northampton: Pell 'long enjoyed the patronage of his noble house'. Not unexpectedly, for a nineteenth-century village G.P., it contains several poems on the deaths of local people (Rev. Henry Gauntlett, Vicar of Olney, and the Rev. John Seagrave, Rector of Castle Ashby) as well as other local subject-matter: *Cowper's Oak* and the title-poem, *Lines written on Over's Hill, Near Olney.* I have chosen a poem which represents his profession. The subject of *The Victim of Consumption* suffered from an illness of which Pell would have been only too aware and whose condition he describes with an expert eye.

The Victim of Consumption

I saw her in the morn of hope, in youth's delicious spring,
Elate and joyous as the lark just bursting on the wing,
A radiant creature of the earth as first it soars on high,
Without a shadow on its path, or cloud upon its sky.

I see her yet–so fancy deems–her dark and waving hair,
Gleaming like shadows upon snow, above her forehead fair,
Her large dark eye of glancing light, the winning smile that play'd
In dimpling sweetness round the mouth Expression's self had made.

I marked the first faint emblems of Consumption's hectic wreath,
The boding smiles that spoke to me of treachery beneath,
Her wasting slenderness of form, her changed yet lustrous eye,
And sadly said my heart, 'O God! and must this fair one die?'

And long she lingered ere the chain that bound her spirit broke,
And long and sorely suffered, ere the last resistless stroke,

That took away all mortal pain and weakness and disguise,
And her soul upborne upon the wings of angels sought the skies.

Yet peaceful was its parting from its wasted tenement,
And much of Heavenly mercy with the painful judgment blent,
And blessed airs from Paradise came wafted through the gloom,
To cheer and to support her in her passage to the tomb.

And now her tenantless remains are decaying in the grave,
And above that narrow dwelling doth the grass unchidden wave,
Yet again shall life and beauty re-animate her clay;
For 'the sting of death is sin'; and that her Saviour took away.

Over's Hill, 1863

THOMAS PERCY
(1729–1811)

One of the most notable 'birds of passage' in the county's annals was the antiquary, poet and divine, Thomas Percy. He was born at Bridgnorth, Salop, in 1729, the son of a grocer, and educated at Christ Church, Oxford, where he took his M.A. in 1753. On 17 November 1753 he was presented by his college with the living of Easton Maudit which from 1756 he held jointly with that of Wilby. He lived at Easton Maudit until 1782 when he was appointed Bishop of Dromore, County Down. He died 30 September 1811. At Easton Maudit he entertained Dr. Johnson, Shenstone and Garrick, and it was here that he completed his monumental work, *Reliques of Ancient English Poetry*, published in three volumes in 1765. It was the result of many years collecting old ballads from every quarter, including a large folio Manuscript which had fallen accidentally into his hands. Despite being attacked by later writers as unscholarly, it was a pioneering work of immense influence. In April 1759 he married Anne Gutteridge of Desborough, and it was to his future wife that he addressed his poem, *Nancy*, first published anonymously (*A Song by T. P--cy*) in Robert Dodsley's *A Collection of Poems* (1758). Burns thought it the finest ballad in the language, and it has been set to music by several composers. In later years he spent long periods at the home of his daughter Barbara at Ecton, glad to exchange 'the turbulence of Ireland for the quiet of Northamptonshire'.

'O Nancy, Wilt Thou Go With Me?'

O Nancy, wilt thou go with me,
    Nor sigh to leave the flaunting town?
Can silent glens have charms for thee,
    The lowly cot and russet gown?
No longer dressed in silken sheen,
    No longer decked with jewels rare;
Say, canst thou quit each courtly scene,
    Where thou wert fairest of the fair?

O Nancy, when thou'rt far away,
    Wilt thou not cast a wish behind?
Say, canst thou face the parching ray,
    Nor shrink before the wintry wind?
Oh, can that soft and gentle mien
    Extremes of hardship learn to bear,
Nor, sad, regret each courtly scene,
    Where thou wert fairest of the fair?

O Nancy, canst thou love so true,
    Through perils keen with me to go?
Or, when thy swain mishap shall rue,
    To share with him the pang of woe?
Say, should disease or pain befall,
    Wilt thou assume the nurse's care,
Nor, wistful, those gay scenes recall,
    Where thou wert fairest of the fair?

And when at last thy love shall die,
    Wilt thou receive his parting breath?
Wilt thou repress each struggling sigh,
    And cheer with smiles the bed of death?
And wilt thou o'er his breathless clay
    Strew flowers, and drop the tender tear?
Nor, then, regret those scenes so gay,
    Where thou wert fairest of the fair?

A Collection of Poems, 1758

JOHN PLUMMER

(1831–1914)

John Plummer's career was one of the most remarkable of all our Northamptonshire poets. The eldest son of a poor master-staymaker, he was born in London on 3 June 1831. When he was five, his family was pauperised and he went to live briefly at St. Albans with an uncle. It was during this time that an illness left him partially lame and deaf. He was educated at Spitalsfield School of Design, but in 1853 unemployment forced the family to move to Kettering where he found work in a stay factory. About this time he began writing controversial pamphlets which brought his name to public attention, and by 1860 he claimed that 'nearly 1500 letters, essays and poems, paragraphs, etc.' had appeared from his pen, many of them in Charles Knight's [Kettering] *Town and County Newspaper.* In 1861 he became English Social Affairs Correspondent of the *Sydney Morning Herald* and after a period as a journalist in London, emigrated (1879) to Sydney with his wife and family, where he became a well-known journalist and editor. He died in Sydney in 1914.

Like his fellow-poet and contemporary in Kettering, John Leatherland (q.v.) his political views changed radically during his time in Kettering, from pro-Chartist to anti-Trade Unionist, but he was always a champion of the working-class man. His *Songs of Labour, Northamptonshire Rambles, and other poems* (1860) was dedicated to Lord Brougham and its subscribers included George Ward Hunt (future Chancellor of the Exchequer), Christopher Hughes (q.v.), Abner Brown (see under Anne & Maria Brown) and George De Wilde (q.v.). It is prefaced by a valuable autobiographical sketch. *Scab! Scab!! Scab!!! or The Combinationists' Logic* was written during the shoemakers' strike at Northampton in 1858 and shows the fervent emotion engendered in working-class circles by the rising trades unions.

Scab! Scab!! Scab!!!
or, The Combinationists' Logic

Hunt him here and hunt him there,
Shop-mates, hunt him ev'rywhere;
Let each sot and drunken drab,
Join the chase, and hunt the 'scab'.
What's his crime? He works for bread,
For little Charley–sick in bed.
Nothing else? His wife is poor;
He fain would make his income more.
Is that all? He will not join
Our ranks, and with us all combine.
He dares to think; and dares be free;
Things which never more must be;

For liberty is all a flam:
The People's progress all a sham:
And Bomba is our model king,
So we with glee will ever sing –
    Hunt him here, and hunt him there,
    Shop-mates, hunt him ev'rywhere;
    Let each sot and drunken drab,
    Join the chase, and hunt the 'scab'.

What of our hearts? Oh! they are stone,
Nor love nor mercy e'er will own.
Our interests? Oh! fudge and stuff;
We pay ourselves, and that's enough.
For our pleasure and our play
We have our shillings four a day.
But are you just? Don't know or care:
Ask me no more, or I will swear!
For law, for justice, or for right,
We do not care a blessed mite!
Not common sense shall be our plan;
We'll rule by force, by fear, and ban;
And woe to him who dares to see
Things in another light than we;
For every thing we say is law:
Now there's my speech, I'll say no more.
    Hunt him here, and hunt him there,
    Shop-mates, hunt him ev'rywhere;
    Let each sot and drunken drab,
    Join the chase, and hunt the 'scab'.

But why do you to him deny
His right the case himself to try?
Because we cannot make him see,
That he ought never to be free
To choose his trade, or do his best
To serve and aid his interest.
Oh! nonsense! what is that to you?
There's work enough for all to do.
Ah! yes; but then we want to keep
It to ourselves, that none may reap
The slightest share; but starve and slave
In workhouse yards, or find a grave.
Nay, this is wrong! Well, wrong or right,
For this I'll clench my fist and fight;

No scholar I, but this I know,
The weakest to the wall shall go.

Hunt him here, and hunt him there,
Shop-mates, hunt him ev'rywhere;
Let each sot and drunken drab,
Join the chase, and hunt the 'scab'.

Songs of Labour, 1860

Plummer prefaced his poem with the following note:

> 'Scab,' 'Black Sheep', &c., are terms applied to those working-men who act against the rules laid down by the generality of Trades' Unions. This [song was] written during the Shoemakers' Strike, at Northampton, in 1858; but it is only fair to state that several Trades' Unions, such as the Bookbinders', of London, and the Manchester Order of Smiths', most earnestly deprecate any such conduct on the part of their members.

Until 1857 the shoe manufacturing industry in Northamptonshire had been unmechanised. Early in November 1857 it became known that two manufacturers at Northampton were using closing machines on their premises. This caused great opposition among shoemakers who 'feared that their introduction would be followed by heavy unemployment and the reduction of wages, and that men who retained their jobs would be compelled to work in factories'. The Northamptonshire Boot and Shoe-Makers Mutual Protection Society was formed (April 1858) and in February 1859 they called on their members to strike. The strike was a failure; it was over by May and caused great hardship. (See *Monsters in Campbell Square!* by Victor A. Hatley, *NP&P*, IV, 51–59.)

15. Bomba. Nickname given to Ferdinand II (1810–59), tyrannical King of Naples. He earned the epithet after he subdued a revolt in Sicily by the bombardment of its chief cities.

26. 'An allusion to the payment received by the "Strike" officials.' (Author's note.)

JOHN POOLEY

(1800–post 1841)

The few facts that I have gleaned about John Pooley's life are as follows: he was born at Kelmarsh on 1 September 1800, possibly the son of Thomas Pooley who was churchwarden at the time. In the 1841 Census return he is listed as aged forty-one, an agricultural labourer, living in the house of Edward Harpole. There is no mention of him in the 1851 Census. In his preface to *Poems, Moral, Rural, Humorous, and Satirical* (1825) he describes himself as an 'untaught peasant', yet it is clear from his poetry that he was well acquainted with the works of Burns, Bloomfield and Keats (to whose memory he wrote a poem). In the preface to *Blackland Farm* (1838) he states that the poem was 'composed for his *own* amusement during labours of the field'. His affection for his 'native place' is evident from the many poems that he wrote about the area. In the poem 'Kelmarsh' he writes:

These are the Scenes where my first days were past
And where, on such, I hope to spend my last:
Here oft beneath the Summer's sultry sky,
From morn to eve the Spud, or Fork I ply;
Or mid the noise of screeming Daws and Rooks,
In pensive mood lean o'er my tasteful Books.

Poems, Moral, Rural, Humorous, and Satirical, 1825

(A Kelmarsh John Clare indeed!) *Blackland Farm* he describes as 'a poem in five cantos, founded on tradition', but I have been unable to ascertain whether the tradition was local or not, or whether *Blackland Farm* is based on a local establishment. (Its authenticity would suggest it was.) It is a fine, racy narrative, full of countryman's humour and keen observation. The following extract, from the second canto, describes an auction at the farm.

from Blackland Farm

(THE AUCTION)

Handbills were quickly spread around,
(Oh, how those things have power to wound!)
'Mid streaming tears which flow around,
And vainly flow;
Like all that man on earth has found,
Or seeks to know.

On ev'ry wall, or alehouse screen,
The sale at Blackland Hall was seen;
The smithy, too, where oft he'd been,
Now told the same,
And (placed some fine large words between)
Shrewd Dobson's name.

Three cart-horses, and one nag-mare,
Two stacks of beans, one ditto tare;
Ploughs, harrows, carts—no worse for wear,
Of Firmhand's make;
With forks and rakes, all new last fair—
A duck and drake;

With things too numerous here to name,
Though oft I've stood and view'd the same,
Beneath those words of rustic fame—
Live and dead stock;
Till to *commence* the sale, you came—
At ten o'clock.

'Twas on the fifth of March, they say,
And on our hero's *bridal* day,
When friends and neighbours took their way
Amidst the storm,
That now raged hard, in wild dismay,
At Blackland Farm.

The first which there to auction came,
Was poor, old Ralph, of well-known name,
On all fours–she was mark'd and lame,
And wind not good–
There, with her poor old tott'ring frame,
The creature stood.

So poor old Ralph, you, then, must go,
Cried Dobson's wife in wild, wild woe–
Who now thy evening meal will throw–
Thy master be?
Soon for the dogs, old Ralph, I trow,
Are you–and I.

No more will Dobson o'er thee stride,
To market gay, or fair to ride;
And spread thy name both far and wide,
As well he might–
No more WILT thou become his pride,
Or talk at night.

Thus raved the poor, old dame aloud,
And sigh'd and sob'd amidst that crowd;
She beg'd she might be there allowed
To see her end–
The poor, old mare some gladness shew'd
At her old friend.

But, to proceed–the sale went on–
And Ralph was quickly sold and gone–
Another now before them shone,
Of humbler pride,
On which their good, old ploughman John,
Was placed astride.

Eleven pounds ten–eleven pounds ten!
Down–down if no one bids again!–
Twelve pounds–twelve pounds fifteen!–
and when,
He's worth it twice–

He's going–going–Mr. Penn,
Come, don't be nice!

Say thirteen pounds–well I don't mind–
He's gentle–sound in limb and wind–
Then down he went, as 'twas designed
For Penn to buy–
When some kind neighbour chanced to find
He'd lost an eye.

The man now blamed the auctioneer,
And swore the horse ten pounds too dear,
When friends thought well to interfere,
As friends will do;
And sold again he was, we hear,
When he made two.

The next they brought was Gaffer Gray–
A good one too, but past his day;
Gaffer had drawn three tons of hay,
On hill-close road;
But now he found his strength give way,
And not his load.

The auctioneer soon spread his fame,
And Gaffer Gray did loud proclaim–
It seems, poor lad, he, too, was lame;
And knew it well;
For, startled at old Gaffer's name,
He tript and fell.

The last was Ball, although not least,
He was a fine, high-mettled beast;
He paw'd the ground, and proudly whisk'd
His gallant tail.
What then?–cried John–what, Ball, thou see'st–
Is but a sale.

'At length arrived amidst the throng'–
(This line is took from Bloomfield's song)–
His heels around he fiercely flung,
And snorted loud;
Then prancing, plunging, reckless sprung,
Among the crowd.

The auctioneer, amidst the fray,
Unluck'ly stumbled in his way;
Prone on the ground outstretch'd he lay,
A spectre pale;
And nearly then had Ball, they say,
Wound up his sale.

Take him away–take him away!
Cried ev'ry one, who'd ought to say–
Thus did the poor, old horse repay,
His master's lot;
When off he straight was drove that day,
And sold *was not.*

The beans and tares, as next, were sold–
Two stacks of new–one ditto old–
Next pigs and kine, with Dobson's fold,
E'en to a tail;
And thus concluded, we've been told,
The first day's sale.

from Canto II, Blackland Farm, 1838

98. Bloomfield. Robert Bloomfield (1766–1823), the 'peasant poet' whose *The Farmer's Boy* (1800) became very popular. (See *'What the visitors had to say': An Introductory Bouquet,* p. 9.)

WALTER POPE

(1625?–1714)

The noted mathematician and astronomer, Walter Pope, was born at Fawsley. His mother was a daughter of the puritan divine, John Dod, and he was half-brother to John Wilkins, later Bishop of Chester. He was educated at Westminster School and Trinity College, Cambridge (1645) whence he migrated to Oxford (1648) where he was nominated to a scholarship at Wadham College. He graduated B.A. (1649) and M.A. (1651) and had a most distinguished academic career. Admitted to a fellowship in 1651, he later served successively as bursar, sub-warden and dean. In 1658 he travelled abroad to Paris and in 1660 succeeded Sir Christopher Wren as Professor of Astronomy at Gresham College. In 1661 he received the degree of M.D. He travelled abroad again in 1664, this time for two years in Italy. One of the original members of the Royal Society, he was elected to the society's council in 1666. He lived for some time in the household of his friend Seth Ward, Bishop of Salisbury, and published a biography of Ward in 1697. In 1687, eye inflammation induced him to resign from his professorship and he retired to Epsom. His later years were passed at Bunhill Fields, London, where he died at a very advanced age on 25 June 1714. He is buried at St. Giles, Cripplegate.

Walter Pope's publications were, as might be expected, of a scientific nature. He contributed to the first volume of the *Philosophical Transactions*

CHARLES KINGSLEY, who spent his boyhood at Barnack. In L. Dickinson's portrait (1862), the famous novelist and cleric looks every inch the 'Squarson'. (Note the fishing-rods and basket.) [National Portrait Gallery]

HENRY KINGSLEY, novelist and poet and younger brother of Charles, who was born at Barnack rectory in 1830. Pen-and-ink drawing by William S. Hunt (1901) taken from a photograph.
[National Portrait Gallery]

of the Royal Society, which includes his joint observations with Hooke and others of the partial solar eclipse of 22 June 1666. *The Wish* is therefore something of an oddity–an occasional *jeu d'esprit,* composed to celebrate his retirement. According to Anthony à Wood, it first appeared as a broadside in 1684; Pope published the fullest and most authentic text in 1697 under the title, *Dr. Pope's Wish.* It became extremely popular, running to a third edition by 1710, and it was even latinised by Vincent Bourne (1728). It is the 'wishing song' sung by Benjamin Franklin 'a thousand times when I was young and now find at fourscore that the three contraries have befallen me'. It has subsequently been much anthologised: *inter alia* in Edward Thomas' *Poems and Songs for the Open Air* (1907), Norman Ault's *Seventeenth Century Lyrics* (1928), Vivian de Sola Pinto's *Poetry of the Restoration* (1966) and the *Oxford Book of Seventeenth Century Verse* (1934).

The Wish

If I live to be Old, for I find I go down,
Lett his be my Fate. In a Country Town,
May I have a warm House, with a Stone at the Gate,
And a cleanly young Girl, to rub my bald Pate.

CHORUS

May I govern my Passion with an absolute Sway,
And grow Wiser, and Better, as my Strength wears away,
Without Gout, or Stone, by a gentle decay.

May my little House stand on the Side of a Hill,
With an easy Descent, to a Mead, and a Mill,
That when I've a mind, I may hear my Boy read,
In tho Mill, if it rains, if it's dry, in the Mead.

Near a sandy Grove, and a murmuring Brook,
With the Ocean at Distance, whereupon I may look,
With spacious Plain, without Hedge or Stile,
And an easie Pad-Nag, to ride out a Mile.

With Horace and Petrarch, and Two or Three more
Of the best Wits that reign'd in the Ages before,
With roast Mutton, rather than Ven'son or Teal,
And clean, 'tho course Linnen at every Meal.

With a Pudding on Sundays, with stout humming Liquor,
And Remnants of Latin to welcome the Vicar,
With Monte-Fiascone, or Burgundy Wine
To drink the King's Health as oft as I dine.

May my Wine be Vermillion, may my Malt-drink
be pale,
In neither extream, or too mild or too stale,
In lieu of Deserts, Unwholesome and Dear,
Let Lodi or Parmisan bring up the Rear.

Nor Tory, or W[h]ig, Observator or Trimmer
May I be, nor against the Laws Torrent a Swimmer,
May I mind what I speak, what I write, and hear
read,
But with matters of State ne'er trouble my Head.

Let the Gods who dispose of every King's Crown,
Whomsoever they please, set up and pull down.
Ile pay the whole Shilling impos'd on my Head
Tho I go without Claret that Night to my Bed.

I'll bleed without grumbling, tho' that Tax should
appear
As oft as New Moons, or Weeks in a Year,
For why should I let a seditious Word fall?
Since my Lands in Utopia pay nothing at all.

Tho' I care not for Riches, may I not be so poor,
That the Rich without shame cannot enter my Door,
May they court my converse, may they take much
delight,
My old Stories to hear in a Winter's long Night.

My small stock of Wit may I not misapply,
To flatter great men be they never so high,
Nor mispend the few Moments I steal from the Grave,
In fawning, or cringing, like a Dog or a Slave.

May none whom I love, to so great Riches rise
As to slight their Acquaintance, and their old Friends
despise,
So Low or so High, may none of them be,
As to move either Pity, or Envy in me.

A Friendship I wish for, but alas 'tis in vain,
Jove's Store-House is empty and can't it supply,
So firm, that no change of Times, Envy, or Gain,
Or Flatt'ry, or Woman, should have Pow'r to unty.

But if Friends prove unfaithful, and Fortune a Whore,
Still may I be Virtuous, though I am poor,
My Life then, as useless, may I freely resign,
When no longer I relish, true Wit, and good Wine.

To out live my Senses may it not be my Fate,
To be blind, to be deaf, to know nothing at all,
But rather let Death come before 'tis so late,
And while there's some Sap in it, may my Tree fall.

I hope I shall have no occasion to send
For Priests, or Physicians, till I am so near mine End
That I have eat all my Bread, and drunk my last Glass,
Let them come then, and set their Seals to my Pass.

With a Courage undaunted, may I face my last Day,
And when I am Dead, may the better sort say,
In the Morning, when sober, in the Evening, when
mellow,
He's gone, and left not behind him his Fellow.

Without any Noise when I've pass'd o'r the Stage,
And decently acted what part Fortune gave,
And put off my Vests in a cheerful Old Age,
May a few honest Fellows see me laid in my Grave.

I care not whether under a Turf, or a Stone,
With any inscription upon it, or none,
If a Thousand Years hence, *Here lies W.P.*,
Shall be read on my Tomb, what is it to me?

Yet one Wish I add, for the sake of those Few
Who in reading these lines any Pleasure shall take,
May I leave a good Fame, and a sweet smelling Name,
Amen. Here an End to my Wishes I make.

CHORUS

May I govern my Passion with an absolute Sway,
And grow Wiser, and Better, as my Strength
wears away,
Without Gout, or Stone, by a gentle Decay.

Dr. Pope's Wish, 1697

28. Observator or Trimmer. *The Observator* was a journal published by Tory propagandist Sir Roger L'Estrange, 1681–87. 'Trimmer' probably refers to the famous pamphlet *The Character of a Trimmer*, by George Savile, Marquis of Halifax, first printed in 1688, but circulated anonymously some years earlier.
35. 'Tho I go without Claret.' Pope's own note on this passage is, 'If that should happen, it would be a shrewd affliction to the Poet.'

THOMAS RANDOLPH
(1605–35)

'The Muses may seem not only to have smiled, but to have been tickled at his nativity, such the festivity of his poems of all sorts.' wrote Fuller of Thomas Randolph (*Worthies*). He was born at Newnham at the house of his mother's parents, the son of William Randolph, steward to Lord Zouch, and Elizabeth, daughter of Thomas Smith of Newnham. He was educated at Westminster School and Trinity College, Cambridge, where he was elected a fellow. At ten he is said to have written a poetical history of the Incarnation, but later turned to more worldly subjects. In 1632 he went to London where he gained the friendship of Ben Jonson and became one of Jonson's favourite 'sons'. He is said to have led a boisterous (i.e. lewd and boozy) life in the capital and when he returned to Northamptonshire in 1634 he was in broken health and heavily in debt. He resided first with his father at Little Houghton and later with his friends, the Staffords, at Blatherwycke where he died of smallpox in March 1635. Sir Christopher Hatton set up a monument to his friend at Blatherwycke with verses by fellow-poet Peter Hausted (q.v.)

Randolph was only thirty when he died and one of the most promising poets and dramatists of his day. His comedy, *The Jealous Lovers,* was published in 1632. It had been acted at Cambridge in the presence of the King along with *The Rival Friends* by Hausted (q.v.). His *Poems: with the Muses Looking-glasse; and Amyntas* appeared posthumously in 1638. He is, in H. J. Massingham's opinion, 'a spirited, manly and sensitive poet, well-salted and full of good phrasing, and his work has poetic gallantry and freedom'. Many of his verses were set to music by his contemporaries, including Henry Lawes, John Jenkins and George Jeffreys, and Benjamin Britten set *A Charm Song* in his songcycle, *A Charm of Lullabies* (1947).

(A Charm Song)

Quiet, sleep! or I will make
Erinnys whip thee with a snake,
And cruel Rhadamanthus take
Thy body to the boiling lake,
Where fire and brimstone never slake;
Thy heart shall burn, thy head shall ache,
And every joint about thee quake,
And therefore dare not yet to wake!

Quiet, sleep! or thou shalt see
The horrid hags of Tartary,
Whose tresses ugly serpents be,
And Cerberus shall bark at thee,
And all the Furies that are three–
The worst is called Tisiphone,–
Shall lash thee to eternity,
And therefore sleep thou peacefully.

The Jealous Lovers, 1632

2. Erinnys. Erinyes: in Greek mythology, avengers of wrong; the Latin Furies. 3. Rhadamanthus. In Greek mythology, one of the three judges of hell; the other two were Minos and Æacus. 12. Cerberus. In classical mythology, the three-headed dog who guarded the infernal regions.

Upon the Loss of his Little Finger*

Arithmetic nine digits, and no more,
Admits of; then I still have all my store,
For what mischance hath ta'en from my left hand,
It seems did only for a cipher stand,
But this I'll say for thee, departed joint,
Thou wert not given to steal, nor pick, nor point
At any in disgrace; but thou didst go
Untimely to thy death, only to show
The other members what they once must do:
Hand, arm, leg, thigh, and all must follow too.
Oft didst thou scan my verse, where if I miss,
Henceforth I will impute the cause to this.
A finger's loss (I speak it not in sport)
Will make a verse a foot too short.
Farewell, dear finger, much I grieve to see
How soon mischance hath made a hand of thee.

Poems, 1638

* Like Herrick, Randolph had the misfortune to lose a finger, evidently 'in a fray', and like him turned his loss to profit by making it a subject for verse. 14. As indeed it has!

An Ode to Master Anthony Stafford*

To hasten him into the Country

Come, spur away!
I have no patience for a longer stay;
But must go down,
And leave the chargeable noise of this great town.
I will the country see;
Where old simplicity,
Though hid in grey,
Doth look more gay
Than foppery in plush and scarlet clad.
Farewell, you city-wits that are
Almost at civil war!
'Tis time that I grow wise, when all the world grows mad.

More of my days
I will not spend to gain an idiot's praise;
Or to make sport
For some slight Puisne of the Inns of Court.
Then, worthy Stafford, say,
How shall we spend the day?
With what delights
Shorten the nights?
When from this tumult we are got secure,
Where mirth with all her freedom goes,
Yet shall no finger lose;
Where every word is thought, and every thought is pure.

There from the tree
We'll cherries pluck; and pick the strawberry;
And every day
Go see the wholesome country girls make hay,
Whose brown hath lovelier grace
Than any painted face
That I do know
Hyde Park can show.
Where I had rather gain a kiss, than meet
(Though some of them in greater state
Might court my love with plate)
The beauties of the Cheap, and wives of Lombard Street.

But think upon
Some other pleasures; these to me are none,
Why do I prate
Of women, that are things against my fate?
I never mean to wed
That torture to my bed:
My Muse is she
My Love shall be.
Let clowns get wealth, and heirs; when I am gone,
And the great bugbear, grisly Death,
Shall take this idle breath,
If I a poem leave, that poem is my son.

Of this, no more!
We'll rather taste the bright Pomona's store.
No fruit shall 'scape
Our palates, from the damson to the grape.
Then, full, we'll seek a shade,
And hear what music's made:

How Philomel
Her tale doth tell;
And how the other birds do fill the quire;
The thrush and blackbird lend their throats,
Warbling melodious notes.
We will all sports enjoy, while others but desire:

Ours is the sky,
Where, at what fowl we please, our hawks shall fly;
Nor will we spare
To hunt the crafty fox, or timorous hare;
But let our hounds run loose
In any ground they'll choose;
The buck shall fall,
The stag, and all.
Our pleasures must from their own warrants be,
For, to my Muse, if not to me,
I'm sure all game is free;
Heaven, earth, are all but parts of her great royalty.

And when we mean
To taste of Bacchus' blessings now and then,
And drink by stealth
A cup or two to noble Barkley's health:
I'll take my pipe and try
The Phrygian melody,
Which he that hears,
Lets through his ears
A madness to distemper all the brain.
Then I another pipe will take
And Doric music make,
To civilize with graver notes our wits again.

Poems, 1638

* Anthony Stafford (1587-?1645), fifth and youngest son of John Stafford of Blatherwycke and author of *Stafford's Niobe* (1611). Perhaps it was to Blatherwycke that Randolph was hasting.
16. Puisne. Junior judge in the superior courts of common law.
36. Cheap. Cheapside, London's principal market-place.
76. Barkley. George, Lord Berkeley (1601-58).

JOSEPH ROWLATT
(d. 1875)

At the time he published his book of poems, *First Fruits*, in 1874, Rowlatt was librarian at the Northamptonshire Mechanics' Institute. The

Mechanics' Institute (est. 1833) was situated in the Corn Exchange building, Northampton, and had for its primary object 'the dissemination of scientific, mechanical, and other useful knowledge among the operative classes. . . . The library contains about 1,300 volumes. . . . The library and reading-room are open daily. . . . Lectures on scientific and other subjects are delivered during the winter season; as also mutual improvement classes in music and the languages' (*Whellan*, 1874). Rowlatt was appointed librarian in 1873 in succession to Henry Law. In the 1873/4 Burgesses' (Electoral) Roll, his residence is given as 31 Ash Street, a turning off Bailiff Street (not a particularly salubrious area of the town at the time). The Mechanics' Institute Minute-book for early 1875 (in Northampton Central Library) suggests that Rowlatt was overworked and in poor health. An entry for 15 July minutes the appointment of Mr. Greenough as librarian on the 'lamented death of Mr. Rowlatt'.

The extract from his long poem, 'Abington Abbey', is a touching tribute to John Clare. It is often thought that Clare was ignored or condescended to at this period, but as De Wilde's essay in *Rambles Roundabout*, Askham's sonnet (q.v.) and Rowlatt's *Reverie* indicate, he was held in high esteem by the discriminating few. *First Fruits* also includes an acrostic *Tribute* to Marianne Farningham (q.v.).

from Abington Abbey*. A Reverie

(JOHN CLARE)

Yet I do mind me of a king of men,
A bright, bright star, though set amid the slough!
In an obscure and lowly village born,
Of humble birth, with yet an heritage
A king might rank among his noblest gifts!
He rose from out his lowly village home,
He shone a star among his fellow men,
Upon his forehead Poesy had set
Her broad distinctive seal, and in his eye,
That large blue eye, so full of love and truth,
The light of genius glowed. Dear simple John,
Would that the foolish world had never plucked
Thee from the heaven remote thou didst adorn,
And set thee in an artificial world,
Something to wonder, stare at, and admire,
Something to please their fashion-sated taste;
And then, when they had wondered, stared their fill,
Back to thy simple home thou didst return.
But ah, that brilliant artificial glare
Shed o'er th'uncultured garden of thy soul,
Had killed the sweetest flowers that grew therein,
And thou didst know it, and thy simple heart

POEMS

UPON

SEVERAL OCCASIONS.

By Mrs. *LEAPOR* of *Brackley*
in *Northamptonſhire.*

LONDON,

Printed: And Sold by *J. Roberts* in *Warwick-Lane.*

MDCCXLVIII.

MARY LEAPOR. Title-page of Vol. 1 *Poems upon Several Occasions* by the Marston St Lawrence-born poetess. Her poems were edited after her death by Isaac Hawkins Browne the elder

JOHN MERRY. Frontispiece to Merry's *Miscellaneous Pieces* showing Moulton Mill where the poet was miller

CHARLES MONTAGU-DOUGLAS-SCOTT, author of *Northamptonshire Songs* and *Tales of Northamptonshire;* a photograph taken in 1899

JOHN PLUMMER,
author of *Songs of Labour, Northamptonshire Rambles and other poems* (1860) who later became one of Australia's leading newspaper editors

THOMAS RANDOLPH,
the poet and dramatist who was born at Newnham and became one of Ben Jonson's poetic 'sons'.
He died at Blatherwycke in 1635 at the age of 30

Grieved for the lovely treasure thou hadst lost.
How sweet a dream that silly world did break!
I see thee standing mid the ripening corn,
Watching the lark soar upward in its flight,
And catching inspiration from its song:
I see thee by the little babbling brook,
Weaving sweet music from the shallow stream,
Rippling and murmuring in its pebbly bed;
Each tiny flower that grew upon its banks,
Or branch that cast its shadow o'er the stream,
Or songster twittering in the willow copse,
Or butterfly or buzzing humble bee,
Is answered by a voice as sweet and pure,
And musical, and innocent of guile,
That speaks from out thy earnest loving heart,
That whispers from the garden of thy soul.
But like a vision of supremest ill,
I see thee standing mute and passionless!
The noble fire lies dead within thy eye,
And in its place sits stolid dark despair!
The strings of that sweet instrument, thy soul,
Lie broken o'er the ruins of thy heart!
The cheerless walls that frown upon thy woe
Are not so desolate as thy sad state;
Reason lies prostrate, and its peerless throne
Doth hold usurping chaos for its king.
Where wander now thy threaded pearls of thought?
For though in after time some feeble gleam
Was shed across the darkness, and again
Thou didst essay to touch the charmed strings,
'Twas but the feeble echo of a harp
Touched by a hand whose skill for aye had fled.

First Fruits, 1874

* Abington Abbey Retreat, opened in 1845, was a lunatic asylum founded and supervised by Dr. T. S. Prichard, who had previously been medical superintendent to Northampton General Lunatic Asylum. Though Rowlatt mentions Clare in his reverie on Abington Abbey, the poet had in fact been Prichard's patient at NGLA.

11. Dear simple John. John Clare. (Author's note.)

JOHN RYLAND

(1753–1825)

John Ryland's father, John Collett Ryland, was Baptist Minister at College Street Church from 1759–86 and also wrote religious verse (there is a pamphlet in the Northamptonshire Studies Collection at Northampton Central Library). John Jnr. was born at Warwick on 29 January 1753 and educated at home. He was by all accounts a precocious child and before he was nine had read and translated the whole of the Greek Testament. In 1781 he was ordained co-pastor at his father's church in Northampton and when his father moved to London remained as sole pastor. Whilst here, he preached 'in numerous villages and country places'. He was a friend of William Carey and Andrew Fuller and with them was co-founder of the Baptist Missionary Society. In 1794 he moved to Broadmead, Bristol, where he died on 25 May 1825. Whilst at Northampton he published several poetry pamphlets. The following poem, written just before his death, is taken from *Hymns and Verses on Sacred Subjects* published posthumously in 1862.

Musings in a Time of Affliction

In that day,
Oh! grant I may
Find mercy, Lord, with thee;
Thro' Him who kept thy holy law,
Without a blemish or a flaw,
Then died upon the tree.

Full of sin,
And guilt within,
No worthiness I plead:
If thou iniquity shouldst mark,
Dismal my prospects were, and dark,
Hopeless my case indeed.

Merit none
Call I my own;
But my demerits vast:
Think of the merits of thy Son!
What he has suffer'd! – he has done!
And I am safe at last.

Vile I am;
But this blest Lamb
His precious blood has spilt;
That blood, thou hast been pleas'd to say,
Can wash the foulest stains away,
And cancel all my guilt.

On him I
Humbly rely,
All other trust abjure;
Jesus, to thee alone I flee:
This hope shall like an anchor be,
For ever firm and sure.

Hymns and Verses, 1862

WILLIAM DRAKE SARGEAUNT

(1859–post 1929)

William Drake Sargeaunt, the son of John Barnaby Sargeaunt (b. 1823) and Elizabeth Drake, was born and brought up at Stanwick and educated at New College, Oxford, where he took his B.A. in 1883. He was Vicar of Bozeat with Strixton from 1892 to 1901, during which time he published *The Banks of Nene* (privately printed, 1900) and *Poems* (Dent, 1902). Afterwards he moved to Stoke Abbott and Donhead St. Mary in Dorset. He married Florence Thursby; their son, Lieutenant-Colonel W. T. Sargeaunt, published an article on the family, 'Sargeaunts and Shoemakers' in *NP&P*, III, 280–1. Sargeaunt was an ardent Liberal and a great friend of the Liberal M.P. for East Northants, Francis Channing (1841–1926).

That he was pleased to return as vicar to a parish close to his beloved Nene is apparent from his poem, *The Banks of Nene:*

With happy presage I return
To fields I count it joy to know . . .
For there my boyish days were spent
In eager-hearted merriment.

His dearest wish was to

Help live again the beauty shewn
Of old in gothic arch and spire,
And music's full harmonious tone
Restore to the four-voicèd choir
From Peter's stately western pile
To lowly Bozeat's pillared aisle.

I have chosen his poem on the whitlow-grass, not only because it achieves a miniature perfection, but also because it may well be the only poem ever written about this remarkably beautiful, but tiny and often overlooked flower.

Whitlow-Grass

Fierce and cold are the winds of March
That play with the delicate twigs of the larch,
And hinder the day when she shall be seen
Decked in her robing of tender green.

A robin the leafless boughs among
Singeth his early matin song,
He alone of the countless choir of May
Carols to welcome the rising day.

The crocuses their cups of gold
Refuse in trembling fear to unfold,
Nor in quest of their sweetness is any bee
Hovering from flower to flower to see.

Penned in the hurdles the huddled flock
Against the frost and boisterous shock
Of winds that scatter sleet and rain
Their thick warm winter coats retain.

For mists hang over the country side,
And their shepherds busy themselves to provide
What yet remains of winter fare,
And patches of snow lie here and there.

But the tiny whitlow-grass on the wall
Nor frost nor furious winds appal,
And ere the warmer days are begun
His little starry course is run.

Poems, 1902

THOMAS VAUX
2nd Baron Vaux of Harrowden
(1509–56)

The eldest son of Nicholas Vaux (pronounced 'Vawkes'), 1st Baron of Harrowden, and Anne, daughter of Thomas Green of Green's Norton, Thomas Vaux was born at Harrowden Hall on 25 April 1509 and educated at Cambridge. He succeeded to the barony on the death of his father in 1523 and in the same year married Elizabeth, sole daughter and heir of Sir Thomas Cheyne of Thenford and Irthlingborough. He attended in Wolsey's train on his embassy to France, later accompanying Henry VIII to Calais and Boulogne, and was created Knight of the Bath on the occasion of the coronation of Queen Anne Boleyn in 1533. Little is known of his life after the death of Henry VIII. His biographer, Geoffrey Anstruther, suggests that 'he probably lived quietly at Harrowden, writing his plaintive songs and singing them to his friends, thus keeping his head on his shoulders and his hands clean' (*Vaux of Harrowden: a Recusant Family*, 1953). It was he who proclaimed Mary I at Northampton on 18 July 1553. In 1556 England was visited by widespread drought followed by plague. Lord Vaux fell victim to it and died in the middle of October 1556; his wife, Elizabeth, died a month later. He is buried 'in Northamptonshire', but nobody seems to know where.

Vaux belonged, with Sir Thomas Wyatt and the Earl of Surrey, to the cultured circle of 'courtly makers' at the end of Henry VIII's reign, but unlike that of his eminent peers, his own work tends to be 'overweighted with a freight of proverbial morality' (Jourdain, in *Memorials of Old Northamptonshire*, 1903, p. 219). His work, however, was greatly admired in his own day and received high praise from his contemporaries:

> Piers Plowman was full plaine
> And Chaucer's spreet was great;
> Earl Surrey had a goodly vayne,
> Lord Vauxe the marke did beat.

Thomas Churchyard, in his
1568 edition of Skelton's Works

> The Lord Vaux his commendation lyeth chiefly in the facillitie of his meetre, and the aptnesse of his descriptions such as he taketh upon him to make, wherein he sheweth the conterfait action very lively and pleasantly.

George Puttenham: Arte of English Poesie (1589)

Though none of his poetry was published during his lifetime, two poems appeared soon after his death in *Songes and Sonettes* (*Tottel's Miscellany*, 1557) and a further fifteen in *The Paradise of Dainty Devices* (1576), both of which ran into several editions and were clearly very popular. Several of his lyrics were set to music during the Elizabethan period, the most famous being *An Aged Lover renounceth Love*, which has been immortalised by Shakespeare in the parody version mumbled by the First Gravedigger in *Hamlet*. An early lute-song setting of *No Pleasure without Some Paine* was published by William Barley in 1596. Three hundred years later, Vaughan Williams made a memorable setting for voice and piano. Vaux's poetry tends to sound pessimistic and gloomy to our ears:

> He is one of the old Catholic nobility, deeply disturbed by the prevailing religious chaos, and singing in the midst of the ruins.

Anstruther: *op. cit.*

The Aged Lover Renounceth Love

I loathe that I did love,
In youth that I thought sweet;
As time requires, for my behove,
Methinks they are not meet.

My lusts they do me leave,
My fancies all be fled,
And tract of time begins to weave
Grey hairs upon my head.

For age with stealing steps
Hath clawed me with his crutch,
And lusty life away she leaps,
As there had been none such.

My Muse doth not delight
Me as she did before;
My hand and pen are not in plight,
As they have been of yore.

For reason me denies
This youthly idle rhyme;
And day by day to me she cries,
'Leave off these toys in time.'

The wrinkles in my brow,
The furrows in my face,
Say, limping age will lodge him now
Where youth must give him place.

The harbinger of death,
To me I see him ride;
The cough, the cold, the gasping breath
Doth bid me to provide.

A pickaxe and a spade,
And eke a shrouding sheet,
A house of clay for to be made
For such a guest most meet.

Methinks I hear the clerk
That knolls the careful knell,
And bids me leave my woeful work,
Ere nature me compel.

My keepers knit the knot
That youth did laugh to scorn,
Of me that clean shall be forgot,
As I had not been born.

Thus must I youth give up,
Whose badge I long did wear;
To them I yield the wanton cup,
That better may it bear.

Lo, here the barèd skull,
By whose bald sign I know
That stooping age away shall pull
That youthful years did sow.

For beauty with her band
These crooked cares hath wrought,
And shippèd me into the land
From whence I first was brought.

And ye that bide behind,
Have ye none other trust;
As ye of clay were cast by kind,
So shall ye waste to dust.

15. Plight = condition.

Tottel's Songes and Sonettes, 1557

No Pleasure Without Some Paine

How can the tree but waste and wither away
That hath not sometime comfort of the sun?
How can that flower but fade and soon decay
That always is with dark clouds over-run?
Is this a life? Nay, death you may it call,
That feels each pain and knows no joy at all.

What foodless beast can live long in good plight?
Or is it life where senses there be none?
Or what availeth eyes without their light?
Or else a tongue to him that is alone?
Is this a life? Nay, death you may it call,
That feels each pain and knows no joy at all.

Whereto serve ears if that there be no sound?
Or such a head where no device doth grow
But all of plaints, since sorrow is the ground
Whereby the heart doth pine in deadly woe?
Is this a life? Nay, death you may it call,
That feels each pain and knows no joy at all.

Paradise of Dainty Devices, 1576

ANN WALTON

(fl. 1810)

Like Elizabeth Brown (q.v.), Ann Walton was a 'cottage-girl poet', though of a slightly earlier generation. I know nothing of her other than the few facts gleaned from the copies of her *Original Pieces on Different Subjects Chiefly in Verse* in the Northamptonshire Studies Collection at Northampton Central Library. This volume was published at 'Harleston, Northamptonshire'; there is no date, but it is probably c1810. On the flyleaf of one copy is the inscription: 'Jane Williamson/Her Book/Janry 21st/1812/ Gave her by Mrs. Walton/of Harlestone/Northampton.' The 'Mrs.' would not necessarily have meant that she was married. (Mary Leapor was often referred to as 'Mrs. Leapor'.) All the items are in verse except for *A Prayer*. I like her poem, *Contemplation*. It has the homely directness and simplicity of the best primitive poetry. The philosophical content is 'Northampton' through and through, reminiscent of our few surviving folk-songs which it closely resembles in language and tone.

Contemplation

Or Serious Thoughts in a Flower Garden

After many a frost and snow
And cold bad winters day
It was into my garden
I happened to stray.
There I again did see
The flow'rs begin to spring
And likewise I did hear
The pretty birds to sing.

'Twas there full in my sight
Upon my flower bed
A snow-drop look'd so white
All with its drooping head.
The patica likewise
Did spring up without fear,
All this to me did shew
That spring was drawing near.

These flowers look'd to me
So very fine and gay
As if they never was
To fade and fall away.
There is people here on earth
I really do believe
Who vainly in their mirth
Themselves as much deceive.

For they will boast and say
O we shall not die yet
But little do they think
Their time on earth is set.
There's no one can withstand
Grim death's resistless dart
When God doth him command
To strike us to the heart.

(God saith) there shall be a time
For all things ever be
But few attempt to find
A time to worship thee.

John Ryland

JOHN RYLAND, Baptist pastor and hymn-writer, who ministered at College Street church, Northampton, between 1781 and 1794

THOMAS VAUX: Holbein's portrait-sketch of the Tudor poet who inspired Shakespeare's gravedigger to song in *Hamlet.* [Windsor Castle, Royal Library, Her Majesty The Queen]

A time for all things here
Allowed is on the earth,
A time likewise for trouble
And a time for mirth.

A time there is for flowers
To look fresh and gay,
A time likewise for them
To wither and decay.
There is a time for man
When he must die also
As quickly each of us
The truth thereof shall know.

We then are like the flow'rs
That quickly fade away,
But still there is preserv'd
For us another day,
And if we do but strive
And do from sin refrain
There is a heav'n above
Where we may live again.

There we again shall bloom
And look so fresh and gay
Just like the rose in june
And the sweet flow'rs in may.
There evermore preserv'd
We ne'er shall fade again
But live in endless bliss
Freed from all care and pain.

Original Pieces, c1810

13. patica. Hepatica: probably *Anemone hepatica triloba*, cultivated as a garden flower in this country since 1573, which flowers from early February onwards.

SIMON WASTELL
(1560–1631)

Simon Wastell was descended from a family who lived at Wastell-(Wasdale-)head, though he may well have been born in Northampton (see *NN&Q*, V, 116-7). He entered Queen's College, Oxford in c1580 and took his degree five years later, married Elizabeth and settled in Northampton. She bore him several children: the register of baptisms at All Saints' Church contains entries for eleven children born between 1592 and 1611. 'Being accounted so proficient in classical learning and poetry, he was made Master of the Free School at Northampton, whence by his sedulous endeavours, many were sent to the Universities.' (Lees: *A Short History of Northampton Grammar School, 1541–1941*, 1947, p. 27.) This appointment took place in c1605 and he remained Master until his death in January 1631. In 1607 he was granted the freedom of the borough in recognition of his services to the vicar of All Saints, Robert Catelin, a puritan who had a long series of confrontations with the diocesan authorities. (See Sheils: *The Puritans in the Diocese of Peterborough, 1558-1610*, 1979, p. 127.)

In 1623 Wastell published *A True Christian's Daily Delight*, a translation of John Shaw's *Biblii Summula* (1621). In 1629 he issued a second, enlarged edition retitled *Microbiblion, or the Bible Epitome, in Verse*: 'The Summe of every Chapter of the Old and New Testaments, set down Alphabetically, in English verse, that the Scriptures we reade may more happily be remembered, and the things forgotten more easily recalled.' Wastell's aim was to fix the history of the Bible in the memory of young people, and to accomplish this he began each stanza with the letters of the alphabet in regular succession. As such the work achieved a certain popularity. George Wither, author of *Hymns and Songs of the Church* (1623) and himself no mean exponent of biblical paraphrase, supplied commendatory verses and Wastell dedicated his volume to 'the Right Honourable, his singular good Lord, Sir William Spencer, Knight, Baron Spencer of Wormleighton'. In the Appendix to the 1629 edition, Wastell printed the famous verses beginning, 'Like to the damask rose. . . .' This poem for many years was attributed to him–indeed Elgar's famous setting (1892) bears Wastell's name. But it is now considered to be the work of Francis Quarles (1592–1644). A pity: it is better poetry than the *Bible Epitome*. I print the opening sequence from *Microbiblion*, letters A–F of *Genesis*, as a sample of Wastell's schoolmasterly versification.

(Verses from Genesis)

At first Jehovah with his word
    did make heaven, earth and light:
The firmament, the moone, and starres,
    the glistering Sunne so bright.

By him the earth was fruitfull made
    and every creature good:
He maketh man like to himselfe,
    and doth appoint his food.

Creation ended, God then rests,
    and sabbath day ordaines:
Plants Eden, and the fruit forbids,
    for feare of endlesse paines:

Dust of the ground was man made of:
    of rib out of his side
The woman: Adam nameth all:
    wedlocke is sanctifide.

Eve by the serpent is deceived,
    they fall most shamefully:
God them arraignes, doth serpent curse,
    and putteth enmitie

Foule Serpent twixt and woman's seed,
    man's punishment's set downe,
Their first cloathing, their casting out,
    The Lord at them did frowne.

Microbiblion, or the Bible Epitome, in Verse, 1629

LEONARD WELSTED

(1688–1747)

If Leonard Welsted is remembered today, it is usually because of Pope's mock eulogy in Book 3 of *The Dunciad:*

> Flow, Welsted, flow! like thine inspirer, beer,
> Though stale, not ripe; though thin, yet never clear;
> So sweetly mawkish, and so smoothly dull;
> Heady, not strong; o'erflowing, though not full.

As one commentator has observed, this criticism, though making allowance for poetic exaggeration, is just. Welsted was born at Abington on 3 June 1688, where his father was rector from 1685–92, and was educated at Westminster (where he was Queen's Scholar) and Trinity College, Cambridge (1707). He then became what today we would term a civil servant, working in the offices of one of the Secretaries of State. By 1725 he was Clerk Extraordinary to Leonard Smelt, Clerk of the Deliveries in the Ordnance Office, and had a house in the Tower of London. In 1730 he had risen to Clerk in Ordinary and in the following year was appointed one of the commissioners for managing the state lottery. His first wife was Frances, daughter of the composer, Henry Purcell. She died in 1724. The only daughter from this marriage died in 1726 which prompted his *A Hymn to the Creator.* His second wife, Anna Maria Walker, was a great beauty, the 'Zelinda' of *A Song.* She died in 1747, just after her husband.

Welstead's genius certainly 'flowed', and from an early age. His poem, *Apple-Pye* was written in 1704 (and published in King's *Art of Cookery,* 1709) and is a precocious effort for a sixteen-year-old. During his lifetime he published numerous odes, epistles, satires and plays. In *The Triumvirate* (1717) he attacked Pope, Gay and Swift, which inevitably led to Pope's retaliation in *The Dunciad* (see above). In 1724 he published a collection of *Epistles, Odes, etc. written on several subjects.* Nichols edited *The Works in Verse and Prose* in 1787. The song, *While in the bower,* was set to music by Henry Carey as *The Nightingale.* He died at his residence in the Tower in August 1747.

The Invitation

Freeman, I treat tonight, and treat your friends:
If, happily, from care your thought unbends,
If Lucy rules not with her jealous sway,
I shall expect you at the close of day.

I give you the rough wholesome grape, that grows
In Tuscan vales, or where the Tagus flows;
Of, if the Gallic vine delight you more,
Of Hermitage I boast a slender store.
This is my wealth: if you have better wine,
Make me your guest; if not, I claim you mine.

Already is my little sideboard graced;
The glasses marshalled; the decanters placed:
The room is cool; the summer-hearth is gay
With greens and flowers, th'exub'rance of the May.
Indulge the bliss this cheerful season brings;
Omit minuter hopes, and joyless things;
Let fame and riches wait. This happy morn,
With Brunswick, peace and liberty were born!
'Tis fit, my friend, we consecrate to mirth
The day, which gave th'illustrious monarch birth:
When the sun sets, we'll break into delight,
And give to gay festivity the night.

Of what avail is fortune unenjoyed?
Or what is life, in anxious hours employed?
Let the dull miser pine with niggard care,
And brood o'er gold, devoted to his heir:
While we in honest mirth send time away,
Regardless what severer sages say.
In cheerful minds unbidden joys arise,
And well-timed levities become the wise.

What virtue does not generous wine impart?
It gives a winning frankness to the heart;
With sprightly hope the drooping spirits arms;
Awakens love, and brightens beauty's charms;
High, florid thoughts th'inspiring juices breed;
Spleen they dispel, and clear the brow of need.

Expect superfluous splendour from the great:
Ragousts, and costly follies served in plate.
And ortolans, from distant regions brought.
In foreign arts of luxury untaught,

I give you only lamb from Uxbridge fields:
And add the choicest herb the garden yields;
Silesian lettuce, with soft Lucca oil,
Delicious blessings of a different soil!

None do our band of fellowship compose,
But know the chasteness of the banquet-rose.
Belmour is ours; Loveless, with humour stored;
And careless Florio, if he keeps his word.
I should exceed your rule, were more allowed:
There's less of mirth than tumult in a crowd.

Remember, time posts on with subtle haste:
Now, as I write, the numbered minutes waste.
Then, Freeman, let us seize the present hour,
And husband the swift moments in our pow'r.
Good-humour bring along, and banish care:
You know your friends; you know your bill of fare.

Epistles, Odes &c, 1724

The poem, originally published in *The Free-thinker*, 29 May 1719, imitates Horace, *Epistles*, I.v. and refers to the King's (George I's) birthday.
39. Ortolans. Small European bird, esteemed as a delicacy.
47. Belmour. Young man-about-town. (Congreve. *The Old Bachelor*.)
47. Loveless. Suitor to 'The Scornful Lady'. (Beaumont and Fletcher. *The Scornful Lady*.)
48. Florio. Witty reference to the lexicographer John Florio (self styled 'The Resolute'), who was parodied as the peasant Holofernes in Shakespeare's *Love's Labour's Lost*.

A Song

While in the bower, with beauty bless'd,
The lov'd Amintor lies;
While, sinking on Zelinda's breast,
He fondly kiss'd her eyes;

A wakeful nightingale, who long
Had mourn'd within the shade,
Sweetly renew'd her plaintive song,
And warbled through the glade.

'Melodious Songstress,' cry'd the swain,
'To shades less happy go;
Or, if with us thou wilt remain,
Forbear thy tuneful woe.

While in Zelinda's arms I lie,
  To song I am not free;
On her soft bosom while I sigh,
  I discord find in thee.

Zelinda gives me perfect joys:
  Then cease thy fond intrusion;
Be silent; music now is noise,
  Variety confusion.'

The Works in Verse and Prose, 1787

The song was first printed in *The Free-thinker*, 25 December 1719.

BENJAMIN WEST
(1740–91)

Benjamin West was the village schoolmaster at Weedon Bec, where he was born and died. He described himself in his poem *A Morning Invitation* as poet of the 'dear Weedonian plains' and elsewhere as 'the Weedonian Bard'. He was highly regarded by his fellow poets in the county and his *Poems, Translations and Imitations* (1780) had a massive list of subscribers. He is referred to in poems by Moulton schoolmaster, William Chown (dedicatory poem to Coles and Furniss: *Poems, Moral and Religious*, 1811, q.v.) and Coles (dedicatory poem to Furniss Jnr.'s *Miscellaneous Poems*, 1841). His daughter married the Weedon Lois poet, Joseph Furniss Snr., and Coles and Furniss wrote an elegy on the death of his son, Benjamin Jnr. (d. June 1809). He was buried at Weedon Bec on 2 September 1791.

Victor Hatley has described West's poetry as 'mostly fustian', but West had the praiseworthy virtue of putting his poetic talents to practical use. In his poem *On the Departure of an Inhuman Taskmaster* he exposes James England, a notorious local ribbon-weaver and silk-manufacturer (see Victor A. Hatley: 'The Inhuman Taskmaster: a Story of Weedon Bec', *NP&P* III, 30-34). He also had a long-running verbal battle with a rival Northamptonshire poet, 'Lapidarius'. Who provoked the argument is uncertain, but West, in his preface to *The Pedantic Hypocrite Exposed* (1786), states that Lapidarius had vented his spleen on West in a series of pamphlets after West had turned down a poem for inclusion in an anthology. West replied with a satire on Lapidarius, published as the Prize Enigma in the widely-read *Gentleman's Diary* for 1786. Lapidarius responded with a pamphlet, *Criticus Unmask'd* and West wrapped up the matter with *The Pedantic Hypocrite Exposed; or The Crick Wolf Exhibited in his proper garb to the Public* (Dicey, 1786). This battle of wits between two local poets seems remote to us today, a tiny storm in a distant tea-cup, but was clearly important to those involved. The identity of 'Lapidarius' is unknown but is almost certainly a stone-cutter from Crick named William Billington. ('Lapidarius' = 'stone-cutter'; West's jibe about 'The Crick Wolf' neatly locates him. I am indebted to Victor Hatley for his help in unravelling this 'Prize Enigma'.) West also turned his hand to musical composition and in 1760 published *Sacra Concerto: or the Voice of Melody*, which contains an introduction to musical theory and forty-one psalm-tunes and twelve anthems 'chiefly intended for the Use of Country Choirs' which he himself had composed. Without appearing unkind, the results can only be described as rather primitive, and one wonders at the musical discernment of those scholars of his who had acknowledged 'the benefit they have received from them'. In taking *A Pastoral* as a sample of his verse, I have chosen a poem which combines West's poetic talent with his love of his native landscape and music.

A Pastoral

Addressed to Laura

Arise, pretty Laura, arise!
Attend to the dictates of love!
See! the lark soars aloft to the skies,
And carols an anthem to Jove.

The dawn's rosy hour to enjoy,
Let's haste to yon jessamine shade;
No dangers our bliss will annoy;
No clamours our quiet invade.

Astride tardy dobbin, the swain
Blithe whistling in concert is found
With the blackbird's mellifluous strain,
That undulates softly around.

The cuckow, thro' meadow and grove
Cornuto derides in her song;
And Philomel warbles her love
The woodlands and vallies among.

With raptures of poetry warm'd,
Deep-musing on pastoral themes;
The bard with such melody charm'd,
Of Pindus and Helicon dreams.

The peasant, with heart-bounding joy,
The fruits of his industry sees
In fields, where the green-bearded rye,
Waves gently before the soft breeze.

By Nen's limpid mirror, the lambs
Frisk wanton along the green mead,
And bleat for their lactary dams,
While Corydon pipes on the reed.

All nature invites us to love:
  Then, Laura, O! bless and be blest,
With heart-soothing pity remove,
  The anguish you caus'd in my breast.

A pledge shall I give to my fair?
  A pair of young turtles receive:–
Then frown,–and I die with despair;
  But smile,–and with transport I live.

Miscellaneous Poems, Translations, and Imitations, 1780

14. Cornuto. Cuckold. 15. Philomel. The Nightingale.
20. Pindus. Range of mountains in Northern Greece.
20. Helicon. The home of the Muses.
28. Corydon. A love-sick shepherd.

JANE WEST
(1758–1852)

The name Jane West is hardly known, if at all, today. Yet in her lifetime she and her *nom-de-plume*, 'Mrs. Prudentia Homespun', were familiar to a wide reading-public. By the time she was forty she had published half-a-dozen volumes of poetry, two tragedies, a comedy and two novels. Her obituary appeared in the *Gentleman's Magazine* and she has an entry in *DNB*. She was born in London 30 April 1758, the daughter of John Iliffe and his wife Jane. When she was eleven, the family moved to Desborough. Entirely self-educated, she was a precocious scholar and began writing verse at the age of thirteen. She married Thomas West, a yeoman farmer of Little Bowden, on 18 November 1782. Her husband's maternal ancestors had been Rectors of Little Bowden for 150 years and Thomas' name crops up in the parish records as churchwarden between 1782 and 1810. The baptism registers at Little Bowden have entries for three children born to them: Thomas (1783), John (1787) and Edward (1794), so Jane was well-qualified to write her major poem, *The Mother* (1809). This is a didactic work, an early nineteenth century Spock and Agony-Aunt combined. Book I, 'Infancy', begins:

> I sing the mother's duties, joys and cares

and goes on to address 'young women to be careful in their conjugal choice' (see the extract below). Her *Poems and Plays* appeared in four volumes between 1799 and 1805. She lived to the ripe old age of ninety-three, dying at Little Bowden on 25 March 1852.

from The Mother

And ye, fair maids! Thron'd in the early pride
Of beauty's reign, fly not alarm'd: my lay
Courts the chaste ears of those who wish to lead
Their willing captives to the honour'd shrine

Of life-endearing Hymen. Ev'n to you
Th'unborn maternal passion pleads to check
The pride of levity, the rash resolve
Of doting, headstrong, eye-directed love.
Is there among your train a youth whose arts
Triumph'd o'er virgin fame; who mocks at faith
Divine and human; who, with boastful air,
Recounts his orgies to the bestial powers,
Bacchus, or Paphian Venus? Tho' his form
Vie with Adonis, tho' in wealth he seem
First born of Plutus, and in fame excel
Alcmena's son, reject his baleful vows,
Give not your future projeny a sire
Whose deeds shall soil the gloss of youthful hope,
Or chill with deadly damps the ardent glow
Of generous emulation. Spare your heart
The pang it must endure, when the apt child
Turns o'er the sacred page, and weeping sees
Its father rank'd in Belial's cursed train,
Or Baal's slave, at emnity with heav'n.
Amid the haunts of guileless infancy,
Sacred to truth, can ye assume disguise
To gloss the crimes your intercessive prayers
Daily bewail? or bid th'ingenuous boy,
Panting with virtuous energy, divide
The sinner from the parent? Modest, fair
And innocent, your lovely daughters bloom.
Must they, with blushing cheeks and wounded hearts,
Fly from the guilty licence of the man
Who gave them being; lest the voice design'd
To utter benedictions, and call down
Unction celestial, should profane their ears
With jests obscene, or vaunting blasphemies–
Satan's accursed dialect;–to God
Most impious, and most horrible to man!

Nor let the coxcomb, forward, pert, and bold,
With swing important, vesture alamode,
Half bred, half civil, half inform'd, half wise,
Uttering quaint nothings, with distorted face,
And gestures from some ouran-outang caught
Seen at a raree-show; a spurious brood,
To Britain once unknown, familiar now
To crowded cities and to rustic burghs:

Let not this prating Dapper-wit, who gibes
At courts and camps, yet parodies their crimes,
Win wondering Cicely from blunt Colin Clout,
The honest son of pure simplicity,
Attractive even in his rustic garb.
No: let her call Audrey and Blowsibel
To strip the jackdaw of his plumes, and toss
His self-invested greatness to the wind.

The Mother, 1810, Bk. I: Infancy

5. Hymen. God of marriage.
13. Paphian Venus. Paphos was a city in Cyprus where Venus was worshipped; hence, illicit love-making.
15. Plutus. God of riches.
16. Alcmena's son. Hercules: his father was Zeus.
23. Belial. Satan.
24. Baal. A god (as lord of a place).
45. Raree-show. A travelling show (originally a peep-show).
48. Dapper. Brisk, lively, clever.
50. Colin Clout. Pastoral name assumed by the poet Spenser.

ELEANOR MARY WESTLEY

(fl. 1900)

Eleanor Westley's *Wayside Sketches* was published in the U.S.A. by the D. W. Robinson Press of Oakland, California. There is no publication date, but the copy in the Northamptonshire Studies Collection at Northampton Central Library has the words 'Put in Aug. 1900' pencilled on it. I have been unable to trace the Northampton connections of this poet. Westley, though, is a common local surname and the dialect of the 'door-knockers' in her amusing poem, *Writing under difficulties,* has a strong Northamptonian ring to it.

Writing Under Difficulties

The house is so quiet, and I am alone,
I will open my desk ere my fancies have flown,
And dipping my pen in the ink–but no more,
For I have to jump up; there's a knock at the door:
'Do you want any sorlt?'

Now why should my fingers so soon have to halt?
I certainly do not require any salt!
Then I take up my pen, write the title quite plain–
Rat-tat–O, confound it! the knocker again:
'Gas bill, please.'

With a sigh I come back to my desk and my pen;
But before I have scarcely had time to count ten
There's a black-looking fiend flings wide open the
door,
And his yelling re-echoes from ceiling to floor:
'Chimly wants sweepin'?'

Another *rat-tat.* Now who can that be?
O, I need not rise up; tis the postman, I see.
Why does he not go? He has something to-day;
And I open the door to find I must pay
'Extra postage, ma'am.'

Now I will write a line: but before I begin
There's a rattle of wheels and a clatter of tin;
With a noise like the screech of a demon in pain
(It is meant for a cry, if he did but speak plain):
'New milk, Oh!'

Let me see, now: where was I? I'm sure I forget;
But it really is no use whatever to fret.
This house must be certainly under a spell;
I have locked up the door, and now there's the bell–
That's the baker, I know.

I have taken the loaf, found my pen on the floor,
When I hear a child's lumbering knock at the door.
'T is a poor little fellow, his jacket all rags,
And his bare, chilly feet on the cold, frozen flags:
'Wood – six a penny!'

The agents, collectors and beggars who call,
I really can't give you a list of them all.
There are men who sell boot-laces, boys who sell
buns
And crumpets and cakes; but the noisiest ones
Cry: 'Evening paper! Fourth dishin!'

And so they keep calling from morning till night.
It is no use whatever attempting to write.
There are broken-down tradesmen with buttons to
sell:
Some knock at the door, some, ring, and some yell,
'Slithers to grind?'

But my bright-glowing fancies, my well-chosen words!
They have all flown away like a wild flock of birds;
And so, having nothing of value to send,
I will bring these inconsequent rhymes to an end–
There's a knock at the door!

Wayside Sketches, c1900

NATHANIEL WHITING

(1612–82)

Though not born in Northamptonshire, Nathaniel Whiting spent most of his turbulent life here. He was born in 1612, 'probably the son of Nathaniel of Desford, Leics.' (*Longden*). He was educated at Queen's College, Cambridge (BA 1631, MA 1635) and was ordained at Peterborough Cathedral but, unable to accept the teaching of the Church of England, turned to nonconformity. He took the living at Lowick in 1645, where he replaced the ejected rector, Robert Lingard, and in the same year was instituted minister at Aldwincle All Saints through the patronage of his friend Sir William Fleetwood of Aldwincle Manor. At the Restoration he was deprived not only of his living but also of his post as headmaster of the local grammar school. After his ejection (1662) he gathered a church around him at Cranford and secured a licence as a Congregationalist at his own house and that of Lady Pickering at Titchmarsh (see John Dryden). Edmund Calamy (*Ejected Ministers*, 1662) describes him as 'not so eminent for his learning as for his holiness and heavenliness. . . . He has a singular gift in comforting the sick.' He died at Cranford 'of a violent fit of the wind' in 1682.

Whiting's life was typical of the turbulent pattern of the seventeenth-century parson. The Church of England clearly did not suit his spiritual needs: 'the door is too narrow for me to enter in', he is quoted as saying (*Calamy, op. cit.*). His dislike of ceremonial is demonstrated by an entry in the church accounts at Aldwincle showing that he sold the Early English font for 4s. 6d. and paid 6d. for 'a basone'. In 1632, whilst at Cambridge, he published some Greek and Latin poems, but his main literary work was *Le Hore di Recreatione, or, the Pleasant Historie of Albino and Bellama*, published in 1637. This long mock-heroic poem (over 4,000 lines) is a novel-in-verse, written in six-line stanzas and interspersed with songs and other lyrics. Considering that he was a 'fullblown Puritan' it is extraordinary that Whiting should have written such a poem, parts of which are Rabelasian in their ribaldry. The following extract is the description of the lovers' feast at a 'straw-thatched' cottage. No romantic pastoral this, but kitchen-sink realism! George Saintsbury in his edition of the poem remarks: 'the description of this meal requires nearly as strong a stomach to read as the meal itself to eat'. Needless to say, Bellama 'could not eat a bit' and Albino, though he ventured, 'was fain to spit'! There is an article on Whiting by a descendent, J. R. S. Whiting, in *NP&P*, IV, 223: *A Seventeenth Century Parson-Poet of Northamptonshire.*

(A Stomach-Turning Feast)

Then, joining heart and hand with easy pace,
They travelled to a paque adjoining near
Where in a straw-thatched roof (an homely place
For such a pair) they entertainèd were,
And what fine cates old Kath'rine could afford,
Was served in state unto an aged board.

Their table with rich damask cloths was spread,
Whose every twist outvied the double cable,
The napkins diaper, of equal thread,
The mourning trenchers clothèd were in sable.
A curious salt cut out o' th' boulder stone–
And for their plate–sincerely there was none.

The dropsied host like to a sew'r did strut,
To marshal every dish; and first did bring
A spacious bowl, to scour the narrow gut,
Of nut brown ale, a liquor for a king.
And says, 'My Bona Roba, drink this bowl,
'Twill clear thy throat, and cheer thy drooping soul.'

Next came the mumping hostess and set down
A lusty dish of milk–sky-coloured blue,
Crumbed with the ludgets of the lusty brown,
Which two months since was piping hot and new;
'Yet 'tis,' says she. 'as savoury in good law
As wheaten trash which crams the ladies' maw.'

This good old crone was troubled so with wind,
Her coats did dance to th' music of her belly.
Next came a barley dumpling whose harsh rind
Was oilèd o'er with a fine tallow jelly
Brought by a mincing Marget, passing trim,
Whose juicy nose did make the pudding swim.

Next came some glotrah (which the ploughman flanks
Joined with a pudding on a holy day)
Brought by a jetting dame, on whom in ranks
And discipline of state whole troops did stray
Of–I forbear to say, lest these rude feet
With queasy dames and lady readers meet.

Last, a tough cheese must lock the stomach's door,
Milked from a cow that fed on naught but burrs,
Had lain five winters on a spongy floor,
To gain an harness and a coat of furs;
    So neatly peopled too, 'twas judg'd a court,
    Such herds of gentles did about it sport.

Le Hore di Recreatione, 1637

2. Pague. Village.   5. Cates. Fine food.
13. Sew'r. Sewer, one who comes before the meat at the table of a king, great man, to place the dishes etc.
19. Mumping. Sullen, churlish.   21. Ludgets. Lumps of bread
31. Glotrah. ?Tongue.   33. Jetting. Ostentatious

GEORGE JOHN WHYTE-MELVILLE
(1821–78)

This remarkable man—soldier, novelist, poet, sportsman and philanthropist—was born in 1821 at Stathkinnes, Fifeshire, the son of J. Whyte-Melville and Catherine Osborne, daughter of the 5th Duke of Leeds. He was educated at Eton after which he joined the army (1839-49), rising to captain in the Coldstream Guards. In 1854, on the outbreak of the Crimean War, he volunteered for active service, serving as a major of the Turkish irregular cavalry. After the war he devoted himself to literature and field sport, 'his days devoted to hunting, his evenings to literary work'. His love of field sports was one of the reasons why he moved to Northamptonshire. In 1847 he married Charlotte, second daughter of William Hanbury, 1st Lord Bateman of Kelmarsh Hall—an unhappy match by all accounts—and they lived at Boughton, where an inn now bears his name. Locker-Lampson has commented that, because he could always afford to hunt the fox, the excitement of the 'chasse aux pièces de cent sous, which stimulates most authors, was denied him', but he was nevertheless a very professional author. Because he did not need the money earned from his writing, he gave all profits to charity, including the working-man's club (1865) named after him in St. Giles' Street, Northampton. He lived for a short time at Wootton Hall before moving to London and finally (when his daughter married) to Tetbury, Gloucestershire. He was killed, as he might have wished, on the hunting-field, in the Vale of the White Horse, on 5 December 1878.

Whyte-Melville's novels on historical and hunting subjects were very popular in the last half of the nineteenth century. They include *Digby Grand* (1853), *Holmby [Holdenby] House* (1860)—set in Northamptonshire at the time of the Civil Wars—and *Market Harborough* (1861)—a contemporary hunting novel set in Fernie and Pytchley country. With Surtees he is considered the finest nineteenth-century chronicler of the hunting scene. As a poet of the chase he is without peer. Indeed, T. H. Ward (*Men of the Reign*, 1885) has described him as 'the Poet-Laureate of the Hunting Field'. His *Songs and Verses* was first published in 1869 and ran into numerous editions. Several of his poems have been set to music, notably by Frederic Cowen (1852-1935). The two poems that I have chosen show his two main literary preoccupations: historical romance and hunting. *A Cavalier's Song* comes from *Holmby House*. The poetic 'charade', *The Bullfinch* needs some explanation. The bullfinch in question is not *Pyrrhula pyrrhula*, but the high thick hedges of the shires:

> A bullfinch fence . . . is a quickset hedge of perhaps fifty years' growth with a ditch on one side or the other, and so high and strong that [one] cannot clear it. (*Quarterly Review*, March 1832).

Possibly they were so called because they looked as if nothing bigger than a bullfinch could force a way through.

A Cavalier's Song*

Ho! fill me a flagon, as deep as you please,
Ho! pledge me the health that we quaff on our knees;
And the knave who refuses to drink till he fall,
Why the hangman shall crop him—ears, lovelocks, and all,
    Then a halter we'll string,
    And the rebel shall swing,
For the gallants of England are up for the King!

Ho! saddle my horses as quick as you may,
The sorrel, the black, and the white-footed bay;
The troop shall be mustered, the trumpet shall peal,
And the Roundhead shall taste of a Cavalier's steel.
    For the little birds sing,
    There are hawks on the wing
When the gallants of England are up for the King!

Ho! fling me my beaver, and toss me the glove
That but yesterday clung to the hand of my love;
To be bound on my crest—to be borne in the van,
And the rebel that reaps it must fight like a man!
    For the sabre shall swing,
    And the head-pieces ring,
When the gallants of England strike home for the King!

Ho! crush me a cup to the queen of my heart!
Ho! fill me a brimmer, the last ere we part,
A health to Prince Rupert! Success and renown!
To the dogs with the Commons! and up with the Crown!
    Then the stirrup-cup bring,
    Quaff it round in a ring!
To your horses! and ride to the death for the King!

Holmby House, 1860

* This is the title that Whyte-Melville gave to the poem when it was re-published in *Songs and Verses*, 1869.

9. Sorrel. Light reddish-brown horse; today it would be called a 'chestnut'.
15. Beaver. Armour to cover the lower part of the face.

The Bullfinch

My first is the point of an Irishman's tale,
  My second's a tail of its own to disclose;
But I warn you in time, lest your courage should fail,
  If you're troubled with either the shakes or the slows,
That the longer you look at my whole in the vale,
  The bigger, and blacker, and bitterer it grows!

Songs and Verses, 1869

ROBERT WILD

(1609–79)

This 'fat, jolly, and boon Presbiterian' (Anthony à Wood) was born at St Ives, Huntingdonshire in 1609, the son of a shoemaker. He was educated at St John's College, Cambridge, where he received his MA in 1639. In 1642 the University of Oxford conferrred on him the BD and in 1661 the University of Cambridge the DD. He was appointed Curate of Aynho in 1639 and in 1646 was 'intruded' by the Parliamentary Visitors as Rector. The story goes that, to gain the benefice, he had to preach a competitive trial sermon against another minister. On being asked the result, he replied, 'We have divided it. I have the Ay! and he has the No!' After the Restoration he was ejected from his living (1662). He died in Oundle, where he was buried on 30 July 1679.

A notable Puritan divine and great anti-papist, Wild was one of the principal journalist-poets for the Presbyterians. In later years, however, he seems to have made his peace with the government and even written Royalist 'Panegyricks'. His *Iter Boreale* (1660: considerably expanded in 1661 and 1688), inspired by General Monck's march from Scotland to London in 1660, became immensely popular. Even Pepys confessed to liking it. The two epitaphs and *Alas poor scholar* come from the much-expanded 1668 edition. *Alas, poor scholar* is a parody of an anonymous poem, *Hollo, my fancy! Whither wilt thou go?* written about 1639. Wild's poem was published first in *Wit and Drollery* (1656) and was probably written in 1641. Many of its contemporary allusions are lost to us today, but it clearly shows the predicament of a would-be man-of-the-cloth in an age of religious turmoil. In the light of Wild's future career, it has a piquant irony.

from Alas, Poor Scholar, Whither Wilt Thou Go?*

In a melancholy study,
    None but myself,
Methought my Muse grew muddy;
    After seven years' reading,
    And costly breeding,

GEORGE WHYTE-MELVILLE, eminent novelist and 'the Poet-Laureate of the Hunting Field', who lived for several years at Boughton and Wootton Hall. [National Portrait Gallery]

ANTHONY WOODVILLE, 2nd Earl Rivers, who was born at Grafton Regis. The picture shows Earl Rivers presenting a copy of his *Dictes and Sayings of the Philosophers* (the first book published by Caxton in England) to his brother-in-law, Edward IV. Woodville's sister, Elizabeth, stands behind her husband; Prince Edward, the future Edward V, is between them. [Lambeth Palace Library]

I felt, but could find no pelf:
Into learned rags
I've rent my plush and satin,
And now am fit to beg
In Hebrew, Greek, and Latin;
Instead of Aristotle,
Would I had got a Patten!
Alas, poor scholar! whither wilt thou go?

Cambridge, now I must leave thee,
And follow fate,
College hopes do deceive me;
I oft expected
To have been elected,
But desert is reprobate.
Masters of colleges
Have no common graces,
And they that have fellowships
Have but common places,
And those that scholars are
They must have handsome faces.
Alas, poor scholar! whither wilt thou go?

I have bowed, I have bended,
And all in hope
One day to be befriended:
I have preached, I have printed
Whate'er I hinted,
To please our English pope;
I worship towards the east,
But the sun doth now forsake me;
I find that I am falling,
The northern winds do shake me:
Would I had been upright,
For bowing now will break me!
Alas, poor scholar! whither wilt thou go?

At great preferment I aimed,
Witness my silk;
But now my hopes are maimed:
I looked lately
To live most stately,
And have a dairy of bell-rope's milk;
But now, alas!
Myself I must not flatter—

Bigamy of steeples
Is a laughing matter;
Each man must have but one,
And Curates will grow fatter.
Alas, poor scholar! whither wilt thou go?

Into some country village
Now I must go,
Where neither tithe nor tillage
The greedy patron
And parched matron
Swear to the Church they owe.
Yet if I can preach,
And pray too on a sudden,
And confute the Pope
At adventure, without studying,
Then ten pounds a year,
Besides a Sunday pudding.
Alas, poor scholar! whither wilt thou go? . . .

Iter Boreale, 1668

* 'Or, Strange alterations which at this time be,
There's many did think they never should see.'

6. Pelf. Wealth.
12. Patten. High-soled shoe, over shoe, or clogs shod with irons to raise the feet out of the mud.
32. Our English pope. William Laud (1573–1645), the anti-puritan Archbishop of Canterbury.
48. Bigamy of steeples. Plurality of benefices, a growing evil in the church at the time.

Two Epitaphs

1. *For a Godly Man's Tomb*

Here lies a piece of Christ; a star in dust;
A vein of gold; a china dish that must
Be used in heaven, when God shall feast the just.

2. *For a Wicked Man's Tomb*

Here lies the carcase of a cursed sinner,
Doomed to be roasted for the Devil's dinner.

Iter Boreale, 1668

MICHAEL WODHULL

(1740–1816)

Michael Wodhull came from an old county family tracing back to the Conquest which had its seat at Thenford for more than 300 years. He was born at the family estate in 1740, son and heir of John and his second wife, Rebeccah, daughter of Charles Watkins of Aynho. He was educated privately at Twyford, Winchester College and Brasenose College, Oxford, where he matriculated but did not take his degree. After leaving Brasenose, 'he retired to his "paternal acres" where he occupied himself in reading, translating, and book-collecting until his death' (*Allibone*). He possessed a large fortune and had a town house in Berkeley Square. In the 1760s he built a new manor house for himself at Thenford, replacing an Elizabethan one near the church. A strong republican in his youth and a keen Whig, he was High Sheriff for Northamptonshire in 1783. In 1761 he married Catherine Milcah, daughter of Rev John Ingram of Welford, Warwickshire. There were no children from the marriage and he died at Thenford on 10 November 1816, the last of the Wodhull line.

Wodhull was a keen bibliophile and had an extensive personal library. After the Treaty of Amiens (1802) he visited Paris to look at the libraries, and was one of Napoleon's *détenus* for some time. He was also a notable translator, the first to translate into English verse all the extant tragedies and fragments of Euripides (1782, 4 volumes). In 1772 he published, for private circulation amongst his friends, his *Poems*. These were reprinted in 1798 and 1804 with his portrait prefixed.

Song

What still does fair Lucy's disdain
Occasion this festering smart;
Cannot Time give relief to your pain,
And heal the slight wound in your heart?

The arrows of Cupid, I know,
At first are all pointed with steel:
But how frail is the strength of his bow!
How fleeting the pang which we feel!

His wings they are shatter'd by Time,
His quiver is soil'd in the dust;
Such, such, is Life's flowery prime,
And Beauty's most insolent trust.

Taste the joys a new passion can give,
With the Nymph that's complying and kind;
Or, learning more sagely to live,
Be blest, and give Love to the wind.

Poems, 1772

ANTHONY WOODVILLE
Baron Scales and 2nd Earl Rivers
(1442?–83)

Knight, man-at-arms, 'Defendour and Directour of the Siege apostolique for our holy Fader the Pope in His Royame of England' (Caxton), scholar and poet, Anthony Woodville was born at Grafton (later Grafton Regis), son of Sir Richard Woodville (who became Earl Rivers in 1466 and was beheaded at Kenilworth in 1469) and brother of Elizabeth, who married Edward IV in 1464. He fought on the Lancastrian side at the Battle of Towton, March 1461, was reported killed, taken prisoner and obtained a pardon. After his sister's marriage, his advancement at court was rapid. He married twice: firstly Elizabeth, daughter of Lord Scales, who died in 1473, and secondly (c1480) Mary, daughter of Sir Henry FitzLewis. He was an accomplished knight–at Bruges, on the occasion of the marriage of the King's sister Margaret to the Duke of Burgundy, he broke eleven lances in the joust–and made several pilgrimages abroad to Portugal, Spain, Southern Italy and Rome. On his voyage in 1473 he was shown a copy of *Les dits moraux des philosophes* and on his return to England began to translate it. This book, *Dictes and Sayings of the Philosophers*, was the first book printed in England by Caxton at his Westminster press (1477). With the death of Edward IV, he fell out of favour. He was ambushed on the road from Northampton to Stony Stratford and within two months was executed at Pontefract, 25 June 1483, the first and noblest of the victims of Richard, Duke of Gloucester (the future Richard III). At the end of Shakespeare's *Richard III*, he appears as one of the ghosts to haunt his fellow-Northamptonian:

> Let me sit heavy in thy soul tomorrow,
> Rivers, that died at Pomfret. Despair and die.

On the eve of his death, Woodville is said to have written the following poem–the only specimen of his poetry to survive, for his *Diverse Balades agenst the Seven dedely synnes* is lost. This balet was published by Percy (qv) (1765) and Ritson (1792). Percy writes: 'We owe [it] to Rouse, a contemporary historian, who seems to have copied it from the earl's own handwriting'. It is written in imitation of Chaucer's poem beginning, *Alone wakyng, In thought plainyng*. It was set to music as a three-part song, possibly by Thomas Fayrfax, in the early sixteenth century. This setting must have been very popular, for it appears in at least five manuscript versions, including the *Fayrfax Book* (BM, Add MS 5465). A modern transcript appears in John Stevens' *Music at the Court of Henry VIII* (*Musica Britannica* XVIII, 1962/1969: No. 107) and the words of the balet are reprinted in the same author's *Music and Poetry in the Early Tudor Court* (1961: Appendix A).

Balet

written during his imprisonment
in Pontefract Castle, Anno 1483

1 Sum what musyng,
And more mornyng,
In remembring
The unstydfastnes;
This world being
Of such whelyng,
Me contrarieng,
What may I gesse?

2 I fere dowtles,
Remediles,
Is now to sese
My wofull chaunce.
For unkyndness,
Withouten less,
And no redress,
Me doth avaunce.

3 With displesaunce,
To my grevaunce,
And no suraunce
Of remedy.
Lo in this traunce,
Now in substaunce,
Such is my dawnce,
Willyng to dye.

4 Me thynkys truly,
Bowndyn am I,
And that gretly,
To be content;
Seyng playnly,
Fortune doth wry
All contrary
From myn entent.

5 My lyff was lent
Me to on intent,
Hytt is ny spent;
Welcome fortune!
But I ne went
Thus to be shent,
But sho hit ment,
Such is hur wone.

Reliques of Ancient English Poetry, 1765

6. Whelyng. Uncertainty. 38. Shent. Disgraced.
40. Wone. Wont (practice).

A Mixed Bunch

A NOSEGAY OF PLACE-RHYMES
A CALENDAR OF RHYMES
CHARMS, PROVERBS AND WEATHERSAWS
LACE-TELLS, SAMPLER VERSE, CHILDREN'S RHYMES
A WREATH OF EPITAPHS
A ROSETTE OF ELECTION SONGS
A FINAL POSY

A NOSEGAY OF PLACE-RHYMES

A Northamptonshire Jingle

Abington, Addington, Boddington, Doddington,
Bainton, Barton, Hinton, Horton,
Elmington, Elkington, Luddington, Loddington,
Slipton, Slapton, Knuston, Norton.

Hannington, Harrington, Overstone, Oxendon,
Gayton, Glendon, Glinton, Weston,
Warmington, Werrington, Hackleton, Piddington,
Moulton, Milton, Easton Neston.

Geddington, Harrowden, Hellidon, Hardingstone,
Brington, Brampton, Braunston, Charlton,
Middleton, Nassington, Duddington, Farthingstone,
Weldon, Weedon, Welton, Carlton.

Ailsworth, Arthingworth, Harringworth, Blisworth,
Astcote, Duncote, Eastcote, Burcote,
Culworth, Greatworth, Theddingworth, Brixworth,
Holcot, Hulcot, Huscote, Murcote.

Barford, Dodford, Cranford, Denford,
Blakesley, Brackley, Catesby, Mawsley,
Heyford, Lilford, Maidford, Thenford,
Daventry, Pytchley, Naseby, Fawsley.

Irthlingborough, Sudborough, Litchborough, Peterborough,
Cogenhoe, Farthinghoe, Furtho, Wadenhoe,
Silverstone, Haselbech, Pattishall, Wellingborough,
Rockingham, Wappenham, Passenham, Stowe.

Kislingbury, Lamport, Kingsthorpe, Middlethorpe,
Brafield, Byfield, Hollowell, Lowick,
Newbottle, Nobottle, Blatherwycke, Thorpe,
Maidwell, Pipewell, Scaldwell, Crick.

I do not know the origins of this ingenious rhyme, with its witty alliterations and humorous groupings. It appeared in *The Northampton County Magazine*, I, 1928, 20.

Brackley breed,
Better to hang than to feed.

This was, of course, Brackley a long time ago when it was a decayed market-town, abounding with poor, and breeding beggars . . .

King's Sutton is a pretty town,
And lies all in a valley:
There is a pretty ring of bells,
Besides a bowling-alley:
Wine and liquor in good store,
Pretty maidens plenty:
Can a man desire more?
There aint such a town in twenty.

Halliwell published this in *Nursery Rhymes and Tales of England* (1845). For another reference to the sweet bells of King's Sutton, see the main GARLAND under W. L. Bowles.

If we can Padwell overgoe, and Horestone we can see,
Then Lords of England we shall be.

If the origins of this rhyme are correct, then it is the oldest verse in the book. The Danes are supposed to have uttered it upon point of battle with the Saxons. Padwell is a spring near Edgcote; Horestone an old stone on the Warwickshire border.

Thorpe and Achurch stand in a row,
Lilford and Pilton and peevish Wadenhoe,
Onicle-Chronicle stands by the waterside,
Islip is nothing but malice and pride.
Thrapston, Whitehorse
Titchmarsh, the Cross,
Clapton, the Clay,
Barnwell, King's Highway,
Armston, On the hill,
Polebrook, In the hole,
Ashton, Blows the bellows,
Oundle, Burns the coal.

I heard this rhyme recited in Wadenhoe as recently as 1974. It appeared in *The Northampton County Magazine*, IV, 1931, 32, sent in by 'A. Milton, Wadenhoe'. He wrote that he remembered his father repeating it to him when he was a child. His father (who died aged 80 in 1924) had known it from *his* boyhood. Most of the references are self-explanatory. 'Onicle' is a local alternative for Aldwincle. Why Wadenhoe and Islip should be specially chosen for nasty remarks, I cannot think.

The wind blows cold
Upon Yardley old.

'Old' is a common Northamptonshire pronunciation of 'wold'.

A CALENDAR OF RHYMES

St. Valentine's Day

Good morrow, Valentine!
Plaze to give me a Valentine.
I'll be yourn, if ye'll be mine:
Good-morrow, Valentine!

Sternberg, 179

Parties of children, going from house to house 'soliciting gratuities', would sing this song or variants of it on the morning of St. Valentine's Day.

May Day

Remember us poor Mayers all,
To hear how we begin
To lead our lives in righteousness
For fear we die in sin.

For if we die, we die in sin,
The Lord will to us say,
Begone, begone, you wicked ones,
For I know not your way.

Awake, awake, you pretty maid,
Awake, and you shall hear;
For Christ hath died for all our sin,
And lovèd us so dear.

So dear, so dear He lovèd us,
Upon the cross was slain;
Bade us leave off our wicked ways
And turn to the Lord again.

Where have you been a-wandering
This day and night astray?
We've been and returned back again,—
Have brought you a branch of May.

A branch of May I've brought you here,
Before your door to stand;
It is but a sprout, but it's well spread about;
'Tis the work of our Lord's hand.

Take your Bible in your hand
And read your chapter through;
When the Great Day of Judgment comes,
The Lord will remember you.

The fields and meadows are so green,
As green as any leek;
Our heavenly father waters them
With his heavenly dew so sweet.

Give me a bowl of your good cream,
And a mug of your brown beer,
For we do not know where we may be
To be merry another year.

Now my story's almost done,
No longer can I stay;
God bless you all, both great and small,
And I wish you a joyful May.

Northamptonshire May-songs are mostly variants of the same basic format and all have a strongly puritanical streak to them. The above is the very full version given by Rev. Abner Brown, Vicar of Pytchley, 1832–51, in *Lyrical Pieces, Secular and Sacred*, 1869 (see page 40). Some versions omit the first five verses and begin with 'A branch [Or "bunch"] of May I've brought you. . . .' (For a full account, and the Polebrook version, see *Baker*, II, 421–9.)

Guy Fawkes Day

Please to remember
The fifth of November,
Gunpowder, treason
  and plot.
I see no reason
Why gunpowder treason
Should ever be forgot.

Umberella down the cellar,
There I saw a naked feller,
Burn his body, save his soul,
Please give me a lump of coal.
If a lump of coal won't do,
Please give me a hapenny,
All around the Market Square,
Up and down the Drapery.

I remember both versions of this November begging-song from my boyhood days in Northampton. The first is a fairly universal ditty; the second clearly local.

St. Catharine's Day

Here comes Queen Catharine, as fine as any Queen,
With a coach and six horses a-coming to be seen;
And a-spinning we will go, will go, will go,
And a-spinning we will go.

Some say she is alive, and some say she is dead,
And now she does appear with a crown upon her head;
And a-spinning we will go, &c.

Old Madam Marshall she takes up her pen,
And then she sits, and calls for all her royal men.

All you that want employment, though spinning is but small,
Come list and don't stand still, but go and work for all.

If we set a-spinning, we will either work or play,
But if we set a-spinning we can earn a crown a day.

And if there be some young men, as I suppose there's some,
We'll hardly let them stand alone upon the cold stone.
And a-spinning we will go, will go, will go,
And a-spinning we will go.

St. Catharine's Day (25 November) used to be observed as a holiday in Peterborough. 'Till the introduction of the new poor laws, the female children belonging to the workhouse, attended by the master, went in procession round the city on St. Catharine's Day. . . . The procession stopped at the homes of the principal inhabitants, begging for money at every house as they passed along' (*Baker*, II, 436). St. Catharine was patron saint of spinners, and spinning was formerly the employment of females at the workhouse.

The Mummers' Play

The mummers performed their folk-play at Tander (St. Andrew's Day, 11 December) or, more usually, Christmas. *Baker* (II, 429–32) quotes a version which she witnessed 'some years since, at the seat of the late Michael Wodhull, Esq. Thenford' (qv). She gives full details of the 'Dramatis Personae' and of their costumes. Here are two typical verses:

BEELZEBUB

In comes old Beelzebub,
On his shoulder he carries a club,
In his hand a dripping-pan:
Don't you think he's a funny old man?
Sweep, sweep, make room for me
And all my jolly company . . .

JACK

In comes I, little Jim Jack,
With my wife and family at my back;
Although my substance is but small,
I'll do my best to please you all.
Roast beef, plum pie –
Who likes it better than I?
I wish you a merry Christmas and a happy new
year,
A pocket full of money, and a cellar full of beer.

CHARMS, PROVERBS AND WEATHERSAWS

Some of these rhymes are in currency outside the county, but all are vouched for within.

CHARMS

Churn, butter, churn,
In a cow's horn;
I never see'd such butter
Sin' I was born.
Peter's standing at the gate
Waiting for a butter'd cake,
Come, butter, come.

Baker, I, 138

A Charm to Prevent a Thorn from Festering

Our Saviour was of a virgin born,
His head was crowned with a crown of thorn;
It never canker'd nor fester'd at all;
And I hope in Christ this never shall.

Sternberg, 155

PROVERBS

Thack and dyke
Northamptonshire like.

Sternberg, 113

Thack = thatch.

A whistling woman, and a crowing hen.
Is neither fit for God nor men.

Sternberg, 156

If you go a birn,
You go a sirn.

Baker, II, 236

birn = borrowing. sirn = sorrowing.

Go day, come day,
God send Sunday.

(Quoted by Thomas Isham of Lamport in his *Diary* for 7 November 1671. It is a proverb directed against clock-watchers.)

WEATHERSAWS

Rain on Easter-day,
Plenty of grass, but little hay.

Sternberg, 189

A swarm of bees in May
Be worth a load of hay;
A swarm in June
Be worth a silver spoon;
A swarm in July
Bent worth a fly.

Sternberg, 22

Ice in November to bear a duck,
Nothing after but sludge and muck.

Current in Wadenhoe, 1989

LACE-TELLS, SAMPLER VERSE CHILDREN'S RHYMES, ETC

LACE-TELLS

Like the sea-shanty and lullaby, the lace-tell is a work-song, sung by lacemakers in traditional areas of lace-making. It was sung not only to while away the time but also to fit in with the patterns and rhythm of work, hence the references to pins and fingers. Here are two local examples, recorded by Thomas Wright in *Romance of the Lace Pillow* (1919). The first comes from Yardley Hastings.

(i) Twenty pins have I to go,
Let ways be ever so dirty
Never a penny in my purse,
But farthings five and thirty.

Betsy Bays and Polly Mays,
They are two bonny lasses:
They built a bower upon a tower,
And covered it with rushes.

The reference in the last line is to taking rushes to church on 'Rush-bearing Sunday'.

(ii) Nineteen long lines hanging over my door,
The faster I work, it'll shorten my score,
But if I do play, it will stick to a stay,
So ho! little fingers, and twink it away,
So ho! my little fingers and twink it away,
For after tomorrow comes my wedding day!

My shoes are to borrow, my husband to seek,
So I cannot get married till after next week,
And after next week it will be all my care
To prink and to curl and to do up my hair.
So ho! my little fingers, and twink it away,
For after tomorrow comes my wedding day!

KNITTER'S RHYME

'The following rude lines are often repeated by knitters during their occupation, and appear to contain a caution against dropping stitches' (*Baker*, I, 354):

Needle to needle, and stitch to stitch,
Pull the old woman out of the ditch.
If you aint out by the time I'm in,
I'll rap your knuckles with my knitting-pin.

SAMPLER VERSE

Jesus, permit thy gracious name to stand,
As the first effort of an infant's hand;
And, while her fingers on the canvas move,
Engage her tender heart to seek thy love;
With thy dear children let her have a part,
And write thy name thyself upon her heart.

Baker, II, 195

This verse is said to have been composed for his wife by Thomas Trinder (1740–94), Principal of College Lane Boarding School (see Appendix A). According to Baker, it was frequently used on their samplers by Northampton children in the early years of the nineteenth century.

WASHING DAY RHYME

They that wash on Monday
    Have all the week to dry;
They that wash on Tuesday
    They have pretty nigh;
They that wash on Wednesday
    Have half the week past;
They that wash on Thursday
    Are very near the last;
They that wash on Friday
    Wash for need;
Thay that wash on Saturday
    Are sluts indeed.

Baker, II, 384

Nobody of course washed on Sunday.

CHILDREN'S RHYMES

(i) To a Ladybird

Cowlady, cowlady, fly away home,
Your house is on fire, your children are gone;
All but one, and that's little John,
And he lies under the grindle stone.

'Repeated by children if one of them happens to settle on the hand, to induce it to take flight; if it does not obey the command, it is thrown into the air.' (*Baker*, I, 149)

(ii) Bird-Boys' Rhymes

Pigeons and crows, take care of your toes,
Or I'll pick up my crackers,
And knock you down backards,
Shoo all away, Shoo away, Shoo.

Away, away, away birds,
Take a little bit, and come another day, birds;
Great birds, little birds, pigeons and crows,
I'll up with my clackers, and down she goes.

Shoo all away, birds and crows,
Never come no more till barley grows.

Shoo all away! all away!
Black-a-top, don't eat all your master's crap
While I lie down and have a nap,
Shoo! all away–all away!

Baker, I, 50

(iii) Oats and Beans

Oats and beans and barley grow,
Oats and beans and barley grow,
Do you or I or anyone know
Where oats and beans and barley grow?

The farmer comes and sows the seed,
Then he stands and takes his ease,
Stamps his foot and slaps his hand
And turns him round to view the land.
  Waiting for a partner,
  Waiting for a partner.

Now you're married you must obey,
Must be true to all you say,
Must be kind and must be good
And help your wife to chop the wood.

'Choosing Partners' was a popular singing-game at parties when I was a boy during and just after the Second World War. For those who do not know the ritual which accompanies the words, see *Northamptonshire Notes and Queries*, I, 163–5. *NN&Q*, II, 161 gives the tune to which the words are sung locally.

A WREATH OF EPITAPHS

Aldwincle All Saints

To Henry Pykering, rector for 40 years: d. 1637, aet. 75. He was John Dryden's maternal grandfather.

Just dealing, meekness, charitye, being such
At Heaven's command he practized very much:
For which Heaven's comfort failed not, when he cryed;
He lived to a full age, yet bewailed he died.

Boughton

Time was I stood where thou dost now,
And view'd the dead, as thou dost me;
Ere long thou'lt be as low as I,
And others stand and look on thee.

Great Brington

To Laurence Washington, Northamptonshire ancestor of the first President of the USA; d. 13 December 1616.

Those that by chance or choyce of this hast sight
Know life to death resignes as daye to night,
But as the sunns returne revives the day
So Christ shall us though turnde to dust and clay.

Canons Ashby

To John Mallbury, d. 5 May 1776, aet 78.

His life was Virtuous, meek, and lowly,
Patient, harmless, kind, and holy;
Free from Malice, void of pride,
So he liv'd and so he dy'd.

Courteenhall

To Richard Ouseley, d. 1599. He came from Shropshire. His first wife, nee Partridge, had no children; his second, a Wake from Salcey, had 12. The last two lines are supposed to be spoken by his second wife who died nine years after him.

A Salop's Osely I, a ruen Partridge woone,
No bird I had her by, such work was with her doone.
She dead I turtle sought, a Wake in Salsie bred,
Twice six birds she me brought, she lives but I am dead.
But when ninth year was come, I slept that was a-Wake,
So yielding to Death's doome, did here my lodging take.

Finedon

To Richard Dent.

Here lyeth Richard Dent
In his last tenement.

Gayton

To William Houghton, d. 17 December 1600.

Neere fourscore years have I tarryed
To this mother to be marryed.
One wife I had & children ten:
God bless the living, Amen, Amen.

Harpole

'Erected by his scholars of Harpole. Sam Leek, died April 18, 1729. Aged 46 years.'

He larned singing far and near
Full twenty year or more
But fatal Death hath stopt his breath
And he can larn no more.

His scholars all that are behind
Singing he did unfold
Exhorting all their God to mind
Before they turn to molde.

Lutton

To Adlard Apreece, d. 2 May 1608, aet 44.

Heare dead alyve Adlard Apreece survyves
Earthes ending Fate whos verute gaynes two lyves.
France knew his learning, Hungary his might,
Farara sawe him worthily dubd knight.
When it diffused in Joye did intertayne
The Austrian Princesse then matcht with Spayne.
Two famous Courtes Great Austrie and Baviere
For his approved service held him deare.
Thus Schoole, Campe and Court him heere honour
gave
Which he brought home for to adorne his grave.

Marholm

To Edward Hunter, d. 9 October 1646. A reminder of the Civil Wars and the destruction of 'popish' monuments by zealous parliamentarians. 'Grassante bello civili' = to the courteous soldier.

Grassante bello civili
Noe crucifixe you see, Noe frightfull Brand
Of Superstition's here; Pray let me stand.

Peterborough

One of the county's most famous epitaphs: to Robert Scarlett, the long-lived Peterborough sexton, the 'King of Spades'. Amongst his many assignments he buried two queens: Katherine of Aragon (1536) and Mary, Queen of Scots (1587). He died in 1591, aged 98. His portrait hangs in the cathedral, showing the old man with the grisly insignia of his trade – a shovel, pickaxe and a skull (see Vaux's poem, *The Aged Lover Renounceth Love*).

You see old Scarlett's picture stand on high,
But at your feete there doth his body lye.
His gravestone doth his age, and death time show,
His office by these tokens you may know.
Second to none for strength and sturdie Limme,
A scare-babe mighty voice, with visage grimme:
He had interr'd two Queens within this place
And this townes Householders in his lives space,
Twice over: But at length his own turn came,
What hee for others did, for him the same
Was done: No doubt his Soul doth love for aye
In Heaven: though here his body clad in clay.

Plumpton

To a young child, Anna Moore, d. 10 July 1683.

The cask decayes, the Jewells fled,
The Soules at Reste, the Rest is dead.

Rushden

To Sir Robert Pemberton and his wife. He was gentleman usher to Queen Elizabeth I; d. 1608.

By God's grace we so evenly were paired
As that in sexes equally we shared;
We had eight children to augment our joys,
For her four daughters and for me four boys.

Sibbertoft

To Anthony Atkyns, d. 1564.

Atkyns priest religious and lerned,
Not haveying where to dwell,
Wanderinge sycke at last here stayed
Tyll deathe did lyfe expell.

Wadenhoe

To John Andrewe, d. 29 March 1629, aet. 63.

Here restes the ashes of ann humble sperrit
Who while he liv'd these graces did inherit:
A pious fervent zeale to serve the Lord,
A conscious care with man to keep his word,
A christian love to all that dwell him nay
And redie still to helpe the poore and needy.
These lines men knowe doe truly of him story
Whome God hath call'd & seated now in glory.

Wicken

To John Jacks, a gardener, d. 1785.

His seeds are sown, his line is now wound up,
The trees are pruned, his knife is also shut.
His hoe is left, and likewise too his shears,
And here he sleeps in peace from all his cares.

Walcote Park

Next to God (and himself) the Englishman reveres his dog. Not unexpectedly, canine epitaphs are quite common and Northamptonshire has its quota. Here is a fine one, inscribed 'on an expensive pyramid in Walcote Park, Northamptonsh. the seat of Tho. Noel, Esq.'

Beneath this turf my fav'rite foxhound lies:
Stop here, ye hoaxers all, and wipe your eyes,
Here mourn with me for lovely Dolphin dead,
The flower of all my pack, tho' not the head;
Of shape exactly fine from head to foot;
To one scent steady, cautious, yet not mute;
To riot or to babbling never prone,
Nor slack on vermin scent to set us on;
Active, tho' not surpassing in his pace;
Brisk and unwearied in the longest chace;
The most determined foe our foxes knew,
Fixed to his point and obstinately true:
Such Dolphin was, whose fame must surely last
As long as sportsmen shall preserve their taste.

A ROSETTE OF ELECTION SONGS

Elections invariably spawn acrimonious and abusive literature. In 1818 a particularly protracted and bitterly contested election campaign took place in Northampton. The original candidates were Earl Compton (Spencer Compton, qv) and William Hanbury, the sitting members, and Sir George Robinson, Bart. Hanbury withdrew after the first canvas in February and Captain W. L. Maberly took his place. Though a minor at the time, Maberly was brought forward under the impression that Parliament would not be dissolved until much later. When dissolution took place earlier than expected, Maberly resigned in favour of Colonel Sir Edward Kerrison, a veteran of Waterloo. The final result, after 13 days of polling, was:

1. Earl Compton	815
2. Col. Sir Edward Kerrison	666
3. Sir George Robinson	639

As a sample of the dozens of songs published as handbills during the campaign, here are three, one for each candidate:

Compton!–Huzza!–For Ever!

Tune–The British Oak

Electors free, give ear, I pray,
My song deserves attention,
Vote for the man who is your friend
Without a place or pension:

Compton is he who will be free,
Support him now or never;
And let your cry thus rend the sky—
Compton—Huzza—For Ever!

With mind serene, and soul sincere,
For freedom firm and hearty;
Fair liberty to him is dear,
No dupe, or tool of party.
And in your cause, you may depend,
He'll do his best endeavour;
Your country's laws he'll well defend,
And those secure for ever.

To Compton then be staunch and firm—
Like him be independent;
Success will crown your hearty votes,
And he's the man, depend on't.
With heart and hand then join his cause,
And it shall ever be, sirs,
That when the votes are added up,
Your Compton first you'll see, sirs.

Compton, an independent Tory candidate, is the same Spencer Compton who was later to edit *The Tribute* (see under Compton in the main *Garland*). First elected in 1812, he remained MP for Northampton until 1820. He later became a Whig.

Kerrison for Ever

By a Lady

Ye freemen of Northampton, come listen to me,
Give your votes unto Kerrison, and then you shall see,
That your borough will prosper—you will not complain
That your labour is lost, or your votes gave in vain.
Then sing Kerrison for ever,
May he win the day.

For that noble hero has fought and has bled
For his King and his Country; and now, instead
Of rewarding his services by honour and fame,
Would you bring in another, and blot out his name?
No! sing Kerrison, etc.

Although he has gain'd so much honour and fame,
You'll not find him proud, or puff'd up with the same;
He stoops to the meanest, ne'er turns from his door
The wretched and needy–he's a friend to the poor.
    Then sing Kerrison, etc.

Kerrison, the wounded hero of Waterloo, was clearly very popular with the ladies, as his final message to his voters indicates:

> 'To the Ladies of N'pton who have honoured me with their smiles and constant attendance after every day's poll, I have to return my warm and grateful thanks.'

A New Song

Round Robinson's banners Electors now range,
    Those banners to Liberty dear;
His Plumpers whom nothing can bribe or can change,
    Shall under their waving appear.

The Green and the Yellow, while streaming in air,
    The Colours which Freedom should prize,
Their union of order and judgment declare,
    Those blessings most dear to the wise.

Let M----ly squander his money away,
    His *Infancy* renders it fit;
But say who can wonder? we see every day,
    That *Boys* have more money than wit.

Sir George Robinson was the Whig candidate.

3. Plumpers. Votes given solely to one candidate at an election when the voter had the right to vote for two or more. Tactical voting meant that you might prefer to withhold your second vote.
9. M----ly. Maberly (see above).

In the 1868 election, Charles Bradlaugh (1833–94) stood for the Northampton seat. Though unsuccessful, he built up a loyal following in the town which finally resulted in his election in 1880. During the 1868 campaign a young Northampton shoemaker, James Wilson, wrote the words for a song, *Bradlaugh for Northampton*, which was set to music by John Lowry. This became extremely popular amongst Bradlaugh's supporters, 'sung and whistled along the streets by boys and men'. If you are prepared to brave the traffic that swirls round Bradlaugh's statue on Abington Square, you will see Wilson's verses inscribed round the plinth. The following version comes from *'Thorough': the late Charles Bradlaugh, MP, and Northampton, a souvenir* (Campion, N'pton, 1894).

Bradlaugh for Northampton!

Electors of Northampton, work!
The day will soon be here,
When you will have to give your votes,
And give them without fear;
For freedom's battle ne'er was won
By cowards in the past,
Nor can it ever be sustained
By men who fear the blast.

Then toil, men, toil in freedom's cause,
Rest not content with vain applause.
Humanity needs better laws–
To win these we'll send Bradlaugh!

'Tis not to tread your churches down,
Nor chapels built by men,
Nor hinder earnest worshippers
On mountain or in glen;
But to give freedom to each thought
That swells the brain of man,
Religious liberty for all,
No State Church in our plan.

Then toil, men, toil in freedom's cause,
Rest not content with vain applause.
The nation needs far better laws–
To win these we'll send Bradlaugh!

'Tis not to rob rich lords of lands,–
Oppress as they would you,
Nor property make insecure,
To feed a lawless few;
But to make way for those to rise,
Who hard yet humbly toil,
And give to all some interest
In Nature's gift, the soil.

Then toil, men, toil in freedom's cause,
Rest not content with vain applause.
Our starving poor cry 'BETTER LAWS';
Then, hail success to Bradlaugh!

Some cowards cry out, 'Heresy!'
Beware! My fellow men.–

That cry's been raised, so hist'ry says,
'Gainst Britain's noblest men.
Say, Is he manly, is he true?
Is he for justice strong?
And will he labour good to do?
Then echo in your song–

We'll toil, we'll toil in freedom's cause,
Nor rest content with vain applause,
But fight determined for just laws–
And make our member, Bradlaugh!

A FINAL POSY

A rhyming advertisement . . . musings of a Salcey oak . . . the rooks' address. . . . We begin and end in the belfry.

Harlestone Belfry Board: Forfeits for Improper Ringing of the Church-Bells

Who turns a bell while light or dark
Shall two pence pay to parish clerk.

Who turns a bell on Sabbath Day
Double the sum at least shall pay.

With hat who rings, or with spurs on,
Must four pence pay, or else be gone.

Ring not till four, nor after nine;
Who keeps worse hours pays twelve pence fine.

Who climbs a wheel, or cuts a rope,
Escape resentment cannot hope.

And who these forfeits will not pay
Presented is the next court day.

Who blots, or scrats, or tears this down,
Will prove himself to be a clown,
And for his fault shall pay a crown.

Baker, II, 327

Similar 'forfeits' appeared at Bugbrooke and Brington. They were more commonly found in barbers' shops – and are still often found in pubs.

A Rhyming Advertisement

In sable Dress, I use the Art,
That's Black; yet uncorrupt my Heart,
No other Care disturbs my Head
Than how to earn and get my Bread.
When Lords and Country 'Squires command,
Myself and Imps are strait at hand;
Smoke condens'd from ev'ry Hole I rake,
Ready Pence for ev'ry Jot I take.
When out at Top my Head I peep,
I 'wake the Maids with *Chimney-Sweep;*
The Cook she brings a friendly Meal,
The Butler waits with Horn and Ale.
In ev'ry Place I'm welcome made,
And brisk pursue my Sooty Trade.

Rhyming adverts are still quite common—they have taken on a new lease of life in TV jingles—but were particularly favoured by advertisers in the late 18th and 19th centuries. The above rhyme appeared in the *Northampton Mercury*, 14 November 1768, placed by local chimney-sweep, Joseph Young. (See Victor A. Hatley: 'Rival Sweeps, 1768', *NP&P*, VI, 340.)

Salcey Oak

On 29 October 1825, the following 'Petition of the Old Hollow Oak in Salcey Forest' appeared in the *Northampton Mercury:*

Great George the Fourth, of Brunswick stem,
Who wears Britannia's diadem;
And Grafton's Duke, whose pedigree
Proceeds from regal ancestry;
And all yore Commoners, whose blood,
Though not so high, may be as good;
All you, in short, who rights maintain
In Salcey's Forest's wide domain,
To vert, or venison, or what not,
Which in that forest may be got,
Whether of high or low condition,
I supplicatingly petition
That you would please to spare my age
From the devouring axe's rage,
Which you've commissioned, so hear we,
To cut down every forest-tree,
That the crook'd ploughshare may invade
Our soil first since the world was made.

Know that I'm monarch of the wood,
And full five hundred years have stood,
And twenty sovereigns I have known,
Successive fill the English throne;
While round me each coveal oak
Has fall'n beneath the woodman's stroke.
But time my trunk has hollow'd wide,
Fit place for hermit to reside,
Or where some Dryad nymph might dwell,
Protectress of my sylvan shell;
And if cut down, *unutile lignum,*
I should be found *non arte dignum,*
Not fit ev'n for the kitchen fire,
Much less for any purpose higher.
Then spare my patriarchal years,
And straight release me from my fears,
By kindly passing a decree
Not to cut down or injure *me.*

QUERCUS

In response the *Mercury* printed this answer of the King, Duke and Commons:

Old Quercus, dissipate your fears,
For we respect your lengthen'd years,
And after reading your petition,
Have come to this our joint decision,
That no rude axe shall e'er molest
Your hollow trunk or tufted crest,
But that a monarch you shall reign
In Salcey's Forest's wide domain,
Till your majestic form decay,
And moulder back to common clay;
Or till your trunk no more can prop
The weight and pressure of your top;
But tumbling down with crashing sound,
Shall prostrate lie, and strew the ground;
Or till some wind's tempestuous gust
Shall lay your honours in the dust;
Or till, perchance, the world shall end,
An event near, as some contend;
Which, when it comes, will ruin bring
To men, and trees, and everything.

Then dread to you no sad event
From the late Act of Parliament;
Since thus your safety we have decreed–
As witness this, our act and deed.

REX DUX PLEBS

The Rooks' Address to the Farmer

The following verse, signed 'W. T., Northampton, 1820', appeared in the *Northampton Mercury*, 29 January 1820:

Oh, do not, with merciless, murdering gun,
Drive us wounded away from your store;
Oh, spare a few grains till the snow is all gone,
Then we will disturb you no more.

Believe not the lie that the scandalous say,
That we seize on the corn in the field;
'Tis the worm and the grub that we there make our prey
That your barns and your yards may be fill'd.

It is not by choice that we come near your home,
But the snow lies so deep on the ground,
And the keen eastern blast through the dark forests moan,
Nor a grub nor a worm's to be found.

The robin you feed with the crumbs from your hand,
Repays you with only a song;
But we will from vermin make clean all your land,
That your crops may grow plenteous and strong.

Ah, how like the world, which so bountiful gives
For some trifling amusement it gains;
While honest industry seldom receives
What it merits, and gratitude claims.

Though singly in song we cannot repay,
Yet together we'll call forth our powers;
And when we all rise in the grand choral lay,
What music is grander than ours?

Then do not, with merciless, murdering gun,
Drive us wounded away from your store:

Oh, spare a few grains till the snow is all gone,
Then we will disturb you no more.

W. T. was an observant naturalist, with enlightened views on *Corvus frugilegus* for his time.

Northamptonshire Bells

Baker (II, 91–2) quotes two Northamptonshire versions of the familiar London bell-rhyme, 'Oranges and Lemons', prefaced by the following note:

> PANCAKE-BELL. The church bell which is rung about noon on Shrove Tuesday, as a signal for preparing pancakes. This ancient custom is still observed in most of our villages. At Daventry, the bell which is rung on this occasion is muffled on one side with leather, or *buffed*, as it is termed, and obtains the name *Pan-burn-bell*. Jingling rhymes, in connection with this day, are repeated by the peasantry, varying in different districts. The following are the most current:–

Pancakes and fritters,
Says the bells of St Peter's.
Where must we fry 'em?
Says the bells of Cold Higham.
In yonder land thurrow,
Says the bells of Wellingborough.
You owe me a shilling,
Says the bells of Great Billing.
When will you pay me?
Says the bells at Middleton Cheney.
When I am able,
Says the bells at Dunstable.
That will never be,
Says the bells at Coventry.
Oh yes, it will,
Says Northampton Great Bell.
White bread and sop,
Says the bells at Kingsthrop.
Trundle a lantern,
Says the bells at Northampton.

> That the bells of the churches of Northampton used also to be rung on this day, may be inferred from the following similar doggerel:–

Roast beef and marsh mallows,
Says the bells of All Hallow's.
Pancakes and fritters,
Says the bells of St Peter's.

Roast beef and boil'd,
Says the bells of St Giles'.
Pokers and tongs,
Says the bells of St John's.
Shovel, tongs and poker,
Says the bells of St Pulchre's.

5. Thurrow. Furrow. 28. St John's. St John's Hospital.
30. St Pulchre's. [Holy] Sepulchre.

APPENDIX A

Select Bibliography of Northamptonshire Poets 1450–1900

I have restricted this bibliography to

—poets who have published in book form
—poets born before 1900.

I have also excluded the numerous minor poets who wrote texts for hymns. Publications, set out in chronological order, are identified solely by their year of publication. Fuller bibliographical details can be obtained from the British Library Catalogue or John Taylor's monumental *Bibliotheca Northantonenis* in the Northamptonshire Studies Collection at Northampton Central Library. In the case of very prolific poets, such as Dryden and Bowles, I have made a representative selection, but have included wherever possible the publications from which the Garland examples are taken.

AKENSIDE, Mark (1721–70)
—*The Pleasures of Imagination*, 1744;
—*Odes on Several Subjects*, 1745.

ALCOCK, Mary (1741?–98)
—*The Air-Balloon; or Flying Mortal*, 1784;
—*Poems*, 1799.

ALLEN, T. S. (fl. 1826–48)
—*The Weathercock and other poems*, 1833;
—*The Parrot and other poems*, 1848.

ARCHER, Ferdinando (1608–1705)
—*The Fall and Funeral of Northampton*, 1677.

ARDEN, William (f. 1767)
—*Elegy on the death of the Duke of York*, 1767.

ASKHAM, John (1825–94)
—*Sonnets on the Months*, 1863;
—*Descriptive Poems, Miscellaneous Pieces, Scriptural, Descriptive, Biographical, and Miscellaneous Sonnets*, 1866;
—*Judith, and other poems*, 1868;
—*Poems and Sonnets, Descriptive, Miscellaneous, and Special*, 1875;
—*Irenia or The City of the Dead*, 1878;
—*Sketches in Prose and Verse*, 1893.

BARCLAY, E. V. ('Colin Clout') (fl. 1906)
—*The Village Wedding*, 1906;
—*The First Love Affair of Miss Emma Jane Brown* (c1906).

BASSE, William (1583–1653)
—Donne's *Poems*, 1633;
—*The Compleat Angler*, 1653;
—*The Poetical Works of William Basse*, ed. Warwick Bond, 1893.

BELCHIER, Daubridgcourt (1580?–1621)
—*Hans Beer-Pot, his Invisible Comedy of See me and See me not*, 1618.

BELL, Thomas (1782–1862)
—*The Ruins of Liveden*, 1847;
—*The Rural Album*, 1853;
—*Winter Evenings at Home*, 1856.

BISHOP, Kate (1869–?)
—*A Life's Requiem and other poems*, 1890.

BOSTOCK, Susan (1862–1948)
—*Spring Notes and other poems*, 1912;
—*The Call of the Uplands*, 1913;
—*The World of Heart's-Delight*, 1930

BOWLES, William Lisle (1762–1850)
—*Fourteen Sonnets, written chiefly on Picturesque Spots during a Journey*, 1789;
—*Banwell Hill*, 1806;
—*The Missionary*, 1815;
—*The Grave of the Last Saxon*, 1822;
—*The Villager's Verse-Book*, 1829.

BRADSTREET, Anne (1612?–72)
—*The Tenth Muse, Lately sprung up in America*, 1650 and 1678.

BROWN, Abner (1800–72)
—*Home Lyrics: Secular and Sacred from a Country Parsonage*, 1859;
—*Lyrical Pieces, secular and sacred. From the Home Circle of a Country Parsonage*, 1869: an extended version of 1859; both include poetry by Annie J. and Maria Sarah Brown, his daughters.

BROWN, Elizabeth (1809?–?)
—*Original Poetry*, 1839.

CAUTLEY, George Spencer (1808?–?)
—*The After-Glow*, 1867;
—*The Three Fountains*, 1869.

CHAPONE, Hester (1727–1801)
—*Miscellanies in Prose and Verse*, 1775.

CHOWN, William (1753–1820?)
–*Original Miscellaneous Poems on Moral, Religious, and Entertaining Subjects*, 1818.

CLARE, John (1793–1864)
–*Poems Descriptive of Rural Life and Scenery*, 1820;
–*The Village Minstrel, and Other Poems*, 1821;
–*The Shepherd's Calendar*, 1827;
–*The Rural Muse*, 1835;
–*The Life of John Clare*, by Frederick Martin, 1865;
–*The Life and Remains of John Clare*, ed. J. L. Cherry, 1873;
–*Poems by John Clare*, ed. Arthur Symons, 1908.

COLES, John (1775–post 1841)
–*Poems Moral and Religious*, 1811 (with Joseph FURNISS Snr., qv).

COMPTON, Margaret (1791–1830)
–*Irene, A Poem, in Six Cantos*, 1833.

COMPTON, Spencer (1790–1851)
–*The Tribute*, 1837.

COOKE, Greville (b. 1894)
–*Poems*, 1933;
–*Jenny Pluck Pears and other Poems*, 1972.

COYLE, Edwin (fl. 1857)
–*Our Book at Home*, 1857.

CUMBERLAND, Richard (1732–1811)
–*Memoirs*, 1807: contains some fugitive verses.

DANIELL, Edward (1790?–?)
–*The Gaol: a collection of poems, and detached pieces. Written in confinement*, 1817;
–*The Woodland Muse*, 1824.

DE BURGH, Emma Maria (?–1851)
–*The Voice of Many Waters*, 1858.

DE WILDE, George James (1804–71)
–*Rambles Roundabout and Poems*, 1872.

DEMPSEY, J.[Mrs] (fl. 1887)
–*The Village of the Well.... Being a Poetical History of Rothwell* (?1887).

DENT, Caroline (fl. 1854–74)
–*Thoughts and Sketches in Verse*, 1854.

DEXTER, Thomas (fl. 1823–4)
–*The Red Well Mill*, 1823;
–*Wellingborough, a Poem*, 1824.

DIXON, Hugh Neville (1861–1944)
–*Wayside Thoughts*, 1930;
–*Pen and Pencil*, 1941.

DODDRIDGE, Philip (1702–51)
– *Hymns founded on various texts in the Holy Scriptures*, 1755.

DOLBEN, Digby (1848–67)
–*Poems*, ed. Robert Bridges, 1911.

DOWNING, James (1781–post 1811)
–*A Narrative of the Life of James Downing (a blind Man) late a private in His Majesty's 20th Regiment of Foot, containing historical, naval, military, moral, religious and entertaining reflections composed by himself, in easy Verse*, 1811.

DRYDEN, John (1631–1700)
–*Heroic Stanzas*, 1658;
–*Astraea Redux*, 1660;
–*Annus Mirabilis*, 1667;
–*Absalom and Achitophel*, 1681;
–*The Hind and the Panther*, 1687;
–*King Arthur, 1691*;
–*An Ode, on the Death of Mr Henry Purcell*, 1696;
–*Alexander's Feast*, 1697;
–*Fables, Ancient and Modern*, 1700;
–*The Pilgrim*, 1700.

EKINS, Jeffrey (1731–91)
–*Poems*, 1810.

'ESTRANGE, H. O. M.' (Home Strange) (fl. 1922)
–*The Angel at the Loom*, 1922: jointly with Helen Agnes Green;
–*Warp and Woof: a Medley of Rhymes*, 1922.

FANE, Julian (1827–70)
–*Translations of Heine*, 1854;
–*Tannhäuser and other Poems*, 1861; written jointly with Lord Lytton;
–*Julian Fane: a memoir*, by Lord Lytton, 1871.

FANE, Mildmay (1602–66)
–*Otia Sacra*, 1648.

'FARNINGHAM, Marianne' (Mary Anne Hearne) (1834–1909)
–*Lays and Lyrics of the Blessed Life*, 1860;
–*Morning and Evening Hymns for a Week*, 1863;
–*Gilbert and other Poems*, 1866;
–*Leaves from Elim*, 1873;
–*The Summer and Autumn of Life*, 1876;
–*Songs of Sunshine*, 1878;
–*Harvest Gleanings and Gathered Fragments*, 1903;
–*Songs of Joy and Faith*, 1909.

FULLER, Thomas (1608–61)
–*David's Heinous Sin*, 1631;
–*A Panegyric to His Majesty*, 1660.

FURNISS, Joseph Snr (1783–post 1841)
–*Poems Moral and Religious*, 1811 (with John COLES, qv).

FURNISS, Joseph Jnr (1821–?)
—*Miscellaneous Poems*, 1841.

GARDNER, Henry (fl. 1890–1910)
—*Poems* (?1898).

HALL, William Charles (1870–1936)
—*Sweet April*, 1938.

HARRISON, George (1876–1950)
—*Poems*, 1921;
—*Poems and Sketches*, 5 vols., 1927–1946;
—*A Wanderer in Northamptonshire*, 1948.

HAUSTED, Peter (1590?–1645)
—*The Rival Friends*, 1632.

HAWTHORN, Herbert J. (fl. 1926–47)
—*Songs of Life and Nature*, 1926;
—*Songs of a Life*, 1947: this incorporates poems from 1926.

HAWTHORN, Joseph (fl. 1880)
—*Poems*, 1882.

HEEL, Matthew (fl. 1840)
—*Poems*, (?1840).

HEMANS, Felicia Dorothea (1793–1835)
—*Poems*, 1808;
—*Domestic Affections and Other Poems*, 1812;
—*The Forest Sanctuary*, 1829;
—*Scenes and Hymns of Life with other Religious Poems*, 1834.

HENSMAN, Arthur (fl. 1883–1903)
—*Poems*, 1903.

HILL, Charles (fl. 1851)
—*A Few Thoughts in Verse on Religious Subjects*, 1851.

HODSON, Septimus (fl. 1782–1824).
—*An Elegy*, 1782.

HOGAN, John (fl. 1842)
—*Blarney: a Descriptive Poem*, 1842.

HOPE, John (fl. 1769–80)
—*Occasional Attempts at Sentimental Poetry, by a Man of Business*, 1769;
—*Thoughts in Prose and Verse started in his Walks*, 1780.

HUGHES, Christopher (1816–post 1874)
—*The Odes, Epodes, Carmen Seculare, and the First Satire of Horace*, 1867;
—*Poems Early and Late*, 1871.

HUMFREY, Nathaniel (1781–1840)
—*Poetical Sketch with other poems*, 1802; Simpson (*Obituary and Records*, 1861) refers to this book in his obituary for

Humfrey (10 October 1840), but I can find no trace of it or any other reference to his writing poetry.

ISHAM, Charles Edmund (1819–1903)
—*The Food that We Live On* (c1878);
—*Delights of Lamport* (ND).

JEFFREYS, George (1678–1755)
—*Miscellanies in Verse and Prose*, 1754.

KEENE, Talbot (1735–1824)
—*Miscellaneous Pieces: original and collected by a Clergyman of Northamptonshire*, 1787.

KINGSLEY, Charles (1819–75)
—*Poems*, 1879.

KINGSLEY, Henry (1830–76)
—*The Boy in Grey*, 1871.

KINGSTON, F. W. (1855–1933)
—*Cedric, or A Soul's Travail. A Tragedy in Five Acts*, 1888;
—*Julian's Vision and other poems*, 1896.

LAYNG, Peter (1712–78)
—*The Judgement of Heracles*, 1748.

LEADBEATER, Thomas (fl. 1908)
—*Verses on various subjects*, 1908;
—*New Poems* (?1909);
—*Humorous Ditties* (ND).

LEAPOR, Mary (1722–46)
—*Poems upon Several Occasions*, 2 vols., 1748 and 1751.

LEATHERLAND, John Ayre (1812–74)
—*Essays and Poems*, 1862.

LETTICE, John (1738–1832)
—*The Conversion of St Paul*, 1765;
—*The Immortality of the Soul*, 1795;
—*Fables for the fire-side*, 1812.

LINNELL, A. (fl. 1822–45)
—*Poems and Extracts* (?1845).

LUCAS, Robert (1747?–1812)
—*Hymn to Ceres*, 1781;
—*Poems on Various Subjects*, 1810.

MARMION, Shakerley (1603–39)
—*Cupid and Psyche*, 1637.

MASON, Jonah (fl. 1830)
—*Albion's Glory and other Poems* (ND: pre-1831);
—*Poems Devotional and Miscellaneous*, 1831.

MATHER, Dora Mary (fl. 1860–76)
—*Poetic Meditations*, 1876.

MAUNSELL, George Edmond (1816–75)
—*Poems*, 1861.

MERRY, John (1756–1821)
—*Miscellaneous Pieces; in Verse*, 1823.

MONTAGU-DOUGLAS-SCOTT, Charles Henry (1862–1936)
—*Northamptonshire Songs and Others*, 3 vols., 1904, 1905, 1906;
—*The Sonnets of Cecco Angiolieri of Siena Done into English Doggerel*, 1925. (Limited edition of 30 copies for private circulation.);
—*Tales of Northamptonshire*, 1936.

MOORE, William (fl. 1787)
—*Poems and Odes*, 1787;
—*An Ode on the Death of Mr Daniel Coales of Weldon*, 1787.

MOUSLEY, William Morris (fl. 1850)
—*Poems, Lyric and Heroic*, 1850.

NICHOLS, William (fl. 1862)
—*My Apprenticeship: a poem*, 1862.

OSBORNE, Richard (fl. 1777–92)
—*Miscellaneous Extracts, Chiefly Poetical, selected from various authors including many original compositions*, 1792.

PAKENHAM-WALSH, William Sanford (1868–post 1935)
—*Fifty Miles Round Sulgrave*, 1929;
—*Through Cloud and Sunshine*, 1932.

PELL, John (1790–1862)
—*Over's Hill, a poem, and other poems*, ed. by Rev T. C. Haddon, 1863.

PENDERED, Mary Lucy (1858–1940)
—*The Book of Common Joys*, 1916;
—*A Pageant of Northamptonshire*, 1933.

PERCY, Thomas (1729–1811)
—*A Collection of Poems*, ed. Robert Dodsley, 1758;
—*Reliques of Ancient English Poetry*, 3 vols., 1765.

PITTAM, John (fl. 1832)
—*Poems*, 1832.

PLUMMER, John (1831–1914)
—*Songs of Labour, Northamptonshire Rambles, and other poems*, 1860.

POOLEY, John (1800–post 1841)
—*Poems, Moral, Rural, Humorous, and Satirical*, 1825;
—*Blackland Farm; a poem in five cantos . . . with other pieces*, 1838.

POPE, Walter (1625?–1714)
—*Dr Pope's Wish*, 1697: published as a broadside, 1684, as 'The Wish'.

QUINCEY, Samuel (fl. 1755–77)
–*Mumbo Chumbo*, 1765.

RANDOLPH, Thomas (1605–35)
–*The Jealous Lovers*, 1632;
–*Poems: with The Muses' Looking-glass; and Amyntas*, 1638.

ROGERS, Samuel (1732?–90)
–*Poems on Various Occasions*, 2 vols., 1782.

ROWLATT, Joseph (d. 1875)
–*First Fruits*, 1874.

RYLAND, John (1753–1825)
–*Hymns and Verses on Sacred Subjects*, 1862.

SARGEAUNT, William Drake (1859–post 1929)
–*The Banks of Nene*, 1900;
–*Poems*, 1902. Includes several poems from 1900.

SCOT, Elizabeth (1729–89)
–*Alonzo and Cora with other original poems, principally elegiac*, 1801. The anonymous editor's preface is signed 'Northampton, June 1801' and most of the subscribers are from Northamptonshire. Most of her life however was spent in Edinburgh or Jedburgh.

SEDGWICK, John (1823–1909)
–*Oremus: Short Prayers in Verse for Sundays and Holy Days suggested by the Services of the Church of England*, 1852.

'SIGNA' (? Bailey) (fl. 1880s)
–*Zeppa or The Woman's Remorse and other poems* (?1887).

SITWELL, Sacheverell (1897–1988)
–*Collected Poems*, 1936;
–*An Indian Summer, poems*, 1982.

SPATEMAN, John (1697–1749)
–*War: a poem in blank verse*, 1745.

STUBBINGS, Henry Watkins (1774?–1824)
–*Miscellaneous Pieces in Prose and Verse*, 1823.

THORPE, Arnold E. (fl. 1886)
–*A Romance of the Sea and other rhymes*, 1886.

TOLSON, Francis (d. 1746)
–*Hermathenae, or Moral Emblems and Ethnic Tales*, 1739.

TOWNSEND, David (1807–97)
–*Lines occasioned by the Death of William Murdin of Little Oakley Who was found drowned in a pond in his close On the 21st of December 1847* (?1847);
–*The Gipsies of Northampton*, 1877;
–*David's Little Books*: a series dated 1847–92;
–*Heroes of Kettering and other records*, 1892. Includes a long narrative poem, 'Little Preacher and Village Preaching'.

TRINDER, Thomas (1740–94)
–*Geographical and Astronomical Definitions so far as they relate to the Use of the Globes*, 1817. (Yes, in verse!)

VAUX, Thomas (1509–56)
–*Songes and Sonettes* ('Tottel's Miscellany'), 1557;
–*The Paradise of Dainty Devices*, 1576.

WAITT, H. [Mrs] (fl. 1865)
–*A Small Collection of Verses and Rhymes on Elegiac and other Miscellaneous Subjects*, 1865.

WALTON, Ann (fl. 1810)
–*Original Pieces on Different Subjects Chiefly in verse* (?1810).

WASTELL, Simon (1560–1631)
–*A True Christian's Daily Delight*, 1623. In 1629, Wastell issued a second, enlarged edition, entitled:
–*Microbiblion, or the Bible Epitome, in Verse*.

WATKINS, Charles Frederic (fl. 1826–68)
–*The Human Hand and other poems*, 1829;
–*The Twins of Fame; or Wellington and Buonaparte. A National Poem*, 1854.

WELSTED, Leonard (1688–1747)
–*The Triumvirate*, 1717;
–*Epistles, Odes etc., written on several Subjects*, 1724;
–*Oikographia: a Poem*, 1725;
–*A Hymn to the Creator*, 1726;
–*The Works in Verse and Prose of Leonard Welsted*, ed. John Nichols, 1787.

WEST, Benjamin (1740–91)
–*Poems, Translations and Imitations*, 1780;
–*The Pedantic Hypocrite Exposed; or The Crick Wolf Exhibited in his proper garb to the Public*, 1786.

WEST, Jane (1758–1852)
–*Miscellaneous Poems, Translations and Imitations*, 1780;
–*Miscellaneous Poems*, 1786;
–*Poems and Plays*, 2 vols., 1799;
–*Poems and Plays*, vols. 3 and 4, 1805;
–*The Mother; a Poem*, 1810.

WESTBURY, Eliza (1808–28)
–*Hymns: by A Northamptonshire Village Female*, 1828.

WESTLEY, Eleanor Mary (fl. 1900)
–*Wayside Sketches* (c1900).

WESTON, Enoch (fl. 1852–76)
–*The Village Queen and Other Poems*, 1852;
–*The Lash and Other Poems*, 1858;
–*The Escape*, 1866;
–*The Shepherdess and Other Poems* (?1876).

WHALLEY, Palmer (1739–1803)
—*The Sick Minister's Short but affectionate Address to his People*, 1802.

WHITEHOUSE, John (1756–1824)
—*Poems: consisting chiefly of Original Pieces*, 1787;
—*Elegiac Ode to the Memory of Sir J. Reynolds* (?1792);
—*Hymn of Thanksgiving, on the Occasion of our Late Victories, and for other signal National Mercies and Deliverances*, 1814;
—*Odes, Moral and Descriptive* (?1816).

WHITING, Nathaniel (1612–82)
—*Le Hore di Recreatione, or, the Pleasant Historie of Albino and Bellama*, 1637.

WHYTE-MELVILLE, George John (1821–78)
—*Songs and Verses*, 1869.

WILD, Robert (1609–79)
—*Iter Boreale*, 1660: considerably expanded 1661 and 1668.

WISE, Charles (1820–post 1905)
—*Northamptonshire Legends, Put into rhyme*, 1905.

WODHULL, Michael (1740–1816)
—*Ode to the Muses*, 1760;
—*Two Odes*, 1763;
—*The Quality of Mankind, a Poem*, 1765;
—*Poems*, 1772.

Wodhull was also the first translator into English verse of all the extant tragedies and fragments of Euripides (4 vols. 1782).

WOOD, Francis (1850?–1906)
—*Echoes of the Night and other poems*, 1885.

WOODVILLE, Anthony (1442?–83)
—*Dictes and Sayings of the Philosophers*, 1477: Caxton's first printed book. Woodville's balet, 'Sum what musyng', was published by Percy in *Reliques of Ancient English Poetry*, 1765.

APPENDIX B

A Gazetteer of Poets and Places

This is pre–1950 (and in the case of Little Bowden, pre–1888) Northamptonshire with the Soke of Peterborough. Surnames of poets represented in the anthology are in capitals. If a poet is associated with more than one place, he/she appears under each.

Abington	WELSTED
Aldwincle	DRYDEN, FULLER, WHITING
Apethorpe	Julian FANE, Mildmay FANE
Ashby St Ledgers	Waitt
Aynho	MARMION, WILD
Barnack	Charles KINGSLEY, Henry KINGSLEY
Barnwell	BELL
Barton Seagrave	EKINS
Blatherwycke	RANDOLPH
Boughton	Downing, WHYTE-MELVILLE
Bowden, Little	Jane WEST
Bozeat	SARGEAUNT
Brackley	LEAPOR
Bradden	Heel
Brampton Ash	Arden, Rogers
Brigstock	KEENE
Brixworth	Watkins
Castle Ashby	CAUTLEY, Margaret COMPTON, Spencer COMPTON
Cold Ashby	Mousley
Cranford	WHITING
Cransley	COOKE
Daventry	HEMANS
Desborough	Jane WEST
Easton Maudit	ALLEN, PERCY, Tolson
Ecton	Whalley
Everdon	Layng

Fawsley	POPE
Finedon	DOLBEN
Fotheringhay	Julian FANE
Geddington	MONTAGU-DOUGLAS-SCOTT, Quincey
Grafton Regis	WOODVILLE
Grafton Underwood	Townsend
Gretton	Abner Brown
Guilsborough	BELCHIER, GARDNER, PELL
Hackleton	Nichols, Westbury
Hardingstone	LUCAS
Harlestone	WALTON
Harrowden, Great	VAUX
Haselbech	ALCOCK
Helpston	CLARE
Houghton, Great	Sedgwick
Irthlingborough	Leadbeater
Kelmarsh	POOLEY
Kettering	HARRISON, Herbert Hawthorn, Joseph Hawthorn, LEATHERLAND, Linnell, PLUMMER, Townsend
King's Sutton	BOWLES
Lamport	Isham
Lowick	WHITING
Marston St Lawrence	LEAPOR
Middleton Cheney	Pittam
Milton Malsor	Dent
Moulton	Chown, MERRY
Newnham	RANDOLPH, Stubbings
Northampton	AKENSIDE, ARCHER, BASSE, Bishop, BOSTOCK, BRADSTREET, CLARE, DE WILDE, Dixon, DODDRIDGE, FARNINGHAM, Hall, Hogan, HOPE, HUGHES, Kingston, LUCAS, Osborne, Rogers, ROWLATT, RYLAND, Trinder, WASTELL, WESTLEY, Weston, Wood
Northborough	CLARE

Orlingbury	Whitehouse
Oundle	HAUSTED, Moore, WILD
Pattishall	LUCAS
Peterborough	Coyle
Potterspury	White
Pytchley	Abner Brown, Anne and Maria BROWN
Rothwell	Dempsey
Rushden	Lettice
Rushton	MAUNSELL
Stanwick	ALCOCK, Cumberland, SARGEAUNT
Staverton	Hill
Sulgrave	Pakenham-Walsh
Thenford	WODHULL
Thorpe Malsor	MAUNSELL
Thorpe Mandeville	Humfrey
Thrapston	Hodson, Mason
Titchmarsh	DRYDEN
Twywell	CHAPONE
Wansford	Barclay
Weedon Bec	De Burgh, Benjamin WEST
Weedon Lois	COLES, Joseph FURNISS Snr, Joseph Furniss Jnr
Weekley	Wise
Weldon	DANIELL, JEFFREYS
Wellingborough	ASKHAM, Dexter, Mather, Pendered
Weston	Sitwell
Whilton	Spateman
Woodend	Elizabeth BROWN
Wootton	WHYTE-MELVILLE
Yardley Hastings	PELL